How to Do Things with Legal Doctrine

How to Do Things with Legal Doctrine

PIERRE SCHLAG AND AMY J. GRIFFIN

The University of Chicago Press
Chicago and London

The University of Chicago Press, Chicago 60637
The University of Chicago Press, Ltd., London
© 2020 by The University of Chicago
Published 2020

29 28 27 26 25 24 23 22 21 20   1 2 3 4 5

ISBN-13: 978-0-226-72610-6 (cloth)
ISBN-13: 978-0-226-72624-3 (paper)
ISBN-13: 978-0-226-72638-0 (e-book)
DOI: https://doi.org/10.7208/chicago/9780226726380.001.0001

Library of Congress Cataloging-in-Publication Data

Names: Schlag, Pierre, author. | Griffin, Amy J., author.
Title: How to do things with legal doctrine / Pierre Schlag and Amy J. Griffin.
Description: Chicago ; London : The University of Chicago Press, 2020. | Includes
bibliographical references and index.
Identifiers: LCCN 2020001832 | ISBN 9780226726106 (cloth) | ISBN 9780226726243
(paperback) | ISBN 9780226726380 (ebook)
Subjects: LCSH: Law—Methodology. | Jurisprudence.
Classification: LCC K212 .S347 2020 | DDC 340/.1—dc23
LC record available at https://lccn.loc.gov/2020001832

Contents

Introduction 1

Chapter One: What Is Doctrine? 10
   I. *The Big Picture* 10
      A. Artifacts 11
      B. Sources of Law 12
      C. Functions 12
         1. Structuration
         2. Defusing, Resolving, or Extinguishing Conflict
         3. Correction
         4. Realization of the Legal System
         5. Reflexivity
      D. Legal Elements 17
         1. Legal Persons
         2. Entitlements and Disablements
         3. Attribution Rules
         4. Transfer Mechanisms
         5. Interests/Harms
         6. Remedies
   II. *Doctrine* 21
      A. The Characteristics of Doctrine 23
      B. The Structured Elasticity of Doctrine 25
   III. *The Itinerary* 29

Chapter Two: Frames and Framing 31
   I. *Entry-Framing* 32
   II. *Broad vs. Narrow Time Frames* 33
   III. *Segmented vs. Continuous Transactions* 36
   IV. *Action vs. Omission* 37
   V. *Level of Abstraction* 40
   VI. *The Theater Metaphor* 47
   VII. *Exit-Framing* 51

Chapter Three: Baselines 52

  I. Baseline Selection Problems 54

    A. Classic Baselines 55

    B. Variations within a Single Baseline 56

      1. Level of Abstraction

      2. Individualization

      3. Multiplicity

  II. Baseline Neutrality Problems 59

    A. Failed Neutrality 60

    B. Denial and Evasion 63

  III. Baseline Collapse Problems 64

  IV. Summary 69

Chapter Four: The Legal Distinction 72

  I. What Do Legal Distinctions Do? 73

  II. Three Criteria for "Sound" Legal Distinctions 77

    A. Conceptual Intelligibility 77

    B. Practicality 79

    C. Normative Appeal 81

  III. The Trade-Offs among the Three Criteria 83

  IV. The Classic Flaws and Why They Matter 84

    A. The Classic Flaws 84

      1. Overbreadth

      2. Underbreadth

      3. Overlap

      4. Discontinuity

      5. False Dichotomy

      6. Incoherence

      7. Vagueness

    B. Why the Classic Flaws Matter: From Form to Substance 85

      1. Waste

      2. Fairness/Equality

      3. Subversion

      4. Efficiency

      5. Rule of Law

  VI. Crafting Legal Distinctions 89

  VII. Where Do You Draw the Line? 90

    A. The Non-ideal World and the Inevitable Trade-Offs 91

    B. Arbitrariness 91

    C. Indivisibilities 92

    D. Dynamic Fields 94

E. Problem Fields and Non-fields: Of Polycentricity and Flux. 95
F. The Slippery Slope 96
VIII. *The Fetishism of the Legal Distinction* 98

Chapter Five: Rules and Standards 100
I. *Defining Rules and Standards.* 101
II. *The Rules vs. Standards Dialectic* 102
A. Deterrence 103
B. Delegation 104
C. Communication / Formalities / Notice. 104
III. *The Substantialized Versions of the Dialectic.* 106
IV. *The Limitations of the Dialectic* 108
A. Of Vices and Virtues. 109
B. The Polycentricity Challenge. 112
C. The Epistemological Twist 114
V. *The Irreducibility of the Dialectic* 116

Chapter Six: Resolving Regime Conflicts. 119
I. *Techniques* 122
A. Hierarchy 122
B. Sectorization 125
C. Policy Judgments 125
D. Balancing. 127
E. Meta-quantification Approaches 129
F. Conflict Prevention Approaches. 132
G. Referral / Deference / Denial 133
H. Channeling 134
II. *Putting It Together* 135
A. Hybrids 135
B. Entailments. 136
C. Summary. 137

Chapter Seven: Interpretation 138
I. *The Interpretive Situation: Recurrent Tensions and Conflicts.* 139
A. The "Legal" in the Legal Text 139
B. The Interpretive Contexts 140
1. Fact-Rich
2. Institutionally Localized
3. Procedural Posture
4. Discernible Specific Consequences
C. The Textual Feedback Loop. 143
D. The Plurality of Contexts. 144
1. The Context of Application
2. The Authorial Context

3. The Addressee Context
4. The Functional Legal Context
5. Contexts Generally
E. Fidelity to the Original Meaning. 148
F. Summary. 149
II. *Textualism*. 149
A. Individuation: What Is the Unit of Interpretation?. 150
B. Intratextual Integrity 151
C. Intertextual Integrity 151
III. *Purposivism*. 152
A. Multiple Purposes 153
B. Selection 154
C. The Structure of Purpose. 154
IV. *Summary*. 155

Chapter Eight: Cluster Logic 156
I. *A Cautionary Note* 156
II. *The Structural Distinction Clusters* 158
III. *How the Clusters Matter*. 163
A. The Clusters as Classic Options 163
B. Nuance: Substituting One Distinction or One Term for Another. 164
C. Cluster Functions. 165
1. Function Tags for the Choice/Coercion Cluster
2. Function Tags for the Public/Private Cluster
IV. *Operationalizing the Clusters: Interaction* 170
A. Combining Clusters. 170
B. The Theatrical Metaphor. 172
V. *The Logic of Dissociation* 173
A. Chaining: Running an Argument through Successive Clusters. 175
B. Cluster Alliances. 176
VI. *Cluster Logic* 177

Coda: The Topics of Doctrine 179

Acknowledgments 185
Notes 187
Index 201

Introduction

Some time ago, the philosopher Alfred North Whitehead offered advice to his colleagues on how to uncover the philosophy of an epoch. Whitehead counseled them to ignore the specific intellectual positions that comprised the great debates of the day. Instead, he suggested that it would be more rewarding to examine the fundamental assumptions shared by the various contending parties. In all likelihood, these shared assumptions would have gone unnoticed and thus quietly shaped the thinking of the entire epoch.[1]

Imagine now thinking about law in this way. What is it about contemporary law that is so close to us, so obvious, so clearly taken for granted that it escapes our notice? To be sure, this question does not beget just one answer, but there is one we wish to focus on in particular: the idea that law as announced by our courts is predominantly expressed as *legal doctrine*.

For contemporary law students, lawyers, and judges, legal doctrine is so clearly *what law is* that this rarely elicits notice or wonder. And thus it is no surprise that as late as 2006, two commentators could begin an article entitled "What Is Legal Doctrine?" by stating:

> Legal doctrine is the currency of the law. In many respects, doctrine, or precedent, **is** the law, at least as it comes from courts. Judicial opinions create the rules or standards that comprise legal doctrine. Yet the nature and effect of legal doctrine has been woefully understudied. Researchers from the legal academy and from political science departments have conducted extensive research on the law, but they have largely ignored the others' efforts. Unfortunately, neither has effectively come to grips with the descriptive meaning of legal doctrine.[2]

This, of course, does not mean that legal professionals overlook doctrine. Indeed, many speak and write of little else. And as we know, they can argue with each other about the content and reach of this or that doctrine at great length. But that underscores our point: one of the effects of all this heated doctrinal argument is that it systematically normalizes—often beyond notice—that law is primarily expressed as doctrine rather than as something else. And for law students, the point must seem obvious: of course, law is doctrine—what else would it be?

Well, the question does yield an answer: there have been (and there remain even today) other competing modes of expression for law.

Go back through the common law far enough (a matter of centuries) and the preeminent form of law will seem less like doctrine and more like old-school *analogical reasoning*. What matters in this expression of law (one still with us) is not the rule of doctrine, but the rule of precedent. What drives the law (or the judicial opinion) here is not the directive-rule form of doctrine, but analogical comparisons of the present case to those of the past.

Go back even further in the common law and the judicial opinions read like little *narratives*. The opinions read something like this: "The parties came to us with a dispute. Each side told its story. We looked at some similar cases and then thought about a number of things. Finally, we arrived at this conclusion. So ordered."

There are other possibilities as well. In some offices of elite law schools, law is expressed less in terms of doctrine or case law analogies or narrative than as *theory*. The latter appears as an idealization and abstraction of the positive law designed to highlight the essential, the worthy, the important aspects of law from all that is ostensibly not (details, tosh, make-weight arguments). Judges are not overly fond of theory, but listen to impassioned theorists and they will tell you that theory is the law of laws—with doctrine and narrative playing merely supporting roles.

In addition to case law analogies, narrative, and theory, law is sometimes expressed as legal pluralism—the notion that law arises not just in official precincts of law where doctrine is so prevalent but rather in other venues of a cultural, religious, material, or practical character.

And then, of course, there is the obvious point that some law issues not from courts, but from agencies (regulations) and legislatures (statutes) and conventions (constitutions). We do not wish to make too much of that, however, for a great deal of the conceptual armature of regulations, statutes, and constitutions is itself the product of doctrinal concepts and doctrinal elaboration.

We mention all these options—case law analogies, narrative, theory, legal pluralism—to show that the predominance of doctrine as the expression of law is not a given, but is something worthy of inquiry in its own right.

In judicial opinions, in the law school classroom, in legal briefs, doctrine is the mainstay.[3]

And doctrine remains the mainstay despite some non-trivial criticism and ferocious attempts at displacement from many jurisprudential quarters— going all the way back to the legal realism of the 1920s and 1930s. Nearly all other contenders (save perhaps the most staunchly escapist interdisciplinary ventures) have drawn an implicit truce with doctrine.

Perhaps, then, there might be something to be gained in taking doctrine seriously by asking, *Just how does one do doctrine?*

That is exactly what we are about in this book. Here we wish neither to praise nor to criticize doctrine but to reveal and, with some luck, to refine those conceptual and rhetorical operations we legal professionals perform with doctrine. We want to make the crucial doctrinal operations explicit, show how they work, how they shape the law that emerges. The aim is thus to develop a more systematic understanding of the doctrinal moves many of us already make intuitively.

As the reader will see throughout this book, doctrinal arguments found in briefs and judicial opinions are very much patterned. Some of those patterns can be traced to the substantive subject (e.g., torts) and its various concerns (e.g., the correction of wrongs, the regulation of risk). That is not our topic. Some of the patterns, however, come from the character of doctrine itself as a form of law. It is the latter that we focus on here.

In part, our interest has been awakened by the "New Doctrinalists" who make the entirely apt point that for all the undeniable influence of legal realism (and its various descendants) in American law schools, it is doctrine that continues to rule in the courts. The New Doctrinalists take this recognition and search to see if there is not a certain substantive rationality to legal doctrine in specific fields.[4] We make a slightly different move here. Where they are focused on *substance*, we are focused on *form*. We look to discern the staying power of doctrine in the *patterns of moves* it repeatedly generates.

As we see it, doctrine is something that must be taught to law students. It is something that judges and lawyers do. The emergence of the New Doctrinalism and its inviting provocations offer the prospect that judges and lawyers might be helped to do doctrine well rather than poorly. It is that possibility that excites us here. For us the questions are these: How might we reconsider the doctrinal enterprise so that it is done in a more thoughtful and deliberative manner? How might we think about legal doctrine anew—so that doctrine (qua expression of law) might be taught straightforwardly in law school—as a particular jurisprudential style that can be thought about, questioned, and taught explicitly?

In other words, we hope to help make the obvious, the taken for granted, the routine, the everyday—what we call "legal doctrine"—visible and thus a topic worthy of consideration. We hope, in short, to make *legal doctrine a subject in its own right*—something to be taught in law schools the same way that one might teach "legal theory" or "negotiations" or "pre-trial practice." Doctrine—the creation, maintenance, and modification of doctrinal concepts, arguments, and legal regimes—we claim is a crucial aspect of law that merits treatment on its own as a distinctive expression of law.

In no way do we wish our project here to be understood as an effort to supplant the more substantive focus of the New Doctrinalism. But we do wish to add our insights about *legal doctrine as form*, where others have already gone some way in contributing their insights about *legal doctrine as substance*. Our project is in that sense a traditional one—an effort to contribute to the *jurisprudence of form*.[5]

We wish to make our presentation in what might be called an "operationalized" way. That is to say, we wish to describe how to construct and take apart legal doctrine, what to take into account, what to consider. We want to make the options apparent. The focus here is on how to do legal doctrine rather than a more detached analysis of doctrine's identity, character, virtues and vices. (It's not that the latter would not be an immensely useful contribution—it's just that, in this work, we are focused on a more preliminary and basic inquiry: reconnaissance precedes analysis and critique.)

Our focus here will be on those "decision points," or "break points," as we call them, where the legal professional has some choice in the matter. Where there is no choice, it would be both presumptuous and useless to offer guidance or advice. But insofar as law does not arrive simply as given on a scene of already established frozen facts (both of us have had enough legal practice experience to appreciate that in litigation, "the facts" are constructed in light of the law and "the law" is constructed in light of the facts), we will offer guidance as to how law can be rendered plastic (and mutable) as well as inert (and steadfast). Indeed, as we see it, rendering the law as fixed, inert, stable, is itself also a creative act (even though jurists rarely present it as such). Of course, in rendering the law plastic or inert, there will be in both cases limits on what can be done.

One way of thinking about this book that may well help the reader is to recognize that we take as our domain (what we want to explore) not those aspects of legal reasoning or analysis that are well described by jurists and scholars. Instead, we try to take as our domain those gaps in the law, those empty spaces in the corpus juris, where the law offers little or no real guidance as to how to resolve matters.

Why? We have some pedagogical hopes here:. Our greatest hope is to rescue law students and lawyers early on from banal understandings of law and law practice inculcated through pedestrian presentations of doctrine. Too often, we have seen even the most intelligent and thoughtful students taken in by a dulled vision of law. This dullened vision presents law as essentially a matter of rule-selection, rule-application, and mundane policy or principle analysis. IRAC is its sign, and boredom is its affect. Doctrine itself is much more interesting than it is often made out to be. And indeed, we are confident that a serious study of doctrine as form—the one we propose here— could lead to all sorts of inquiries about the relation of doctrine to theory, narrative, rhetoric, politics, economics, cognitive orientations, and so on.

As one of us has observed on several occasions, it is one of the primary functions of courts to shut down disputes and accordingly, whether deliberately or not, to shut down thought. Law, *as expressed by judges in the stylized forms known as judicial opinions,* thus has this irreducibly anti-intellectual aspect. Shutting down thought, however, is most emphatically *not* the primary function of the university or the law school. In fact, more like the contrary. To be sure, as law teachers, we must professionalize our students, which perforce means standardization (and some shutting down of thought). But we cannot just leave them there wondering what has happened to them. If we, and the law school, belong in the university, then we must strive to give students the resources and the repertoire to reflect on (and even to dispel) that standardization. Our main function as we see it is to incite wonder, puzzlement, skepticism—in short, thinking.

It is tragic that law students should embark upon their legal career with a blinkered view of their chosen profession simply because the education they receive leads them to a narrow and wizened understanding of what law is. It is tragic because while practice will be an able corrective for some of the unavoidable limitations of law school training, this is one harm that is likely to go unredressed by the hard shock of actual law practice. Law is a noble profession, but serious law teaching is necessary to ferret out its greater possibilities. Law guards its secrets zealously. The trick, in law school as elsewhere, is not to settle for too little—but to keep expectations high.

In this book, we presume that the reader already knows quite a bit about law and has already acquired the sorts of reasoning skills typically learned in the first year of law school: deduction, induction, analogy, how to distinguish and reconcile cases, how to perform policy analysis, make principled arguments, and so on. We presuppose this foundation and attempt to build on it.

Our approach here rests on viewing legal doctrine in the context of argument. Indeed, we see doctrine as a creature of argument—a creation produced by increasingly careful fashioning of directives in light of a variety of concepts, considerations, policies, principles, and values thought relevant (more on this in chapter 1, "What Is Doctrine"). With regard to doctrinal argument, we wish to reveal two major views—the first, highly conventional, the second, not.

The first view: we see doctrinal argument—whether in legal briefs, oral hearings, or law review articles—as technical and highly context-specific. This means that, for legal professionals, there is no way around the arduous work of mastering the factual and legal details. There is no hidden formula, no easy shortcut. The only substitute for hard work is . . . hard work. Excellent lawyers know this. They think and act accordingly. In serious litigation, against competent opponents, winging it, faking it, or the like is *not* ever an option.

The second view: if one thinks about doctrinal argument, one discovers that it exhibits certain recurrent structures and moves across the corpus of the law. One discovers that there is more commonality across the various fields and specialties of law than one might first have thought. For all the incredible variety and variations of legal doctrine (law school is still a ninety-unit, three-year affair in the United States), one discovers the same kinds of concepts, problems, challenges, and arguments across fields and specialties: whether to use a rule or a standard, how to discern intent in an institutional actor like a legislature, a corporation, a crime syndicate. All of this is to say that doctrinal argument is stylized: it is patterned and stereotyped. It is true that the doctrinal terminology changes from field to field—from torts to contracts, from antitrust to secured transactions—but even as the *semantics* may change, the *grammar* remains much the same.

To claim as we do that contemporary legal argument is indeed highly stylized and stereotyped prompts a question: Why is this deeply patterned aspect of doctrine so seldom apparent to law students and legal professionals? There are many reasons for this, of which we will mention only two.

First reason: because the doctrinal structures and moves are often expressed in different terminology across substantive areas—property, corporations, torts—the commonalities and the shared rhetorical logic often go unrecognized. By way of example, a law student can easily go through law school without ever realizing that "consent" bears a certain similarity to "assumption of risk" or that "concerted action" is a close cousin of "conspiracy," or that . . . (and so on).

Second reason: the doctrinal structures and moves are almost never taught in any *explicit comprehensive manner*—not in law school (and not anywhere else). "Legal doctrine" is not a course in most law schools. It is not treated as a subject matter. Instead, it is tacitly treated as if it were a weight-less and universal *form* of law capable of conveying whatever *substance* one might wish law to carry.[6] Viewed in this way, it is, of course, no surprise that law students, teachers, lawyers, and judges in the US proceed immediately to talk about matters of doctrinal substance.

No doubt there are other reasons why American law teachers have largely eschewed attempts to make the broad patterns of legal doctrine visible—preferring instead to tether their teaching to the contextual and substantive doctrinal idioms of specific judicial opinions. There is clearly value to this approach, but its overriding dominance in the law school world brings with it considerable downsides. One main downside of the heavy pedagogical reliance on judicial opinions in law school is that it has been ghastly-hard for law students to get any sense of overarching patterns (or even to realize that there are various overarching patterns to get in the first place).

The work here aims to begin redressing these shortcomings.

For us, the intellectual, professional, and political rewards of mastering the implicit structures and moves of doctrinal argument seem obvious. On *the intellectual level*, one simply cannot understand the meaning or the role of *the parts* without grasping the broader patterns and movements of *the various wholes* to which the parts belong. On *the professional level*, the rewards seem if anything even more transparent: the work here lays out not only the crucial pivots and axes on which the success and failure of doctrinal arguments turn, but also the array of structural possibilities from which the advocate can choose. On *the political level*, the work reveals law to be a far grander, more exciting, though also possibly more precarious and more controversial enterprise than we might typically think.

The work, as will be seen, aims to be compact and to the point. It is forward-leaning and spare in its use of examples. It strives to convey a great deal of material as succinctly as possible. To suggest, then, that what follows is dense is an understatement. The reason for this economy of expression is that in addition to laying out the basic doctrinal structures and moves (how they work and not), the aim here is also to provide an argument resource. Indeed, once one has finished reading the work here, it becomes useful as a prompt—a checklist of possibilities and limitations. It is a spur and a guide to brainstorming for the judge crafting her opinion, for the lawyer writing his brief, for the legal academic contemplating her article, for the law student writing his paper.

There is one bit of irony in all this—namely, that, for all our insistence on the stylized and stereotyped character of legal argument, the fundamental lesson here is that law is a creative enterprise (much more so than law school and judicial opinions typically lead us to believe). In this regard, it will help the reader considerably if she abandons at the outset the commonplace fiction that law is merely something *we have* (and *to be found*), and instead becomes open to the view that law is also simultaneously something *we do* (and *to be created*).

It's important, of course, not to overstate that creativity. Both of us worked for some time as litigators in law firms before entering the legal academy. Our experience is that the plasticity/fixity ratio or the determinacy/indeterminacy ratio in law practice is arranged very differently in practice and in law school. It is not that law school classes have lots more freedom, while law practice has lots more constraint. Rather, it's that the ratio, or if you want, the mix, of freedom and constraint is arranged differently. One will experience certain kinds of constraints in practice that are absent in the typical law school classroom—a rich (not a spare) set of constraining legal authorities, an identifiable flesh-and-blood set of decision-makers, the reality of a (fearsome?) opposition, and more. One will also experience certain kinds of freedom in practice that are absent in the typical classroom, where the student is generally not free to say things like "I would rather deal with this as quasi-contract or maybe a torts case than as a contracts matter" or "Well, that issue really doesn't matter all that much because the P.R. aspects are such that the defendants have to settle no matter what they do." (Try that one on a professor.) The point here is that the sources and character of both freedom and constraint differ from law school to practice. It's not that one is more "free" or more "constrained" than the other. It's just that the freedom/constraint ratios are distributed differently across different matters.

The work here, as will be seen, generally eschews normative prescriptions as to which is "the better approach" to any given legal task (e.g., how best to interpret a statute). It's not that we have a shortage of opinions on the matter. It's just that we are trying to avoid the prescriptive voice as much as possible. Such a voice would get in the way of the overarching aim, which is to reveal the possibilities and limits of doctrinal exegesis and to reveal the kinds of doctrinal tools available. The work here is not for these reasons any less value-laden.

In this regard, we wish to disclose one overriding objective. We would very much like to help nudge the state of the art in judicial opinions beyond its present condition. In our experience (and consider that as legal academics, we are as close to being "professional readers" of judicial opinions as anyone can be) judicial opinions, on the whole, engage in way too much dogmatism, question-begging, skirting of the issues, and evasion of contrary arguments. This is bad enough on its own. But a further consequence is that, both in style and structure, the contemporary judicial opinion lacks vitality as well as credibility. In virtue of both its form and its rhetoric the contemporary judicial opinion reads like a facsimile of an antiquated art form that may once have been vital, but long ago stopped trying. This is not a personal complaint: our students notice.

How then to read this work? Well, read it all the way through from beginning to end. Or start with whatever chapter seems most pertinent. Or use the highly detailed table of contents to hone in on a particular issue or problem. Or use the table of contents to browse. The book is organized in outline form, but much of it is modular (the parts and subparts can largely stand alone).

Some of the footnotes are labeled "Further Reading." These are intended to guide the reader to a ruthlessly abridged set of excellent readings on the subject—often in allied disciplines, such as rhetoric, cognitive science, and so on. We apologize in advance to the authors of the many other excellent works that we have not listed. Some of the footnotes are labeled "Elaboration." These are brief capsule discussions of the matters discussed in the text. Finally, we've prepared an extensive set of exercises for those who wish to use the text in teaching; those exercises are available in PDF at https://press.uchicago.edu/sites/legal_doctrine.

Pierre Schlag and Amy J. Griffin
Boulder, Colorado
September 1, 2019

What Is Doctrine?

A good question—that one. So, what is it? The question begets an easy answer and a more complicated one. For the easy answer, begin with the usual sources. *Black's Law Dictionary* defines doctrine as "[a] rule, principle, theory, or tenet of the law."[1] In this limited sense, doctrine coincides with what law students often refer to as "black letter law"—the substantive content of judicial opinions cast in the form of a rule or a principle. Sometimes the doctrine is stated explicitly in a judicial opinion. Sometimes, the doctrine has to be constructed by the reader out of the raw materials of the judicial opinion itself—the recitation of facts together with the issue and holding, and perhaps even the rationale and the procedural posture of the case.

But of course there is much more to be said. To describe doctrine in a more meaningful way, we need to provide some context, structure, and terminology. Once we've established a framework, we can examine both the function and the form of doctrine. Specifically, we want to know: What is the role of doctrine in the big picture of our modern legal systems, and what are doctrine's key characteristics? The answers to these questions will then be used to launch us into a quick descriptive overview of the inquiry: *how to do things with legal doctrine.*

I. The Big Picture

Our modern legal systems can be described in terms of certain crucial forms (a cautionary word: this is but an impressionistic sketch, and very far from comprehensive):

Artifacts (e.g., rules, principles, policies)
Sources of Law (e.g., constitutions, statutes)

Functions (e.g., defusing conflict, minimizing harm/friction)

Elements (e.g., persons, entitlements, attribution rules)

These forms are so commonplace that we seldom think about them. They matter, in the same way that language matters: like language itself, they enable, channel, and limit the ways in which we think and do law. If you need an image, think of these *implicit forms* as constructing the very architecture of law.

A. ARTIFACTS

These are some of the major recognized "artifacts" of modern legal systems:[2]

Concepts (e.g., "common carrier")

Directives (e.g., "A contract requires consideration")

Principles (e.g., "no liability without fault")

Policies (e.g., "Tort law aims at optimal deterrence of accidents")

Values (e.g., "fairness")

Considerations (e.g., "administrative convenience")

Interests (e.g., "privacy")

Many legal professionals think of these artifacts as distinct. That is sometimes a useful way of thinking about them—though it is important to recognize that they are often intertwined into different hybrids (e.g., multifactor tests that are combinations of both policies and legal directives). While jurists and scholars will not always agree on shared definitions for these artifacts (many might resist calling them "artifacts"), most accounts will look something like the following:

A *concept* in law is a generalized legal idea (e.g., personal jurisdiction).

A *directive* is a rule or standard that takes the form "If X (the trigger), then Y (the response)."

A *principle* states a generalized preexisting obligation (e.g., "No person can profit from his or her own wrong").

A *policy* states a generalized objective to be achieved or avoided (e.g., the policy of minimizing accidents).

A *value* is a context-transcending moral, political, or aesthetic concern (e.g., justice, equity, mercy).

A *consideration* is a matter worthy of being considered in legal decision-making (e.g., the efficacy of a rule).

An *interest* is a concern that matters to one or more of the relevant parties to a dispute (e.g., the interest in privacy).

The classic simple image of these artifacts goes something as follows: judicial opinions often articulate directives and delineate their scope through the identification of the relevant facts and an affirmation of the holding, and the rationales. The rationales, which serve both to *justify* and to *delineate the scope* of the directive, are usually articulated through the invocation of principles, policies, and values.

The artifacts are related in that, generally speaking, they can all be deployed to modify, extend, and contract each other. They can also meld into and subsume each other in all sorts of hybridized ways.

B. SOURCES OF LAW

The authorized formal sources of state law are well recognized and require no great elaboration here:[3]

    Constitutions
    Statutes
    Ordinances
    Regulations
    Common Law

Typically, these are presented in a hierarchy (in the order above). However, once one examines the way judges, lawyers, and academics actually use and interpret these sources of law, the picture becomes more complicated. We discover, for instance, that the common law has sometimes been used as a referent or even baseline for constitutional interpretation.[4] We also discover that statutes are often read in ways "sensitive" to (with deference to) already promulgated administrative agency regulations. The general point here is that while judges and lawyers will, as a *formal matter* (in opinions, briefs, etc.), generally honor the hierarchy of sources of law, they will often, as an *informal matter*, take into account inferior sources of law.

Obviously, while these might be considered the only *formal* sources of positive state law, there are a multitude of other sources of law that routinely find their way into and through the formal sources. To list just a few examples: legal reasoning, legal interpretation, social morality, tradition, political commitments, and so on.

C. FUNCTIONS

A modern legal system must perform certain basic functions, and doctrine (at least in our current systems) is instrumental to all of them.[5] These functions, while familiar to judges and lawyers (though perhaps in different terms), require some elaboration. The set described below is extremely *minimalist* in two senses. First, it is far from exhaustive: one can imagine other important functions that a modern legal system must perform. Second, the set below is morally and politically minimalist—so much so that one can imagine a legal system satisfying all these conditions and being nonetheless utterly reprehensible from a moral or political standpoint.

1. Structuration

A modern legal system must provide some sort of structuring that enables various parties to operate and achieve desirable ends and avoid undesirable ones. Implicit here is that the legal system is organized and patterned. It must institute a standardized and sometimes technical language that allows actors—particularly legal professionals—to *communicate* with each other and to reliably signal to each other intentions, plans, and goals, and to allocate tasks, responsibilities, and entitlements. It is a kind of language designed to perform routinized legal actions and tasks and to address routine social, economic, and political frictions. Particularly important in achieving structuration, is *channeling*—the routing or triage of various parties, problems, issues, and so on to the "appropriate" institutions, discourses, and personnel (private and public). Indeed, the more complex, intricate, and variegated a society and its legal system, the more important this second-order "referral" function becomes.

Structuration here refers to the creation of a general system that enables the participants to move within and adjust to the system in ways that are variously considered just, effective, efficient, orderly, and so on. In other words, the legal system must be one that provides a sufficiently clear, predictable, knowable structure so that persons can get on with their lives, tasks, and projects. The rule of law (understood as a commitment to publicity, notice, generality, and the like)[6] is but one specification of the kind of structuration required.[7] Justice is another. (There are more.)

2. Defusing, Resolving, or Extinguishing Conflict

Once explicit conflicts or disputes arise, a modern legal system must, if possible, resolve or, at the very least, defuse such conflicts and disputes (the ex post aspect—meaning "after disputes arise"). A legal system must also strive to resolve or defuse disputes by preventing them from arising in the first place (the ex ante aspect—meaning "before disputes arise").

A legal system that fails *entirely* to defuse conflicts is one where the processes of law would nonetheless end in violence or other forms of self-help.

Such a legal system would, in such circumstances, be largely superfluous. Arguably, this would not be a modern legal system at all, but rather the juridical equivalent of what is called in international relations "a failed state."

A modern legal system must strive to minimize harms arising from conflicting activities. The idea is to prevent conflicts or disputes from arising in the first place, by effectively creating legal regimes that minimize such conflicts. There are obvious ways to minimize friction:

> *Isolation*: the separation of the parties or activities that create the conflict through command and control devices, property regimes, and more
> *Regulation*: the constraint or specification of the activities through licensing, certification, predistribution review, product specification, liability regimes, and more

One of the techniques for defusing conflicts is to channel them through legally defined pathways that neutralize the incendiary motivations that drive conflict. The legal system funnels and translates highly partisan, emotion-fraught, drama-driven, incendiary confrontations into more detached, rationalist, procedure-driven, technical disputes.[8] The legal system in many ways strives to contain, channel, and reduce confrontations to much narrower disputes that are, in the Weberian sense, formally rational and disenchanted.[9]

3. Correction

One key function of a modern legal system is to rectify perceived failures (unfairness, injustice, inefficiencies, oppressions, etc.). Involved here is the deliberate intervention of the legal system—whether triggered by legal officials or private parties. Correction and rectification are mentioned only briefly here, though they comprise huge aspects of the legal system and correspond closely with lay conceptions of the essential functions of law.

Correction always depends upon some baseline ideal (a value or a state of affairs) that is perceived to have been violated in some way and thus requires a legal intervention. Many of the great disputes among citizens, jurists, and scholars focus on this aspect of the legal system. Often the disputes elicit contested views as to what the ideal baselines ought to be (justice? efficiency?), and what counts as a cognizable violation requiring legal redress.

4. Realization of the Legal System

The "realization" (i.e., the making real) of the legal system involves inscribing its categories and logics within the political, social, and economic realm.

Viewed *solely* from the standpoint of realization (and, relatedly, efficacy, legitimation, and domination), modern legal systems can be described in terms of various stages of development.[10] We describe three stages here but could easily depict stages with greater granularity. In the first stage, positive laws are enacted on paper and applied by able and willing legal officials to citizens who obey for instrumental reasons (e.g., the carrot and the stick, the "Holmesian Bad Man"). In the second stage, both legal officials and the citizenry obey the law—precisely because they understand that law poses obligations for them (e.g., internalization). The third stage, the most advanced, is achieved when both legal officials and the citizenry unconsciously deploy legal categories and logic, not just because they are the law, but because they are experienced as simply the way things are (e.g., naturalization). There is, in short, a forgetting that everyday categories such as employees, banks, insurance companies, universities, are inter alia *legal categories* organized, at least in part, in accordance with legal logic.

A modern legal system will tend to develop toward the third stage. (No modern legal system, however, depends solely on third-stage realization.) However, localized regressions can happen—lapses back into the second or first stage. Legitimation then kicks in. Legitimation here is the political / moral representation of law as justified (to legal officials, the press the citizenry, etc.) in terms of ostensibly worthy attributes: reason, order, fairness, justice, and so on. Legitimation assists in the process of realization: appeal to worthy attributes makes it easier to accept juridification. Legitimation also fills the gap when realization by other means has not worked. The most effective form of domination for a legal system is the third stage—when the effects of law are no longer experienced or seen as such: rather, they are experienced or seen as just the way things are. This is a stage beyond political legitimation. There can be no direct challenge to law because law is not even perceived to be implicated.

5. Reflexivity

One thing that a modern legal system must do is take cognizance of its own character, actions, operations, and so on so as to effectively discharge other functions and yield change, adjustment, harmonization, and self-correction.[11]

In different words, law needs to be not only directive with respect to what the government, persons, and parties are supposed to do. It also needs to be directive with regard to itself. It needs to recognize what changes, if any, are required in the form and substance of law and provide processes through which legal change can be instituted.[12]

These functions are sometimes mutually supportive. Thus, for instance, it might be that defusing conflict ex ante not only helps to defuse conflict ex post, but helps as well to lessen the need for correction or rectification. In terms of the *sociological success* of a modern legal system, the ultimate would be to achieve synchronicity among all functions. (Note that this might be perfectly horrible from many other angles—the moral, the political, etc.).

Much of the time, however, the various functions will be in tension with each other. Most obviously, correction/rectification is likely to be seen as interfering with structuration (in the simple sense that correction/rectification claims seem to require a "restructuring"). In turn, structuration (a society-wide project) will sometimes conflict with defusing conflict (ex post) in the simple sense that the achievement of the latter may well require abandoning the structure.

> *Example: This will seem very abstract, but consider the arguments that can arise in a tort case. The plaintiff may argue that we need a liability rule that will minimize the sum of accident and accident avoidance costs (defusing/extinguishing conflict—ex ante). The defendant may respond that it would be unfair to depart from existing legal rules. (correction/rectification) and that a new rule will upset expectations and thus create uncertainty (structuration). Moreover, this negative effect on structuration may well require a disruptive adjustment of behavior (realization/efficacy/legitimation/domination). And so on.*

Perhaps the most vexatious aspect of legal doctrine is that all these functions must operate both at the level of legal analysis and at the level of power. Doctrine is thus at once a vehicle of legal power and legal intelligence (and not surprisingly, what is sometimes necessary for one interferes with the other).

Legal arguments sometimes gain different traction among various parties because those parties accord different value or import to these reciprocally interfering functions. Differences in the weight placed on principles, policies, and values among judges, lawyers, and law students often turn upon these very high-level (but often unarticulated) commitments.

Moreover, these functions do not necessarily correspond cleanly to the prevalent or dominant policies, principles, and values that are recognized in a particular field of law such as torts or contracts. In sharp contrast to *nesting* (the repetition of the same argument forms at different levels of legal analysis),[13] here the important point is exactly the reverse: the set of functions applicable at the very high level of law writ large need not (and often are not) repeated at the level of policy, principles, and values pertaining to a particular field. There will often be a kind of *disjunction* among levels rather than a clean correspondence or the repetition we associate with nesting. (See the coda.)

Doctrine, as the dominant form of legal currency, is critical to all of these high-level functions. It provides much of the structure to resolve or defuse conflicts, corrects perceived failures, realizes and develops the legal system, and provides means for the system to self-correct.

D. LEGAL ELEMENTS

Functions are very high-order ends of a modern legal system. They are served by a great many causes of action and defenses described across the corpus of the law, and all of these claims and defenses are explained, animated, elaborated on, narrowed, or expanded by doctrine. The elements that comprise causes of action are described here separately from the functions because it turns out that any given cause of action can serve several different functions simultaneously. Think of a simple cause of action in negligence or breach of contract and consider how each arguably discharges several of the functions described above. It would be cleaner, of course, if each function had a discrete set of corresponding causes of action, but that's not the way it works.

Fundamentally, law breaks down into some characteristic set of very basic kinds of legal elements, including definitions and specifications of the following:

Legal Persons
Entitlements and Disablements
Attribution Rules
Transfer Mechanisms
Interests/Harms
Remedies

Causes of action are defined *through the doctrinal specification* of each of these terms and their specific configuration in a particular cause of action.

Here are some of the classic ways in which law specifies each of these elements.

1. Legal Persons

For our purposes, to be a "legal person" means *no more than that* a party can sue or be sued in law. Obviously, different persons (e.g., corporations, minors, and citizens) have different entitlements and disablements. It would be appropriate then to talk about *degrees of* personhood as opposed to a simple person/non-person distinction. But having registered that point, let's put it aside and consider instead a very brief typology of persons.

First, there are the so-called natural persons, whether they are citizens, immigrants, or foreign nationals. Recognize that insofar as the law is concerned, "personhood" is a *legal* term (which may or may not coincide with our lay beliefs or intuitions). Consider that in the United States it is principally the use of the term "persons" in the Fourteenth Amendment to the US Constitution that does the work of recognizing human beings as persons. (Prior to the Fourteenth Amendment, slaves were not considered persons but chattel property.[14])

Second, there is the obvious creation of so-called artificial persons: institutions such as corporations, partnerships, and so on. Also included here are the definitions of various governmental institutions: the federal government, the states, and their various subdivisions.

Third—and this is the most malleable and thus most interesting category—there are the opportunities to *construct persons or the (near-)functional equivalent* for purposes of litigation: conspiracies, concerted action, joint liability, joint and several liability, alternative liability, and various civil procedure mechanisms such as joinder, class actions, and so on. These are all different legally recognized (there are many more) ways of constructing a person.

In sum, we have then the following:

"Natural Persons" (e.g., persons, citizens, immigrants, refugees, foreign nationals, enemies, enemy combatants, felons)

"Artificial Persons" (e.g., corporations, states, Congress, agencies, partnerships, municipalities)

"Construct-a-Person" (including *legal recipes* for constructing persons: conspiracy, acting in concert, joint venture, apparent authority, class action, joint and several liability)

Non-persons (e.g., neighborhood, friendship, a contract)

In order to charge a person in the legal sense with responsibility for some wrong (e.g., a crime) or in order to determine whether the person has effectively effectuated a transfer (e.g., a gift) it is often required that the person have certain characteristics, such as the following:

Requisite mental state (e.g., general intent, specific intent)
Capacity
Competency
Authority (actual or apparent)

The positive law specifies which persons (e.g., corporations, minors, married persons) are (or are not) entitled and are (or are not) disabled from performing certain actions legally defined. Accordingly, one way to limit or extend entitlements and disablements is to tinker with the definitions of those entitlements and disablements. An alternative approach is simply to tinker with the basic definition of the person.

2. Entitlements and Disablements

In the crisp legal world of the famous legal thinker Wesley Newcomb Hohfeld, the four fundamental correlative jural relations are the following:

Right ⟷ Duty
Privilege ⟷ No Right
Power ⟷ Liability
Immunity ⟷ Disability

There is a great deal to say about these relations—the correlative entitlements and disablements. It is far more than can be addressed here, and so we will not even try—leaving the reader with the option to go elsewhere.[15] Hohfeld's jural relations are by design incomplete. The recognition of entitlements (e.g., rights) and disablements (e.g., duty) requires ascription of substantive content: For instance, A has the privilege to do *what* precisely? Possibilities include the following:

Use his land
Walk down the street
Petition the government

In addition, the predicate conditions for the entitlement need to be specified. A's privilege arises or attaches by reason of *what?* Possibilities include the following:

Status (e.g., marital status, citizenship, bona fide purchaser for value)
Acts or omission (e.g., acceptance, undertakings, promises, negligent acts)
Ritual performance and legal ceremonies (e.g., delivery of seisin, oath, notarization, consideration)
Satisfaction of conditions specified in private agreements (e.g., contracts, wills, trusts, charters)

3. Attribution Rules

These are rules for attributing some act (e.g., negligent omission) or some legally cognizable consequence (e.g., harm) to some legal person. Classic attribution rules include the following:

Causation requirements ("but for," "alternative liability," "natural and probable consequences," "substantial factor," "would have . . ." "could have . . .")

"direct/indirect causation," "reasonable foreseeability," and more). Note, however, that the choices in law are not endless. Part of the knowledge of the lawyer, of course, lies in knowing which test applies when.

Imputed responsibility for self and others (agency/principal, respondeat superior, aiding and abetting, etc.).

There are two major ways to expand or contract the scope of attribution. The most obvious way is to tinker with the causation or imputation tests. Another way of accomplishing the same objective, however, is to redefine the person—through a *construct-a-person* strategy. In *Summers v. Tice* (the quail hunters tort case)[16] one of the two hunters was responsible for shooting the plaintiff, but as there was no evidence as to which one, the burden of proof against either—the preponderance of evidence—was not met. The court's approach—alternative liability—redefines them as one entity (and puts the burden of proof on each defendant to exonerate himself). This effectively secures the plaintiff's meeting of the burden of proof: there is a 100 percent chance that the pair did it.

4. Transfer Mechanisms

These rules govern the transfer of interests from one legal person to another (e.g., property, child custody):

Private agreement (e.g., contracts, wills, delegation)
By operation of law (e.g., intestacy, escheat, taxes)
By judicial proceedings (e.g., probate, attachment)
Self-help

5. Interests/Harms

Not all interests are protected. Not all harms are redressable. There are certain characteristic interests and harms recognized by law. Among them are the following:

Bodily
Real, personal, and intellectual property (tenancy, copyright, trade secrets, fixtures, etc.)
Economic (benefit of bargain, loss of business, etc.)
Cognitive (emotional distress, pain and suffering, etc.)
Reputational (personality, products, organization, etc.)
Privacy (invasion, disclosure, false light, etc.)
Prospective (advantage, future harm, etc.)

Associational (wrongful death, consortium, etc.)
Group (equality norms, antidiscrimination law, etc.)

6. Remedies

Remedies is a very complex subject. But once again, there are certain obvious recurrent elements to define the kinds of redress available:

Damages (benefit of bargain, actual loss, nominal, punitive, treble, etc.)
Declaratory judgment
Injunction (restraining orders, TROs, cease and desist orders, stays, etc.)
Mandatory injunction (mandamus)
Specific performance
Structural injunction (retention of jurisdiction)
Settlement (ADR, mediation, consent decrees, etc.)
Conviction (penalties, fines, imprisonment, etc.)
Special writs (coram nobis, etc.)
In rem remedies (confiscation, condemnation, attachment, foreclosure, etc.)
Self-help
(And so on . . . for quite a while)

This description of artifacts, sources, functions, and elements is but one way of describing law at the very big picture level. In this view, then, doctrine is in the form of various *artifacts* comprising multiple *elements* (creating causes of action, defenses, procedures, etc.) all resting on one or more *sources of law* to serve the *functions* of our modern legal systems. We use this as the foundation for a more complex answer to the question we asked at the start of this chapter: What is doctrine?

II. Doctrine

We borrow from William Twining and David Miers's notion that legal doctrine typically takes the form of a *rule* or a *principle*.[17] As we see it, at the most abstract level, doctrine follows the formula "If this, then that." It has a *trigger* (the "this") and a prescribed *response* (the "that"). Sometimes, of course, the *response* is more implicit than explicit.

> *Example: Many doctrines are stated in the declarative form, leaving the response in part implicit. For instance, consider the doctrine of consideration in contract law. That doctrine states that an agreement is enforceable as a contract only if consideration is provided. The trigger aspect is clear (an agreement). The response aspect has both explicit and implicit aspects. If, explicitly, the response is*

"This is not a contract," implicitly, the legal professional will be able to spin out a number of consequences: not only is this agreement not a contract, but it cannot be enforced in a court of law as a contract; it cannot serve to support a cause of action seeking damages for breach of contract, a defendant sued under breach of contract would be entitled to a motion for summary judgment, and more . . .

To be more specific in our conceptualization, a doctrine prescribes that if in circumstances X, a class of persons Z engage (or do not engage) in behavior of type Y, then Q will (or will not happen). This too is an abstract formula, and obviously actual doctrine is filled out in greater detail. Predicate *mental states* can be specified. *Conditions* can be added. Potential *claimants* can be described and limited. And so on.

By tinkering with the definitions of each of the elements (described earlier in this chapter) we can produce a tremendously intricate set of different causes of action and defenses. To give but one example here, causation (which is one kind of rule of attribution) is variously defined in terms of "but for," "natural and probable consequences," "substantial factor," "would have . . ." "could have . . ." "direct/indirect causation," "reasonable foreseeability," and more. The set of available choices is admittedly limited. But, complexity—in fact, tremendous complexity—arises from the fact that *at the doctrinal level* it is one test that applies *here* (e.g., the "could have" test of equal protection race discrimination) and another one *there* (e.g., the "but for" test in negligence law). And the expert knowledge of the lawyer lies in knowing which test applies when.

> *Example 1: The Fruit of the Poisonous Tree doctrine. This judicially created doctrine prescribes that a criminal defendant* (person) *can exclude evidence from trial* (remedy) *if it was obtained as the result of police illegality if the evidence is not sufficiently attenuated from the initial illegality* (attribution rule). *The doctrine serves to "safeguard"*[18] *Fourth Amendment rights* (interest) *through its deterrent effect, even if it is not recognized as a constitutionally required rule.*

> *Example 2: Vicarious liability. An employer* (person, status) *is liable for an employee's tortious acts* (disablement) *if those acts occurred within the scope of employment. The tortious acts need not have been directly authorized so long as they arose naturally or predictably from the employment context* (attribution rule). *The employer then is responsible for providing the remedy for the harm that occurred.*[19]

The form of doctrine thus ranges from the very simple to the very complex.

A. THE CHARACTERISTICS OF DOCTRINE

We next look beyond this formulaic description of doctrine to better take stock of its character. Five characteristics are key to doctrine as most legal professionals understand it. Doctrine is the following:

General
Directive
Authoritative
Judge-Made
Interlinked

First, doctrine partakes in *generality*. It is not radically particularist (though, of course, there are some doctrines that permit ample discretion and a great deal of particularism). Typically, however, doctrine sets forth classes of persons, classes of activities or acts, and general consequences; its validity and scope extend beyond any single case.

Second, doctrine is *directive*. While it may not require or forbid parties to do anything, doctrine is nonetheless directive in that it spells out consequences: this is a function of doctrine's "If this, then that" structure. Make no mistake, we are not invoking the discredited "command theory" of law. A lot of law is simply permissive. But given the "If this, then that" structure of doctrine, persons paying attention will generally follow the law where the rewards achieved or the pain avoided warrants conformity or compliance. The doctrine of consideration in contract law is a good example. That doctrine does not require parties to provide consideration in their agreements. It does tell them, however (and this is the directive aspect), that if their agreement does not provide consideration, it is not enforceable in court as a contract.

Third, doctrine is generally believed to guide, constrain, or, at the extreme, determine judicial decisions. In this sense, doctrine is *authoritative*. Among legal academics (far less so among judges) there is considerable controversy about when legal doctrine can or does (and if so how) determine outcomes. But clearly doctrine plays a role, whether it is merely that of guiding a decision or something more. And where it is authoritative, doctrine is itself a reason for a court or decision-maker to rule in a certain way. It is even a reason for a party—a person or citizen—to justify his or her behavior. ("Why were you going so slowly?" Because the speed limit was 15 mph.") Doctrine is also sometimes authoritative in the sense that its specifications prescribe legal relations or a legal state of affairs. Thus, in property law, the delivery of a deed for a piece of land is constitutive of transfer. ("How do you transfer land?" Answer: by executing and delivering a deed.) Now, none of this is to say that a doctrine relevant to some issue or case will necessarily prevail and rule the day. It may be set aside for some other more important doctrine or for a variety of other considerations. But the general idea (no more than that) is that a doctrine is supposed to rule over its domain. Doctrine is supposed to be the driving force of law. Judges almost always understand doctrine in this way. It is for them, almost the "natural" form for law—if not at the beginning of legal analysis, certainly by its end. Legal academics, by contrast, tend to be a bit more skeptical and more circumspect. (This has a lot to do with the divergent job descriptions of the two occupations. A bit more on this later.)

A fourth characteristic of doctrine is that it is *judge-made law*. Not just the expression of common law, but also the judicial elaboration of constitutional, statutory, or regulatory law. Notice, by way of example, the *different sources of law* for the doctrine stated in the following examples:

1. If, but for the defendant's negligence, the plaintiff's harm would not have occurred, then the defendant's negligence is a cause in fact. (*common law*)
2. Under the Sherman Act, agreements subject to "the rule of reason" are illegal if they unreasonably restrain trade. (*statute*)
3. Under the rational basis test of the equal protection clause, legislation is constitutional if the statute is "rationally related" to a "legitimate governmental interest." (*constitution*)
4. A person seeking relief from a court must have clean hands. (*equity*)

For our purposes, we are not overly concerned here with pinning doctrine down to judicial pronouncements. But the idea that it is judges who formulate doctrine is fairly common. Thus, few legal professionals would call a statute or a constitutional provision "doctrine."

Fifth, a key feature of legal doctrine is that it is *interlinked* in numerous ways. We will elaborate this particular idea later, but for now, the basic idea at least can be made clear. Sometimes a single doctrine looks very much like a stand-alone, off-the-shelf piece of law. Consider the doctrine of consideration again. On first impression, this bit of doctrine can easily seem like an independent proposition. But its relationship with other doctrine quickly becomes apparent. First, consider the *trigger*: "an agreement." This signals that not just anything can be a contract—an *offer* alone won't do nor will a *command*, for that matter. Second, lots of implications attach to the *response* "This is not enforceable as a contract" (no contract requirement to perform, no damages from breach on the contract, etc.). One would have to know a lot of law—one would have to be legally trained—to know what all the legal consequences might be. This is the *interlinking of doctrine*. Doctrine is not simply made up of words and phrases. Those words and phrases are *legal—*

which is to say, they are always interlinked and infused with meanings arriving from other precincts of law. It's all interconnected in complex, occasionally nuanced, and very often under-recognized ways. By the time this book is finished, that last sentence (barely comprehensible now—if at all) will not only make sense, but will brim with meaning. (We promise.)

For now, the point is to set aside the idea that doctrine is easily usable (let alone understandable) as a stand-alone proposition. This, by the way, is why many law professors have a certain disdain for "black letter" statements of the law: black letter law makes doctrine appear to be stand-alone, self-sufficient, and off the shelf. To be sure doctrine can be represented this way. Reducing doctrine to black letter law is always a theoretical possibility. An advocate can, in various ways, get a judge to focus single-mindedly on just a single doctrine. But at the same time, this sort of reduction is only one of the possibilities of doctrine (not all). The legal realist Thomas Reed Powell perhaps put it best when he reportedly said, "If you can think about something which is attached to something else without thinking about what it is attached to, then you have what is called a legal mind."[20] This is a humorous way of putting the matter, but be advised: Powell's aphorism is stone-cold serious. Realize as well that some judges and scholars will insist on doing precisely what Powell ascribes to the legal mind. And that too will be law. We caution against a possible mistaken impression. Because black letter law seems so fixed, so static, it is easy to imagine the interlinking of doctrine as the gateway to flexibility and choice. In some senses, it is. But the interlinked character of doctrine is a source of not just freedom, but constraint.

Note that the first three of these characteristics (*general, directive, authoritative*) would likely be used in the definition of anything labeled as a rule or principle in its conventional sense. And of course, the most common understanding of doctrine is as "rules" or "principles." But doctrine is the unique product of its setting. It can be understood only in the context of its perpetual creation by judges, creating not a static set of rules but an evolving web of interrelated doctrines (*judge-made* and *interlinked*).

B. THE STRUCTURED ELASTICITY OF DOCTRINE

One key to understanding doctrine lies in appreciating the tension between its structure and its elasticity. On one hand, doctrine is seen as systematized and set. Law students and their professors often refer to doctrine as "black letter law." That is a revealing expression: the term "black letter law" is derived from the name of "a heavy, ornate, early printing type"—black letter.[21] The use of the term to describe doctrine intimates that such law has the same sort of certitude and endurance as that of black letter text in an era when printed text was not so easily created and revised. While that is not our view of doctrine in general (black letter is only one of its possible expressions), it is important to recognize that for some (many?) legal professionals, doctrine = black letter law.

Our view is that while doctrine is patterned and recursive (we hope we are beginning to make that clear), it nonetheless holds many creative possibilities (which is what largely motivates this project).

In the very narrow field of active unsettled lawsuits, judges use doctrine in order to resolve a particular dispute. But even in that relatively narrow sphere, the context in which doctrine is invoked can vary dramatically. Consider the impact of judicial hierarchy: a trial court judge might use doctrine quite differently from an appellate judge. Trial court judges frequently rely on doctrine without ever putting it into written form—using doctrine as invisible guidance for a given ruling from the bench. In a written opinion, a trial court judge (or mid-level appellate judge) uses doctrine not just to speak to the parties, but to speak to an eventual appellate judge audience. The doctrine is used as explanation and justification for the judge's decision.

Supreme Court justices sometimes use doctrine quite differently from every other judge in the nation—they can and do create new doctrine on a regular basis, with no higher judge available to pass judgment. Unlike lower-court judges, judges on the highest court in a jurisdiction may freely criticize and discard doctrine. Justices at this level use doctrine to persuade one another, and to communicate with lower courts and the general public. Similarly, consider the interrelationship between doctrine and different branches of government. Doctrine created when a judge interprets a statute might be a direct message to the legislature even as it serves to resolve a single dispute. Doctrine might be created by a court in rebuke to executive action, or in deference to agency action.

Then too the character of the jurisdiction may affect the use of doctrine. A judge in a state with a small population may have much less doctrine to work with than, say, a judge in California, and this might lead the former judge to treat existing doctrine differently than the latter. Doctrine from one jurisdiction might be used as support for a policy decision in another. Might federal judges treat doctrine differently than state court judges? It's certainly possible. Every part of the scene likely matters, including the identity of the judge.

Advocates in the litigation context are largely making use of doctrine to persuade judges to reach a particular legal outcome. In that formal judicial litigation context, the use of doctrine is policed by judges and their clerks, or at least it can be. Here, a lawyer has an ethical obligation to cite applicable binding precedent, or risk sanctions from the judge. But the use of any other sort of doctrine—any non-binding doctrine—is the choice of the attorney. And even the use of binding authority can be strategic. A litigator's decision to file a summary judgment motion might make sense even if the applicable doctrine doesn't dictate a result in the client's favor. Doctrine in this scenario might be secondary to the relative resources of the parties.

Consider the many (many) differences among advocates. It is a vast over-simplification to imagine a single prototypical attorney who uses doctrine in one way. It is quite likely that criminal defense attorneys use doctrine differently than civil attorneys, and that government lawyers use it differently than private lawyers. For example, an attorney with a burdensome case load who encounters the same legal issues repeatedly (a public defender, perhaps) may rely on stock doctrinal propositions. The identity of the client matters (her goal, her wealth or other means of influence), audience matters (the forum, the particular decision-maker), and the amount of money the attorney is charging probably does as well. The legal profession, mirroring the clients it serves, is a stratified one.

And of course doctrine is not only used in the formal litigation setting. Legal negotiation and client decision-making of all sorts happen "in the shadow of doctrine."[22] In this context, an attorney might use doctrine as a weapon to force another party to act in a particular way—to stop a party from acting or to induce a party to act. Or doctrine might be used as a shield—to protect one party from another. As a bargaining chip in negotiations or as a preventative tool to avoid litigation or prosecution. As information to convince a party to concede to a term in a transaction.

Lawyers regularly use doctrine to predict judicial outcomes and advise their clients accordingly. Every time a lawyer advises a client, it is likely that doctrine looms somewhere in the picture. Doctrine is used as a predictive tool, as knowledge, as background. Lawyers compose demand letters, offer letters, letters of resignation, contracts, and every other imaginable legal document under the influence of doctrine. The doctrine might be used offensively, defensively, or in a reconciliatory manner. In each instance, litigation might be imminent or only a distant possibility—in either case the courthouse is the ultimate formal means of enforcement. It's just that the power of the doctrine extends far beyond the courthouse to influence the behavior of parties regardless of their proximity to litigation. In these contexts, lawyers police one another.

What is the relationship between the lawyer, the doctrine, and the legal strategy? How does the advocate's ethical responsibility to zealously represent her client affect her use of doctrine? Is an advocate required to take advantage of doctrine's elasticity on behalf of her client? The obvious differences between the role of an attorney and the role of a judge must lead to differences in the way that doctrine is used by each.

Arbitrators and mediators may use doctrine in a very different way from other legal decision-makers. Most obviously, in the arbitration or mediation forum, parties may or may not be bound by doctrine. An arbitrator may consider doctrine nothing more than gentle guidance, and could be bound by some other authoritative source (like the Bible). A mediator might consider doctrine to be much less important than the parties' own stories, or not. The parties in such forums adapt doctrine to the particular circumstances.

Doctrine can be used as an educational tool, to draw attention to an issue. It can be created or deployed as a call for legislation, as support for an elected candidate's platform, as propaganda in a culture war. It might be used as a very blunt instrument by a non-lawyer ("I have a right to free speech!") or as a highly refined technical argument by a lawyer crafting a demand letter.

All of this is to say that doctrine is elastic and host to a great deal of pluralism. We could stay with the conventional conceit that it is merely the perspective or the context that changes while the doctrine remains the same. But we think that changes in perspective and context make us recognize aspects of doctrine that we would not otherwise glean, and thus change the doctrine itself (in the same way that the third or the fourth reading of a great literary work changes its meaning).

What is doctrine? Doctrine is a mansion, an organism, a topography, a network, a recipe—choose your image, schema, or metaphor.[23] Realize, of course, that not all of them will take. Doctrine is not chocolate. Or at least, you will not get very far with that one. But a plurality of images, schemas, metaphors will work—some better than others. And as they do their work, doctrine will emerge looking quite different from one vantage than from another. In turn, however, the resulting perspectives generally rest on shared, professionally inculcated experiences and appreciations of our legal system. These experiences and appreciations are rarely consciously articulated. We would have to talk about the aesthetics of law.[24]

Even as we insist on the creative possibilities of doctrine, we wish to emphasize its patterned and recursive character. So yes, there is elasticity, but it is a structured elasticity or an elastic structure. Notice that there is nothing surprising about this: think trees, spider webs, and so on. Moreover, in the world of doctrine neither structure nor elasticity is constant. The two may be in tension, they may also be mutually reinforcing. Homogeneity is not the thing here—banish the thought.

III. The Itinerary

As mentioned in the introduction, we hope to contribute to doctrinal argument by providing an account of what can be done with doctrine when there are choices to be made. In other words, our domain, our subject, is all the points, the places, the opportunities, where the substantive doctrine seems to leave openings for argument. We deal with the gaps and inconsistencies—the break points as we often call them. Our effort is to highlight both the structured and the elastic character of those openings and to show as well how to make them happen or how to shut them down (for that too is a creative enterprise).

We start with idiosyncratic chapter 2, "Frames and Framing," which is all about how to frame factual transactions so as to yield what is known as "a theory of the case" and thus prepare a narrative that allows for the deployment of *this set* of doctrines (over here) as opposed to *that set* (over there). We also discuss how to frame the law and the doctrine.

We then move to a discussion of baselines in chapter 3. Baselines become very important when the doctrine at hand leaves relatively unspecified a particular term or phrase. Much of law deals with deviations from baselines. When baselines are underspecified, problems and choices emerge. Famously, the Fifth Amendment prohibits the taking of private property without just compensation. The term "property" has bedeviled interpreters of this amendment. Just what is the baseline conception of property? What was considered "property" at the time of the nation's founding? Is this a closed or open conception? Are contemporary analogues to be treated as property? What's the baseline? From this relatively simple baseline selection problem we move on to some other classic difficulties.

We begin to think about what distinguishes the domain of one doctrine from another competing or conflicting doctrine in chapter 4, "The Legal Distinction." In this chapter, we consider all the major ways in which legal distinctions can be attacked, supported, and created. We see the legal distinction as a crucial aspect of doctrine for the simple reason that it is the legal distinction that demarcates the scope of one doctrinal regime from another.

This then yields consideration of rules and standards, the familiar dialectic in chapter 5. In this dialectic, classic arguments are marshaled in favor or against either the "bright line rule" or the "flexible standard." This is a classic doctrinal dispute that has now yielded a huge number of publications. We consider how the arguments for and against rules and standards can be deployed, how they work and do not, and whether and when they make sense.

Chapter 6, "Resolving Regime Conflicts," surveys the variety of techniques used by courts (and other officials) to resolve conflicts between different doctrinal regimes, policies, principles, and values. Only a limited set of basic techniques can be used: hierarchies, balancing, process approaches, and so on. Here we set forth the major techniques, describing their strengths and weaknesses.

Chapter 7, "Interpretation," examines the ubiquitous challenges of interpretation across the legal system. Indeed, if there is a mother of all doctrine (not saying), interpretation is it. Interpretation is one of the main vehicles through which the meanings of legal imperatives are elaborated by judges. Our discussion of interpretation focuses on just two of the main interpretive methods used by judges—textualism and purposivism. These techniques are used to derive or ascribe meaning to a variety of different legal sources: statutes, constitutions, case law, documents, and so on. This is hardly an exhaustive treatment (quite the contrary), but it deals with perhaps the principal schism in the interpretive world of law. Our effort is not to argue for or against any form of interpretation, but again to show how the techniques can be successfully deployed or broken down.

Chapter 8, "Cluster Logic," is inspired by the work of Chaim Perelman and Lucie Olbrechts-Tyteca on rhetoric and that of Duncan Kennedy on legal structuralism. Here we return to legal distinctions to claim that there are some (like choice/coercion, public/private, form/substance, etc.) that surface over and over again in field after field. Why hasn't this been more noticed? Because these major distinctions appear with different terms in the various fields. We collect the various terms to show the import of these major distinctions. And we show that a great deal of doctrinal argument is governed by these clusters, their deployment, and the various ways in which they can be privileged (or not) vis-à-vis each other.

In the coda, we return to considering doctrine as a topic. By this point, we hope to have demonstrated both its structured and its elastic character (and the various ways in which each can be intensified to yield different outcomes). We reflect upon what our various takes (frames and framing, baselines, etc.) reveal about the character of legal doctrine.

Frames and Framing

Judges and lawyers are routinely called upon to "apply the law to the facts." This is one of those common phrases that seems to describe an operation that is exceedingly simple. It is anything but simple. The question of *how* the law is to be *applied* to the facts is often a complicated one that allows for a great deal of rhetorical creativity—certainly far more than the key terms ("facts," "law," and "apply") would seem to suggest.

Here we will be concerned with just one of these creative aspects—namely, the recurrent aesthetic frames that lawyers and judges use to give facts and law a certain legal attitude. These aesthetic frames mediate (are interposed) between facts and law. These frames are extremely important precisely because a great deal of legal analysis depends upon which frames are actually selected to characterize the facts and the law. As will be seen, the choice of frame often has a significant legal and rhetorical effect on the legal conclusions reached. So the choice of frames is outcome-sensitive. That is to say, a preferred outcome can affect the selection of the frame. Oddly, however, apart from such outcome-sensitivity, the choice of frames often seems rationally ungrounded. This is to say that the choice of frames seems arational or even irrational. (More on this later.)

Below, we will discuss three familiar framing options key to the construction of the factual transaction to be submitted to legal analysis:[1]

Broad vs. Narrow Time Frames
Segmented vs. Continuous Transactions
Action vs. Omission
Level of Abstraction

While not exhaustive, these framing options are among the most frequently encountered in law. In any legal dispute, the framing possibilities are considerable, and much has been written about how to harness the highly persuasive power of narrative in legal advocacy or decision-making. We've chosen the examples we discuss in depth as emblematic.

In addition to these familiar framing options, three other aspects of framing will be discussed:

Entry-Framing (Prefiguration)
The Theater Metaphor (Kenneth Burke's Dramatistic Method)
Exit-Framing (Abandonment)

At the outset, it is worth noting that some of the framing issues discussed below are well known among some legal professionals. Sometimes the frames selected are deployed self-consciously. And sometimes not. Regardless, it is important to learn to recognize when the aesthetic frames are (or can be) brought in play. Why? First, the choice of a frame will influence what doctrines can be engaged, what kinds of legal arguments can be advanced, and what legal issues can be raised. This works in reverse as well—effective framing of facts is not chosen randomly but is guided by the law that is available. Second, the way in which the relevant factual transaction is framed will often influence how one feels about the case—whether one is more favorably disposed toward one side or the other.

I. Entry-Framing

At the very beginning of a legal text—say, a judicial opinion, a brief, or a law review article—the text begins to enframe the reader and to enlist his or her faculties in a quest, a task, a challenge. Whether it be a scene, an action, a problem, or yet something else, the text elicits the reader's attention. This is *entry-framing*, and it matters very much.

Among other things, entry-framing allows the author to elicit certain kinds of readerly attention (and inattention) as well as readerly hopes (and anxieties).[2] It is a question of putting certain audience faculties and orientations on high alert, while lulling others to sleep. Louis Althusser called this "interpellation"— the calling forth of a particular self, oriented and motivated to undertake certain ideologically structured roles, tasks, functions (and crucially, not certain others).[3] In entry-framing, an entire genre can be elicited. We could reprint the beginning paragraphs of a brief, a judicial opinion, or a law review article, and any well-trained legal professional would be to tell which is which.

In the main, entry-framing involves foregrounding and backgrounding. Certain issues, problems, questions, actors, agencies, and action, will be placed front and center. Others will be set backstage or even left offstage.

What is at work here is often called *prefiguration*—the performative instal-lation of views and commitments (metaphysical, ontological, moral, and more) of the audience to accept the truths that will, without irony, be derived therefrom.[4] When entry-framing and prefiguration are well done, the reader or audience will not even notice, but instead will be carried along in the un-interrupted flow of the author's prose. When prefiguration is badly done, the reader or audience notices that it is being "set up"—framed, as it were, to accept the author's arguments and conclusions. Persuasion falls flat.

II. Broad vs. Narrow Time Frames

So, what caused the Great Recession in 2008? The answer to this question will depend upon, among other things, what we mean by "recession" and "cause." But putting that aside, it also depends upon what time frame we use to de-cide. In fact, we could create a timeline. The longer the timeline, the more potential causes we have, and, indeed, the more the recession appears to be the result of long-standing processes (the cycles of capitalism, financial de-regulation, technological advances, the rise of the credit economy, etc.) The shorter our time frame, the easier it is to associate the cause of the recession with a number of discrete actions performed by readily identifiable actors (the banks, the mortgage lenders, the derivatives, etc.).

In law, it is also possible to characterize a transaction as happening within a very narrow time frame or instead a broadly expansive time frame.[5] And this can greatly affect the outcome. Perhaps the most obvious example is the battered woman defense that is sometimes used to argue self-defense in crim-inal cases. The classic scenario is of a woman who is repeatedly assaulted by her partner and who one day kills him. The controversial case arises when the homicide occurs sometime—say, several hours or days—after the last assault. Can this be considered self-defense or not?

If one takes a narrow time frame—the very moment at which the homi-cide occurs—then arguably there is no threat to the woman at that moment, and self-defense is not available. If, however, one takes a broad time frame— the continuous exposure of the woman to threats of assault—then the homi-cide occurs during the period of an ongoing threat, and self-defense becomes a much more plausible claim. In this scenario, interestingly, the indications are that a new doctrine (battered woman self-defense) was created at least in part to extend the relevant time frame. So it's not just that the contraction or extension of time frames will affect the doctrines that can be brought to bear. It is also the case that doctrines can be explicitly created to include or exclude certain time frames.

Choosing broad or narrow time frames allows for different characteriza-tions of the transaction in ways that can affect the choice of law applicable (and the conclusions reached). Consider the famous McDonald's coffee case in which McDonald's was initially held liable for selling coffee that burned an elderly woman who placed the cup in her lap while a passenger in a car. She was originally awarded punitive damages of $2.7 million.[6] Proponents of tort reform used this case as a poster child to ridicule and condemn excessive tort lawsuits. Now, if viewed in this narrow time frame (which was often the way the story was recounted), the award does seem extraordinary. But if we take a broader time frame and consider that in the ten years prior to the incident McDonald's had received over 700 reports of people burned by its coffee and nonetheless continued to require its franchisees to serve coffee at 180–190 degrees Fahrenheit (this will produce third-degree burns in a matter of sec-onds), then the punitive damages no longer seem so outlandish.

Broad time frames allow the advocate to portray a transaction as the un-folding of a narrative: personal history can be included, events can be linked, patterns presented, motivations developed, entourage introduced, and so on. The broad time frame thus allows the development of cultural narratives.

A narrow time frame, by contrast, plucks out an event from a narrative line and thus strips it of cultural meaning, allowing the law's narratives (e.g., people are presumed to act with free will) to play a more important role. It is arguably absurd to speak here in quantitative terms about the relative import of cultural and legal meaning in characterizing the facts (particularly because culture and law are not independent of each other). And yet, if one can put this well-warranted skepticism aside for a moment, it does seem as if there is a relation here: as the time frame is extended, more "cultural stuff" becomes available to present the transaction as a coherent cultural narrative. By contrast, as the time frame is shortened, the transaction becomes a brute event stripped of cultural meaning, thus leaving intelligibility and meaning to be fashioned and supplied by the law's account of human motivation (free will, rational actors, etc.).

Broad and narrow time frames can also affect the theory of the case. Con-sider, for instance, the famous torts case of *Palsgraf v. Long Island Railroad.*[7] The plaintiff, Ms. Palsgraf, was injured by an exploding box of fireworks on a railroad platform. The plaintiff's lawyer developed his theory of the case within the limits of a relatively narrow time frame. The relevant transaction, according to the plaintiff's lawyer, began with a third-party passenger trying to climb onto a moving train carrying a package. The lawyer argued that it was the railroad guard's negligence in pushing a passenger onto a moving train that caused the passenger's package of fireworks to fall down and explode, thereby causing vibrations that in turn caused a scale to fall apart roughly twenty-five or thirty feet away, where the plaintiff was standing. The plaintiff sustained bodily injury. Justice Cardozo denied liability on a zone of danger rationale—namely, that the risk posed by the guard's negligence was to the third-party passenger (different person) and his package (different interest damaged), not to Ms. Palsgraf, standing many feet away.

Over the years, it has been pointed out that the plaintiff's lawyer might have done much better to pick a somewhat broader time frame for his theory of the case. He might have argued that the railroad's negligence lay in not securing the scale strongly enough to keep it from falling down. The securing of the scale (or the failure to do so in a reasonable way) is, of course, something that would have occurred long before the train, the passenger, and Ms. Palsgraf even entered the station. According to this theory of the case, the railroad was arguably negligent because vibrations from incoming and outgoing trains could quite foreseeably dislocate the scale. The fact that the scale was ultimately shaken loose by explosives (not a train's vibrations) would not negate the railroad's liability, or so the argument goes, because it was still within the scope of the risk posed by the insecure scale that some vibration would jolt it loose. Certainly, if the plaintiff's lawyer had selected this broader time frame, then Ms. Palsgraf, standing right by the scale, would have been within the *spatial ambit* of Justice Cardozo's zone of danger.

As will be seen below, changing the time frame can be used to alter conclusions about whether an action is voluntary or coerced. This matters because in law whether an action is deemed voluntary or coerced can affect liability or culpability. Voluntariness will usually imply blame and responsibility on the part of the voluntary actor, while coercion will usually imply blamelessness and exculpation on the part of the coerced actor.

How then does changing time frames allow for showings of voluntariness or coercion? As a general matter (not always), a broad time frame will make it possible to trace what seems to be a blameless or involuntary action back in time to a voluntary choice or action (such as the choice to drink excessively, the choice to drive a car knowing that one has a heart condition, the choice to limit product quality control, the choice to cut the research and development budget, etc.). Similarly, it is often possible (not always) to trace a seemingly intentional choice and action back to some coercive external force (such as the threat of grave bodily harm, the risk of freezing to death, etc.)

Again, of course, the selection of broad and narrow time frames responds to both rhetorical and legal considerations. This "tracing back" of an action to a choice or instead to a coercive force is not something that can be discerned from the action itself. It is rhetorically constructed. A word of caution is warranted here: it is possible for an advocate to engage in what might be called overkill—overdoing an insistence on choice or coercion to a degree that is unpersuasive. In the context of time frames, overkill happens when an advocate insists on a frame that is too narrow or too broad to be believed by the decision-maker. There are no recipes, no algorithms here. This is rhetoric, not science.

III. Segmented vs. Continuous Transactions

The *Palsgraf* case mentioned above serves to illustrate another framing issue—often very important to the outcome of a case. Consider that if one starts with Cardozo's description of the sequence of events, it seems as if one has many steps to follow in tracing the harm (the scale falling on Ms. Palsgraf) back to the initial negligence (the porter pushing the passenger onto the train). First, there is the guard's initial negligence in pushing the passenger. Then, there is the package falling down. Then, there is the package exploding and causing serious vibrations. Then, the scale comes undone as the result of the vibration. Then, it falls on Ms. Palsgraf who is thereby injured. Now, this multistep description is an example of a segmented transaction: the occurrence is described as a sequence of many distinct steps from origin to end point. Notice how this multiplication of discrete successive steps serves to attenuate the foreseeability of the accident and thus appears to attenuate the causal responsibility of the initial act for the final conclusion. The sequence of events seems so odd as to seem unforeseeable.

Contrast Justice Cardozo's segmented description of the transaction with that of Justice Andrews, which seems more continuous. Justice Andrews, in talking about proximate cause, invokes images of tributaries flowing into rivers, of rocks thrown into ponds producing ripples that go on endlessly. This imagery arguably invites a different framing of the action in *Palsgraf*: the guard let loose a negligence flowing uninterruptedly out toward the world, whereupon it encountered and injured Ms. Palsgraf. For this, the guard and the railroad are responsible and, thus, justly liable. From the Andrews perspective, the particular steps in this transaction are of no moment—there is a continuous flow from the initial negligence of the defendant to the plaintiff's harm. If we are to cut off liability (on grounds of proximate cause), then we can only do so, according to Andrews, by relying (somewhat arbitrarily) on grounds of policy and expediency, by refusing to follow the causal chain.

While segmented vs. continuous transactions can be combined with broad and narrow time frames, they are not the same thing. What is at stake with segmented vs. continuous transactions is whether a given time frame is broken up into segments or is treated as unitary.

The consequences of doing one or the other can be dramatic. There are some rules of thumb here. By definition, a segmented framing will break a transaction into a sequence of discrete events, whereas a continuous framing will aggregate a sequence of events into a unitary transaction.[8] Breaking a transaction into discrete segments will generally multiply the sources of harm or injury, allow for breaks in the chain of causation, provide for discrete points at which liability can be cut off, and tend to subdivide the harm or injury sustained into different aspects. Continuous framing, by contrast, makes causation seem unbroken, renders any cutoff of liability arguably arbitrary, and tends to unify the harm or injury sustained into an indivisible whole. (These are general rules of thumb, not fixed truths by any means.)

Notice that the persuasiveness of a segmented or continuous framing depends upon contextual, rhetorical, and legal considerations. Accordingly, the selection of a frame is subject to overkill—overdoing it to a degree that is unpersuasive. Hence, if an advocate overdoes the breakdown of a transaction into too many discrete parts, everyone will catch on, and the argument will appear overly specific, contrived, and thus unpersuasive. Similarly, if an advocate grossly overlooks a sequence of seemingly discrete events in favor of a continuous flow, the argument will seem overly abstract, an effort to hide something through generality, and will be unconvincing. How much is too much segmentation or too much continuity? That turns out to be a matter of context, rhetoric, and law.

Notice that it is possible to combine broad and narrow time frames with segmentation vs. continuous framing. Thus, the segmentation and the continuity can refer specifically to time periods (as opposed to events). Breaking down a broad time frame into a series of discrete events is what allows lawyers and judges to attribute some act or harm to different agents. It is what allows the law professor to break down transactions into the familiar "$T_1, T_2 \ldots$" (or "time 1," "time 2 . . .") contexts. This happens a lot in criminal law and tort law, where the court has to examine a series of distinct (though related) acts to see if any trigger liability.

IV. Action vs. Omission

As a theoretical matter, a party's conduct can be described as either an action or an omission. We can say that the driver was driving carelessly (an action), or we can say that he failed to pay attention (an omission). We can say that he drove through the stop sign (action), or we can say he failed to apply pressure on the brake (omission). Most conduct is susceptible to description in this way as action or omission. Sometimes, of course, one or the other description will seem morally or descriptively obtuse. Imagine, for instance, a fight in a back alley. Which is likely to be the better description of the incident? The defendant struck the plaintiff in the head with the bat, or the plaintiff failed to move his head away from the downward trajectory of the defendant's bat?

The description of a party's conduct as either action or omission does not always matter. But often it does. Generally, if the objective is to ascribe responsibility, liability, or culpability to a particular party, then framing the transaction as an action rather than an omission is likely to be more persuasive. Likewise if the point is to establish a change in legal relations (i.e., from unmarried to married, no contract to contract). Indeed, a tremendous number of legal formalities (e.g., consideration) are described in law as actions, not omissions.

So why is that? In part, it is because an action tends to spring out of the context as a *distinct* occurrence, at a *particular* point in time, authored by a *definite* agent. In accordance with the theatrical metaphor (to be discussed later) an action appears to be the definite contribution of a specific actor to the scene. It is thus relatively easy to attribute to that specific actor choice, blame, or responsibility for that definite contribution. An omission, by contrast, is the recognition that something didn't happen. Accordingly, an omission is not necessarily distinct from the background or context; it tends to be ongoing and attributable to several, perhaps even many, agents, and perhaps even to the background itself. To put it metaphorically, absent special relations between the parties, omissions do not distinguish themselves. There is no differentiation from the background, the other agents, other moments in time.

To illustrate, consider a rescuer who starts to save a drowning person on a crowded beach (an action) as contrasted with the failure of all beachgoers to rescue the drowning person (omissions). In the first case, we have a distinct act that we can analyze substantively and evidentially for liability or culpability. In the second case, just *what* and *whose* omission do we analyze, and how do we know what to say about it? Nothing happened—the beachgoers just lay there. Perhaps they didn't see the problem. Perhaps they didn't care. Perhaps they thought someone more appropriate or adept would rescue the drowning person. A performance, by contrast, always says something. Actions tend to reveal the actor's motivations. A conscious act seems to reveal a certain intention as well as direction. An omission, by contrast, seems mute. We ask, "Why didn't X do anything?" and the omission reveals nothing: he wasn't paying attention, he had more important things to do, he didn't like the victim, he didn't know, or he was doing something else. Who can tell?

Accordingly, the law itself often seizes on action to predicate liability, culpability, or more generally a change in the relation of the parties. Consider, for instance, how these key actions are seized upon in various areas of law to predicate liability, culpability, or a change in legal relations:

Actus reus (generally a requirement for criminal liability)

Overt act (a requirement for conspiracy)

Signature (often a requirement to give legal effect to a will, a trust, a documentary transaction)

Delivery (often a necessary element for the transfer of property)

Filing (often a requirement for triggering hearings, motions, etc.)

Swearing (a requirement for the rendition of testimony)

Now, it is important not to overstate the importance of action vis-à-vis omission. For one thing, as will be seen later, the action/omission distinction is neither metaphysically secure nor experientially perspicuous. For another, there are some contexts where omissions are routinely and noncontroversially actionable. Failure to perform contracts, to file taxes, to respond to summons, and so on are examples of situations where omissions are obviously actionable. But, of course, these are instances where a body of law effectively provides that a failure to perform some *specific* action in response to the occurrence of some *specific* event in some *specified* legal relation will bring about legal consequences. The interesting question, of course, is how, when, and to what extent we will read or construe the law to require affirmative obligations to perform so that a failure to perform becomes actionable.

There is an obvious political aspect here. Indeed, the more one sees the human community as interconnected and interdependent (a left or progressive stance), the easier it is to find reliance, an undertaking, an agreement, or a special relation that will give rise to affirmative obligations. Formalities (e.g., explicit contracts), in accordance with this political view, might well be deemed unnecessary; the dependence and obligations can simply be inferred from cultural forms and meanings. Thus, it has been argued that a company that has employed citizens for generations has arguably induced reliance on the part of its workforce.[9] The company owes something to the community and cannot simply shut down or pull up roots without taking care of its laborers.

By contrast, the more one sees human beings as independent atomistic individuals (a right or libertarian stance), the more reticent one will be to infer affirmative obligations in the absence of formalities (e.g., explicit contracts). Community and culture are seen as artificial constructs composed of many independent individuals, and, accordingly, it would be a mistake to infer from such thin concepts (community or culture) any strong affirmative obligations. Thus, it has been argued that the quasi-contract cause of action should be extremely limited and that there should be no duty to rescue—neither in tort nor in criminal law.[10]

With regard to the action/omission or act/failure to act distinction, the problem lies in the difficulties posed in reading the culture as to which is which. Sometimes, of course, it is pretty easy: if a driver claims that he went cruising through the stop sign merely because of his failure to apply pressure on the brake (an omission), we will have no practical difficulty setting aside this argument by pointing out that what matters is that he ran the stop sign (an action). If, then, he points out that he was simply not paying attention to the stop sign (an omission), we will have no practical difficulty pointing out that what matters is that he was driving carelessly (an action). If he points out that his driving was merely a failure to use public transport (an omission), we will have no difficulty pointing out that it was his affirmative decision to get in the car and drive (an action). The point is that often we are already so committed to viewing something as an action (or as an omission) that there is no point in arguing the contrary.

But not all cases are easy. Consider the famous *Moch Co. v. Rensselaer Water Co.* case in which a waterworks company contracted with the City of Rensselaer to supply water.[11] Water was to be furnished to the city—including for use at fire hydrants. Water was also to be supplied to residents and industries at a reasonable rate. While the contracts were in force, a fire broke out and spread to the plaintiff's warehouse; the plaintiff then sued the waterworks company, claiming that the company did not furnish water in sufficient quantities or with sufficient pressure to extinguish the fire. Justice Cardozo denied liability, offering a distinction between "withholding a benefit" and actively "working an injury."[12] The question, he said, "is whether the putative wrongdoer has advanced to such a point as to have *launched a force or instrument of harm*, or has stopped where inaction is at most *a refusal to become an instrument for good*."[13] This attempt to resolve the action/omission distinction is but a restatement of the same and is of very little (if any) analytical value in this context. One can just as easily characterize the waterworks company's conduct in one way as the other.

V. Level of Abstraction

The level of abstraction (also called the level of generality) is perhaps the most pervasive and most perplexing framing issue in law. The expression, as its name indicates, refers to the relative abstraction or concreteness, generality or particularity, at which a lawyer or a judge apprehends or casts the transaction, the law, or the issues. We focus first on levels of abstraction with respect to the law.

Perhaps the most ubiquitous example of the level of abstraction in the modern common law system involves "broad and narrow" case holdings. The idea, relatively simple, is that the holding in an opinion can be stated at different levels of abstraction. Here is an illustration of broad and narrow case holdings offered by Herman Oliphant, a famous legal realist thinker, in 1928:

> A's father induces her not to marry B as she promised to do. On a holding that the father is not liable to B for so doing, a gradation of widening propositions can be built, a few of which are:
>
> 1. Fathers are privileged to induce daughters to break promises to marry.
> 2. Parents are so privileged.
> 3. Parents are so privileged as to both daughters and sons.
> 4. All persons are so privileged as to promises to marry.
> 5. Parents are so privileged as to all promises made by their children.
> 6. All persons are so privileged as to all promises made by any one.[14]

Here is another example of the broad and narrow case holdings problem, taken from the famous case of *Brown v. Board of Education I*.[15] In that case the Supreme Court decided that separate but equal is "inherently unequal" and, accordingly, unconstitutional.[16] But what precisely is the right recognized by *Brown v. Board of Education I*? If we read the opinion on its own (i.e., bracketing subsequent history) we have the following possibilities:

ABSTRACT
    A right to integrated education
        A right to redress of all the noxious effects of segregated education
            A right to be free from both de jure and de facto educational segregation
                A right to have intentional dual school systems dismantled
                    A right to have official dual system rules and policies no longer enforced
                  CONCRETE

As one descends in the level of abstraction, the scope, intensity, and value of the right recognized decreases.

Consider another famous example: in *Griswold v. Connecticut*, the Supreme Court struck down a Connecticut statute that prohibited the use of contraceptives.[17] Again, the level of abstraction of the right in question was left somewhat unclear by the opinion in that case. If we put subsequent history aside, we can conceptualize the right recognized in that case as follows:

ABSTRACT
    A generalized right to privacy for all private matters
        A right to be free from government regulation of private sexual
        and family matters
            A right of married couples to be free from government
            regulation of private family planning matters
                A right of married couples to use contraceptives in
                the privacy of their bedroom
                   CONCRETE

Why does the level of abstraction matter? The answer is straightforward: a high level of abstraction will generally (substance aside) lead to a broader, more inclusive scope, while a low level of abstraction (substance aside) will lead to a narrower, less inclusive scope. Questions about the appropriate level of abstraction for a holding arise just about any time a party argues that a particular precedent is applicable. Consider a defendant arguing that a search occurred under the Fourth Amendment when an officer inserted a key into the door of the defendant's apartment, simply to see if the key fit.[18] The defendant argued that a previous decision, where a court held that putting a key into an automobile lock was not a search, should not control. Is the earlier decision applicable to any property with a lock owned by the defendant (automobiles, apartments, houses)? Or do we proceed at a lower level of abstraction and consider the character of the property and its relation to privacy? In the apartment case, the defendant argued that he had a greater privacy interest in his apartment than he would in a car, so the previous holding about the keys and the automobile should not control.

Clearly judges and other decision-makers routinely make decisions about levels of abstraction. But as with the other framing options we have discussed, there is not a whole lot to be said about what level of abstraction to use in any given case.[19]

And accordingly, normative arguments about levels of abstraction often feel infirm. Justice Scalia, for instance, advanced the idea that in fundamental rights cases the Court should "refer to *the most specific level* at which a relevant tradition protecting, or denying to, the asserted right can be identified."[20] The reason for this approach, according to Justice Scalia, is to avoid "arbitrary decisionmaking" in which judges "dictate" their own values. The main problem with Justice Scalia's approach, of course, is that "avoiding arbitrary decisionmaking" is not itself a constitutional standard (let alone, a very specific one). The relevant constitutional standard is whatever the Constitution requires or authorizes. In turn it does not take much imagination to recognize that sometimes what it requires is rather abstract and general, while at other times it is rather concrete and specific.

If justifying the appropriate level of abstraction is difficult (and it is), so too is the more rudimentary task of merely specifying the appropriate level of abstraction. To be sure, we can invoke notions such as general and specific, or abstract and concrete, but ironically these also lack precision. Sometimes the only thing we can do is urge others to be more specific and concrete or, in the alternative, more general and abstract. But doing that (without more) amounts to little more than saying, "Go in this direction." (That statement, however, doesn't tell us how far.) What we clearly cannot do, however, is deliver specific instructions as to how to achieve the appropriate level of abstraction.

Nonetheless, in some instances, the appropriate level of specificity or generality might be an explicit part of the doctrine. Consider the doctrine of qualified immunity for public officials: officials are not entitled to immunity if the constitutional right violated was "clearly established" at the time of the conduct. The Supreme Court has "repeatedly told courts . . . not to define clearly established law at a high level of generality."[21] Similar analysis takes place in the habeas context, where one of the requirements for relief in the Antiterrorism and Effective Death Penalty Act of 1996 (AEDPA) is "an unreasonable application of clearly established Federal law, as determined by the Supreme Court of the United States."[22] The "clearly established" language here sets up the same strategic battle over descriptions of Supreme Court holdings: plaintiffs seeking habeas relief will cast holdings broadly so that they include the wrong they are alleging, while the government will seek to cast holdings narrowly so they do not.

Or consider foreseeability analysis in a negligence claim, where a plaintiff must prove that the harm that took place was reasonably foreseeable. A common issue in such cases is the level of abstraction at which the harmful act should be characterized. For example, should a landlord have foreseen that the child of a tenant would take a very large rock from debris on the property and throw it out of a third-floor window?[23] One can imagine the landlord's argument that he could not possibly have foreseen that a child would actually carry one of the large rocks on the property to the third floor and throw it out of a window, causing injury to a second child. But the court concluded that the appropriate level of abstraction with which to characterize the harm was "getting hurt by a large rock thrown by another child" (as opposed to "getting hurt by a large rock thrown by a child from the third floor") and that such a harm was certainly foreseeable. Notice the familiar dialectic with foreseeability: if you want to make something seem foreseeable, describe it very abstractly; if you want to make it seem unforeseeable, describe it very concretely. Of course, advocates and decision-makers know the trick and are unlikely to be taken in. And, of course, what matters ultimately is that the transaction be described only in those factual terms relevant to the legal claim. In this regard, does it matter that the rock-throwing child was only ten years old? That the rock weighed eighteen pounds? One might think that the reason opinions often fail to specify the level of abstraction stems from poor drafting. That may well be true sometimes, but not invariably so. The underspecification of the level of abstraction in a given case is often simply a function of the fact that law (and its language) simply does not allow full specification. Part of that is the vagueness and imprecision of language itself. Part of it, however, has to do with the relations of law to itself—its various permitted forms of self-reference. If a doctrine can be understood simultaneously in terms of and yet also in isolation from its various principles, policies, values, goals, considerations, and interests, then specifying the level of abstraction becomes a difficult business. Any later interpreter of law will always have the possibility of invoking or excluding something (a principle, a policy, a countervailing consideration, etc.) in such a way as to upset the earlier efforts to specify the level of abstraction. Whether and when such efforts will prove *convincing* to the decision-maker is, of course, a different matter.

There is an even more simple way in which the level of abstraction is often underspecified: readers of statutes or judicial opinions will have different views about how to interpret them. Some readers will read an opinion for its *narrowest possible meaning*, while others will read the opinion for *its general implications*, and yet others will avoid precommitments to generality or its absence. As to which is the correct approach—that question too escapes definitive answer. The answer will depend among other things upon (1) the legal and factual context and (2) the jurisprudential commitments (what counts as law) of the interpreter. Both of these, in turn, are themselves not fully specified or indeed capable of full specification.

The important point here is that the level of abstraction problem is not merely a technical problem of language (though it is that). It is also a jurisprudential problem: it implicates and is implicated in one's theory of what law is or should be (and in turn the way that the *is* and the *should* relate to each other in law). The level of abstraction affects and is affected by one's theory of law: the proper approach to interpretation, legislative history, precedents, history, tradition, and so on. The annals of law are quite conflicted on this score. One can easily find authorities and justifications for the view that decisions should be narrowly framed and context-specific. But one can just as easily find authorities and justifications for the view that a decision needs to be decided on general principles that transcend the immediate factual context.

The level of abstraction problem plays a role not simply in the characterization of law and issues, but in the characterization of the transaction—the facts of the case. Let's turn to the First Amendment flag-burning cases by way of illustration. In those cases, typically, a dissenter burns or desecrates a flag to protest some action of the government. Now, how is the "burning of the flag" supposed to be described factually? What's going on here? Consider some possibilities:

ABSTRACT
    Political speech
        Desecrating a political symbol
            Destroying a flag
                Burning a piece of cloth
                    CONCRETE

Which is the appropriate description of the transaction for purposes of First Amendment analysis? It's not clear. And yet, clearly, the choice of characterization matters. If the dissident is engaged in political speech, then that would seem to suggest that the expression is protected by freedom of speech. If, on the other hand, the dissident is merely destroying a flag, then the question seems to be more debatable.

Characterizing the underlying transaction at a particular level of abstraction has nearly limitless possibilities and is obviously highly strategic—for an advocate seeking to persuade a decision-maker, and for a decision-maker seeking to justify her decision. This decision about the appropriate level of abstraction is just one of the kinds of framing choices discussed above, and all of these framing choices overlap. A broader view of the transaction is likely to incorporate a longer period of time; a narrow concrete view might be more likely to focus on distinct segments of a transaction. Choices about the characterization of the act, the scene, the agent, and so on are likely to involve choices about the level of abstraction. It might be helpful to think about all of these decisions as part of a production—like that of a movie or a play. Every aspect of that production is a decision: what to include, what to leave out, whether to provide a 20,000-foot view or an up-close and personal shot, how to depict the characters, where to start the story, and where to end it. Every aspect of a legal case must be presented — it exists only as it is presented in the course of litigation, and that involves making choices at every turn.

A different kind of challenge posed by the level of abstraction problem is to maintain roughly the same level of abstraction in describing competing values, interests, policies, and principles. Suppose we are going to identify the various values on both sides of the flag-burning scenario. Here is a preliminary take:

On One Side: Freedom of Speech Values and Considerations, in No Particular Order
Political speech
Dissent
Symbolic expression
Use of the flag to express dissent
Use of this flag to express dissent
Use of all government symbols to express dissent

On the Other Side: Government Interests, in No Particular Order
This flag
Flag as symbol of national solidarity
Meaning of the flag to all citizens/veterans
All American flags
All flags
This particular piece of cloth

It's not hard to see that, depending on the level of abstraction, we could produce different outcomes. If what is at stake is a tension between political speech generally and the preservation of this flag in particular, it's not hard to see that the speech interests will win. If, by contrast, the tension revolves around the use of this particular flag to express dissent as against the flag as a symbol of national solidarity, then the government interest becomes more weighty. These comparisons or juxtapositions are sufficiently skewed that it is easy to anticipate the result. At the same time, of course, it seems obvious that these particular comparisons or juxtapositions are tendentiously asymmetrical and thus unacceptable: they seem both to trivialize one side of the issue (through concretization) and to inflate the other (through abstraction). But the fact that we may agree on this (assume we do) does not tell us precisely what would be an appropriate way to frame the issue for a court. To figure out what is wrong doesn't necessarily tell us how to get things right.

We need to answer the crucial question: How can we tell that the various considerations on both sides are each stated at the same level of abstraction? We might say that we ought to take cognizance of competing values, interests, policies, principles, and values at roughly *the same* level of abstraction.

This is easily said, but less easily done: How do we tell when we are operating at the same level of abstraction?[24] The most one can say is "approach the question abstractly" or "approach the question more concretely." This is not nothing—but it's not a lot.

VI. The Theater Metaphor

A trial can be analyzed as a kind of theater: the courtroom as scene; the witnesses, parties, and lawyers as agents; the direct and cross-examination as action (and so on and so forth). The idea that a trial itself is a kind of theater (or that it can be analyzed as such) is perhaps obvious. Less obvious, but equally important, is that the analysis of the underlying transaction at issue (e.g., an accident, a homicide) can also be viewed in theatrical terms.

What is significant here, for our purposes, is that competing accounts of the transaction can themselves be analyzed by thinking about them in explicitly theatrical or dramatistic terms. Kenneth Burke, the great American thinker of rhetoric, proposed that social, political, and literary accounts of human action can be analyzed in terms of various theatrical elements and their relations (or ratios, as he called them). Table 2.1 shows Burke's key theatrical elements.[25]

Thus, in framing a transaction, it is possible to give different accounts that ascribe causality or responsibility to the various different elements: action, scene, agent, agency, and purpose. Consider, as an extended example here, the gun control debate. One side sums up its position with the slogan "Guns kill people." The other side answers back, "People kill people." The first position (guns kill people) ascribes causality to the presence of an *agency*, which if removed from the *scene*, would prevent the *action*, the killing, from occurring. The second position (people kill people) ascribes responsibility to the *agents* who will use any *agency* on the *scene* to produce the *action*, the killing. For the first position (guns kill people), the essential element is the *agency* (the gun). For the second position (people kill people), the essential element is the predisposition of the *agent*.

TABLE 2.1. Burke's Key Theatrical Elements

Act	What was done?
Scene	When and where was it done?
Agent	Who did it?
Agency	How was it done?
Purpose	Why was it done?

Notice the way that there is room, aesthetically and rhetorically speaking, to see things either way. We can pursue the arguments at great length. The anti-gun people can point out that the *agency* (the gun) is so easy to use and so lethal that it is appropriate to treat it differently from other possible instrumentalities of harm. Meanwhile, the pro-gun people can respond that actors who kill are motivated by such virulence that they would inexorably find some other agency—a knife, a paperweight, a rock, and so on—to kill.

The anti-gun people and the pro-gun people can elaborate their arguments by changing the focus on a different set of agents, actions, and scenes. For instance, the anti-gun people can switch things around so that we are now dealing with a different kind of hypothetical action: an accidental shooting or suicide. They can point out that the lethal character of guns means that the availability of guns creates many preventable accidental and senseless shootings. The pro-gun people can switch the focus as well by changing the character of the scene and the action: self-defense. Indeed, that is precisely what the pro-gun people do when they argue that "when guns are outlawed, only outlaws will have guns."

The important point here is a simple one—namely, to recognize that the aesthetic/rhetorical attribution of causal efficacy to different theatrical elements (e.g., *agency*, *agent*, or *action*) can advance (or hinder) different conclusions about what caused what.

> *Example: Consider the fall of the Soviet Union. It can be ascribed to an agent (Gorbachev) and an instance of the "Great Man theory of history."* [26] *Or it can be described in terms of a set of actions—an economically destructive arms race with the United States. Or it can be described in terms of a scene—the collapse of a culturally and politically demoralized infrastructure. It all depends on what elements of the theatrical metaphor—scene, agent, agency, action, purpose—are emphasized.*

By way of a more detailed illustration, consider the obscure (but wonderfully evocative) tort case of *Verduce v. Board of Education*, whose facts help show how the theatrical metaphor might be played out in law. [27] In that case, the plaintiff, Rosalie Verduce, enrolled in a non-credit course called the "Hunter College Opera Workshop" in New York City. The class put on a performance of the opera *Xerxes* directed by the defendant teacher, Mr. Turnau. During a rehearsal, Turnau directed Verduce to make a "haughty exit" without looking down. This involved stepping twenty inches from the stage down to the auditorium floor. Verduce protested that to step off the stage without looking down would be dangerous. Turnau told Verduce that her failure to follow his direction would result in loss of the part. Verduce then stepped down and twisted her ankle. The injuries led to the lawsuit.

Now, in terms of the applicable tort law, there are a number of relevant doctrines. One question is whether Turnau's actions were themselves a breach of the standard of reasonable care. Second, there is the question of whether under the doctrine of primary assumption of risk the voluntariness of the students' enrollment in the class somehow *lessens the duty owed* to Verduce. Third is whether Turnau can avail himself of an *affirmative defense* of secondary assumption of risk. Fourth, there is the question of whether Verduce was contributorily negligent in any way. These are the significant legal claims floating around. The thing that is interesting about this case is the way in which the framing of the case affects the conclusions reached.

Notice that the evidence here is susceptible to all sorts of different characterizations in light of broad and narrow time frames, segmented vs. continuous transactions, actions and omissions. We will disregard all that and organize the analysis in terms of some (not all) of Burke's theatrical elements. The idea here is that (1) by according a particular element a certain characterization and (2) by emphasizing that element, it is possible to attach responsibility to the plaintiff or to the defendant.

There is an agent/agent relation here between Turnau and Verduce. What is the nature of this relation? It can be characterized as teacher/student and director/actor. The former relationship implies an asymmetry of knowledge, expertise, and responsibility (up to a point). This can affect the reasonableness calculus inasmuch as Turnau could think of other options more easily than Verduce—a ten-inch platform, taking off her shoes? This framing of relation as teacher/student matters. It cuts in Verduce's favor in that Turnau's superior position makes it easier to find his behavior more unreasonable than her behavior. On the other hand, the director/actor relationship arguably cuts in favor of Turnau because as director he has responsibilities to the play— artistic excellence and all that. Perhaps a haughty exit actually is required?

But now we get to *scene*. What is the scene here? It can be described in a variety of ways: it is an opera, a workshop, a rehearsal. The opera aspect seems to be the scene most favorable to Turnau because it allows him to say that the scene (the opera) requires certain behavior—notably, the haughty exit. Meanwhile, the characterization of the scene as a rehearsal seems most favorable to Verduce. Indeed, if this is merely a rehearsal, surely it is possible to bypass the "haughty exit" until Verduce is trained, rendered more confident, or allowed to do something else. There is no urgency or real need in a rehearsal. Notice too another scene—namely, New York City (legendary venue for desperate aspiring artists.) It would be interesting to know to what extent this workshop and the later play performance were purely an affair for amateurs and novices or instead an important venue for an actor in the local scene. Either way, of course, there are arguments to be made on both sides. If we are talking about a workshop for amateurs and novices, then the actors are prone to coercion by a director because they lack experience (there is a knowledge asymmetry between the director and the actors). If we are talking about professionals, the actors are susceptible to coercion for a different reason: the stakes (i.e., a job, a role) are high.

Now consider how to frame the *agency*—namely, the twenty inches between stage and auditorium floor. This agency was arguably in the control of the defendant, who, if we frame him as possessed of superior knowledge and expertise, could have devised some other exit mechanism (e.g., a ten-inch platform, no shoes, a haughty exit to the side of the stage).

One of the things that will be unavoidable in this litigation is to deal in some way with *purpose*: Was there a valid non-trivial educational or artistic purpose served in requiring the haughty exit? Notice that identifying the purpose would help reveal the benefit in the cost-benefit version of reasonable care. And if there was no benefit to be gained from a haughty exit from a twenty-inch platform, then clearly Turnau was negligent.

What exactly was the nature of the *action* here? What exactly was being done (1) when Turnau told Verduce that she must step down and (2) when Turnau told her that otherwise she would lose the part? Was this coaxing, coaching, admonishment, intimidation, threat, coercion, or what? And whatever it was, can we say it was required by the scene, by the play, by the class? And what about her action—was she protesting, negotiating, expressing a lack of confidence, fear, or what?

All of these inquiries about agent, scene, agency, action, and purpose can be developed by counsel for Verduce and Turnau to facilitate or frustrate conclusions about reasonableness, unreasonableness, voluntariness, coercion— all of which may be relevant to the ultimate legal conclusions about whether there is or is not liability. Notice how rich the possibilities are here. In part, that is because the choice of how to describe one element (e.g., scene) will affect other elements (e.g., agent). It is all quite interactive in precisely the way that a piece of theater is interactive.

Burke's dramatistic theory is considerably more sophisticated than this brief introduction allows. Among other things, when we start linking one dramatistic term to another (say, scene and agent) we can tease out the philosophical possibilities. Does scene determine agent? Do agents construct scenes?

VII. Exit-Framing

As its name implies, exit-framing is the frame the author leaves with the reader or the audience. Doctrinal argument aims to be transformative. It aims specifically at making it difficult for the judge or decision-maker to rule for the other side, and easy to rule for one's own. This means that there is movement in doctrinal arguments—whether they are contained in judicial opinions, briefs, or law review articles. The idea is to start with an entry frame acceptable to the reader and bring him or her along to a different exit frame. This is true even for those who argue for the status quo: they hope to make the case for maintaining the existing regime *stronger and more compelling*.

What then can be said about the exit frame? When it's well done, the reader or the audience has been moved to a new position, a new orientation, a new frame. It is as if the reader or the audience were now on a new stage— looking out at a new scene, perhaps populated with new characters, or attended by new agencies, and motivated by a sense of new urgencies, primed for some different kind of action.

And when it's badly done, it falls flat.

3

Baselines

In legal analysis, disputes often turn upon a claim that a party's conduct is an unlawful *deviation*. The question is, A deviation from what precisely? The answer: A deviation from some applicable norm—some controlling statute, some relevant doctrine or the like. How does one tell whether there has been an unlawful deviation? Well, very often, the norm itself specifies the baseline very clearly, and accordingly no real issue arises.

> *Example 1: Did the defendant exceed the speed limit? "Yes, he was going over 55 mph—the speed limit for that stretch of road." Here, 55 mph counts as the baseline, and there is no difficulty identifying it.*

> *Example 2: A "revocation-on-divorce" statute automatically voids a spouse's beneficiary designation upon divorce. Here the baseline will be clear nearly all the time—to wit, a valid divorce.*

> *Example 3: In many jurisdictions, two witnesses are specified by statute as the baseline for a valid will that is not in the testator's handwriting. Fewer than two witnesses and the will is not valid.*

Specific baselines can be not only statutory, but constitutional or regulatory or common law. For instance, the US Constitution specifies thirty-five as the minimum age qualification for the Office of President; traditional common law rules provide that a person under eighteen lacks the capacity to enter into a contract. When a numerical value is specified, the baseline (at least as to that aspect) generally leaves little room for debate. So far so good then: no significant baseline problems.

Often, however, the applicable norm will not be fully clear in describing the relevant baseline. Specificity will have gone on holiday. Ambiguity reigns. Vagueness suffuses the scene. Whatever the problem, the advocates and the decision-maker are left wondering, Well, what is the baseline here? In litigation, this actually happens a lot.[1]

The US Constitution is rich with provisions that do not specify concrete baselines. Insofar as it does not "partake of the prolixity of a legal code . . . and only its great outlines should be marked," underspecification is definitely a constitutional strong suit (the "broad outlines").[2] In turn, this underspecification leads to disagreements about the appropriate baselines. For instance, the Fifth Amendment provides that "private property" shall not be "taken" for public use, without just compensation.[3] In order to decide whether an unconstitutional taking has occurred, some *baseline* conception of "private property" seems to be required. Indeed, it is only if "private property" has been *taken* that the provision comes into play. The challenge here is that there are several plausible candidates for the baseline conception of "private property." These may lead, depending upon the context, to different conclusions about what is and what is not a taking. One possibility, for instance, is to say that the baseline for a taking is limited to whatever was generally conceptualized as private property at the time the Fifth Amendment was ratified. Another possibility is to say that the baseline for a taking is whatever is considered today as private property (at common law or in statutes). And, of course, there are other possibilities. The general point, though, is that the various options will, at least in some cases, yield different conclusions as to what counts as a taking.

When a baseline is vague or not specified, attorneys have an opportunity to advocate for a favored baseline and to challenge less favorable ones. Examples of underspecified baselines abound. If a statute prohibits "unfair competition," what is the baseline that establishes fair competition? If a statute allows a defendant to expunge his criminal record when he has "lived an honest and upright life," what is the baseline for such a life? (Interestingly, according to one court it is impossible to live an honest and upright life while in prison.[4])

Notice one important exception to all this. It's not clear that in every case where we seek to identify a wrong, we need to have an explicit baseline. The "one case at a time" common law approach of juridical decision-making allows courts to make determinations such as "*This* is unconscionable, *this* shocks the conscience, *this* is . . ." without defining a baseline. The rationale for this approach is simple and well known: "Whatever the baseline may be (there can be disagreement) *this* conduct is so over the top, so clearly unacceptable by any (reasonable? conceivable?) baseline that we can say it's a wrong. Full stop." Notice that the same pattern can also arise when we are talking about conformity with a baseline. There too it seems sometimes possible to say: "We don't really know what the baseline is, but we are convinced that this case conforms with whatever the baseline might (reasonably? conceivably?) be." In the world of doctrine, these sorts of ad hoc determinations seem suitable only (if at all) in extreme cases. The closer we get to the proverbial boundary, as it were, the more likely we are to demand a specification of and justification for a baseline.

It is in these circumstances that the baseline problems begin. There are three such major problems, which we will call "baseline selection problems," "baseline neutrality problems," and "baseline collapse problems." Each problem is more troublesome than the prior one.

I. Baseline Selection Problems

When the law is not sufficiently specific and thus leaves some range of possible baselines from which to assess a potential deviation, the question arises: which baseline to pick and why? In short, the judge or decision-maker must find some way to select and justify one baseline at the expense of the others.

This matters considerably because the choice of baselines can greatly influence outcomes. In constitutional law, for instance, it often matters greatly whether the relevant baseline is the original understanding (e.g., public meaning at the time) or tradition (e.g., "the collective conscience of our people") or other bodies of law (e.g., cosmopolitan reference to foreign constitutional law). In contract law, it matters whether the meaning of contractual terms is determined by reference to the subjective agreement of the parties, the four corners of the document, the course of dealing among the parties, established industry practice, or yet something else. Indeed, in every field of law, there will be some norms or terms that are sufficiently vague or underspecified, allowing a baseline selection problem to arise.

The relationship between baseline selection and interpretation (see chapter 7, "Interpretation") is worth noting here. Whether *a baseline selection problem* arises (or not) will often depend upon what the work of *interpretation has wrought.* Thus, for instance, in principle, a baseline selection problem can be resolved by doing interpretive work and making a convincing case that a text that once seemed underspecified is upon further examination actually clear: lo and behold, it provides for baseline X. Or, conversely, interpretive work can be deployed to show that a text that seemed clear on first impression is in fact underspecified and thus presents a baseline selection problem. Once an official decision-maker decides upon a baseline (rejecting all other competitors), that may well suspend interpretation problems that might otherwise arise. Baseline selection problems and the work of legal interpretation have a significant interactive relationship.

A. CLASSIC BASELINES

Depending upon the specific legal context, baselines could be just about anything—anything that can count as the "normal" state of affairs or the "starting point" from which we can assess deviations. Despite this open-endedness, there are certain stereotyped baselines that are invoked repeatedly to provide the framework for legal analysis. The following are some of the most common sources of baselines:

Borrowing from Other Bodies of Law: When a key legal concept remains un-derspecified in one field of law, judges and other officials sometimes "import" the missing content from other fields of law. In constitutional law, for instance, the terms "liberty" and "property" used in the Fifth and Fourteenth Amendments' due process clauses have been notoriously dif-ficult to specify. Some legal thinkers have argued that *common law rights* at the time of the founding of the US Constitution should be used as the baseline to give content to these terms. Similarly, a state court might use common law as the baseline when a statute's silence on an issue is unclear (for example, does rape require "force"?).

Expectations: Sometimes the expectations of the parties serve to provide base-lines. Expectations can be used as a way to specify baselines in all sorts of legal contexts: what counts as property, whether the defendant had a duty, what the parties contracted, and so on. As a baseline, expectations will almost always be attended by an implicit or explicit qualification of reasonableness, as in the phrase "reasonable expectations."

Tradition/History: Tradition and history are often used as baselines. Refer-ences to both are made in constitutional law (e.g., "the collective con-science of our people") to furnish a frame of reference for the specification of constitutional rights. For instance, whether public property counts as a "public forum" under First Amendment doctrine depends on tradition. Likewise, the old common law rule that presumes a mother's husband is the legal father of a child born into the marriage is based on traditional societal norms.

Custom/Customary Practice: Custom involves a settled social practice that persists over time and gives shape to the performance of various tasks, ac-tions, and so on. (As such, custom might be seen as a subset of tradition/history.) Custom is used, for instance, in tort law to inform the standard of care for physician malpractice. Similarly, prevailing professional norms are used as the standard for judging whether a defendant has been deprived of effective assistance of legal counsel. Consensus in the medical community is used to determine whether medical treatment is necessary under the Eighth Amendment. Custom might be deemed relevant in any number of other contexts. Should donning and doffing uniforms count as "work time" in an employment law case? No, said one court, in part because that would disregard long-established customs.[5]

Course of Dealing: This typically refers to the settled practice among two or more parties who have some protracted relations—such as the ongoing contractual dealings between merchants. Again, this too might be considered a subset of tradition/history.

Good Faith/Reasonableness/Common Sense: These concepts are often used in actual statutes, opinions, and so on. Even when the concepts are not specified, advocates and decision-makers often invoke these ubiquitous standards as baselines to evaluate potentially deviating performance or behavior.

Status Quo: This might be understood as an extremely vague term that encompasses all or some of those above. The status quo is the sort of baseline that is often not explicitly identified. Consider, for example, a court's conclusion that the in-court identification of a defendant was constitutional because there was nothing "unusually suggestive" about it.[6] The implicit baseline here is (an ironic) status quo where apparently the usual amount of suggestiveness is acceptable.

Status Quo Ante: This would be the status quo existing *before* the challenged action or activity at issue occurred.

All of the above are used, depending upon the context, as baselines for legal analysis. They are used as the frame of reference (the "normal" state of affairs or the starting point) to assess whether there has been some actionable deviation. Notice that all of these sources are used as baselines, and yet ironically they can often present their own baseline challenges and issues in turn.

B. VARIATIONS WITHIN A SINGLE BASELINE

With regard to many of the baselines above (and others not mentioned here) certain characteristic difficulties recur. It is important to attend to these because they may influence, in any given context, not only what kind of baseline to select (e.g., expectation of the parties, custom, reasonableness), but also what content to give to a specific kind of baseline (*minimal* expectations, *reasonable* expectations, *maximal* expectations—what precisely?).

1. Level of Abstraction

The baselines all work ostensibly to give more specific content to some underspecified term (i.e., liberty, safety, etc.). The question is, How much specificity should the baseline provide? Suppose that in assessing what counts as "cruel and unusual punishment" under the Eighth Amendment of the US Constitution, we decide to use, as our baseline, whatever was considered cruel and unusual punishment at the time of the nation's founding. That may help, but it will not answer all our questions. Indeed, we can then wonder whether we should simply take the list of cruel and unusual punishments as *closed* at the time of the founding. Or do we instead try to discern or distill some *concept* of cruelty and unusual punishment from that list? If so, do we then try to *transpose analogically* what was considered cruel and unusual at the time of the founding to what might be considered cruel and unusual in our contemporary society? If *punishment A* was cruel and unusual in the late eighteenth century, do we look for what its analogue (i.e., *punishment B*) might be in contemporary circumstances? These possibilities (and more) describe different ways of setting the level of abstraction pertinent to the same baseline (namely, the punishments deemed cruel and unusual at the time of the founding). It matters, of course, because in some cases the possibilities would lead to different outcomes. (See generally the discussion of level of abstraction in chapter 2, "Frames and Framing.")

2. Individualization

Closely related to the level of abstraction problem is the *problem of individualization*. Suppose in a given tort case, we decide to use "the reasonable person in the circumstances" standard (as indeed we do in the US for ordinary negligence cases). What circumstances (age, health, mental capacity, superior training, inferior training, gender, experience, familiarity, or the like) will we take into account in terms of defining the reasonable person? Over time, common law courts have produced many different answers to these types of questions. The reasoning supporting the line drawing has not always been terribly satisfying.

Courts thus retain the power to nudge baselines in one direction or another. Courts may implicitly refuse to consider actual individual circumstances by specifying only certain characteristics as worthy of recognition.

Example: The reasonable person test in negligence law admits of certain types of individual characteristics (youth, blindness, deafness, etc.) but not certain psychiatric conditions (depression, mania, or obsession).

Sometimes, of course, the individualized conditions are themselves qualified by individualized additions. For example, terms of probation must ordinarily be such that individuals of "ordinary intelligence" can understand them. A court might put a gloss on this baseline ("ordinary intelligence") by adding that a probationer is not left to understand probation conditions on his own, but presumably has the help of a probation officer and the court. Hence, it is that the ordinary intelligence baseline becomes the ordinary intelligence with the help of an expert baseline.[7] Often, of course, advocates and decision-makers differ about how to specify the individualizing condition. Consider the "reasonable observer" baseline for determining under the establishment clause whether a challenged government act has the effect of endorsing religion. Justice O'Connor's "reasonable observer" is one who is "aware of the history and context of the community and forum in which the religious display appears,"[8] while Justice Stevens objected to O'Connor's "ideal human" as "a being finer than the tort-law model" and thus "singularly out of place in the Establishment Clause context."[9]

3. Multiplicity

Sometimes baselines turn out to be *fixed* (relatively unchanging over time, parties, geography, etc.), *closed* (the set cannot be contracted or expanded), and *unitary* (there is only one version of the baseline). But this too does not always hold. Sometimes, particularly when baselines remain somewhat abstract, the baseline is not fixed or closed or even unitary. Consider "the expectations of the parties" as a baseline. Sometimes, the decision-maker will be lucky enough to discover that the expectations of the parties are similar, perhaps even identical. But often, the two parties—being somewhat adverse in interest—will have different expectations. Then too if the parties deal with each other over a protracted period of time, their expectations may change. Or consider custom. With that baseline, it often turns out that there is not a single custom, but rather several customs. And, again, here too the customs may change over time. A legal rule can be reversed on the basis of a changed baseline. At common law, alcohol providers were protected from liability for damages caused by an intoxicated patron; eventually some courts reversed that rule, reasoning in part that what was foreseeable had changed—the baseline thus changed along with social mores.

There are two important points to bear in mind here. The first is that the choice of which kind of baseline to select (e.g., custom, expectations) may be affected by the degree to which the various baseline options suffer problems associated with the level of abstraction, individualization, and multiplicity. The second point is that even after a particular kind of baseline has been selected (e.g., custom) it remains possible to argue for different substantive variants of that baseline: the level of abstraction, substantive individuation, and multiplicity all point to ways in which different variants might be created. And, of course, technological, cultural, and economic changes can so affect behavior that an old baseline ceases to play its intended role. Thus, legal protections for privacy (including baselines) have been overwhelmed by tremendous reductions in transaction costs in gaining information about people.[10] Competition (in the form of rent-seeking, arbitrage, networking, branding, sliming, etc.) likewise affects the social meaning and efficacy of baselines.

II. Baseline Neutrality Problems

When selecting a baseline, an advocate or decision-maker aims to avoid choosing in an arbitrary way. For some legal thinkers (many, actually) this has meant choosing a baseline that is deemed to be "neutral"—in the sense of non-political, non–value laden, and non-biased. For a long time in American law, it was believed that such "neutral" baselines existed. Perhaps the most significant example was the view that the common law is neutral, while government regulation is not. Unfortunately, no one has been able to explain successfully (short of a dogmatic natural law theory) why this would be so: the "common law," after all, is just as much state-created, distributive, and consequential as "government regulation."[11] No one can deny that insofar as effects are concerned the law allocates wealth and power. Indeed, in its effects, the law is (among other things) an elaborate system of subsidies and penalties.

Nonetheless, the persistent tendency remains in American law to label certain baselines as neutral (in the sense of non-political, non–value laden, and non-biased), while others are deemed political.

The associations (vertical) and dissociations (horizontal) of these baselines, shown in table 3.1, are tendentious, however. It is true that if there is going to be a deviation, then it has to be a deviation *relative to something*—in law, to a baseline. But what perspective would allow us to deem a particular baseline neutral? Could we be assured that this perspective (whatever it may be) would itself be neutral? Neutral relative to what . . . baseline? Once there is a choice to be made between competing perspectives and the choice has to be constructed in the instant action, it is not at all clear how legal

TABLE 3.1. Ostensibly Neutral/Political Baselines

Ostensibly Neutral Baselines	Ostensibly Political Baselines
non-intervention	intervention
status quo	change
common law	legislation
free market	government regulation

neutrality might be possible. To be sure, one might adopt approaches to safeguard against arbitrariness, caprice, or randomness, but that falls far short of achieving neutrality.[12]

Now, of course, everyone is convinced that legal decision-makers should not decide for A against B on the grounds that A is a valued family member, pays hefty bribes, or is a pleasant fellow. But to think that these are inadequate grounds (as we and most legal professionals do) is hardly the same as having an adequate, let alone a robust, concept of neutrality.

Perhaps the closest thing to choosing a neutral baseline would be to flip a coin. Even then, this is arguably nonsense because there are rarely only two options or only one way of characterizing the given options. Moreover, even if flipping a coin were seen as neutral, it is not clear that it would be seen as legal (in the sense that it is *law* that drives the decision, as opposed to some random tie breaker).

A. FAILED NEUTRALITY

Why and how is neutrality in any strong sense of the term at times unreachable? Here several arguments may play a role. Insofar as they are arguments, they will sometimes seem convincing, while at other times, not. One thing is clear: it is important to distinguish these arguments because they are not all as clearly applicable in all circumstances.

> *Non-referentiality*: In table 3.1, the terms in the left-hand column might be viewed as artificially severed from the terms in the right-hand column. That is to say, "non-intervention," "common law," and "legislation" are not stand-alone identities securely insulated from the effects and implications of their opposed term. Let's face it, the content and character of the common law *today* are very much a function of legislation (and other sources of enacted law). These other sources of law (legislation, constitutional law, treaties, and regulation) have contributed to making the common law what it is. The common law has evolved (and not) because of the content and character of these other sources of law. The content and

character of our ostensibly neutral common law have thus been shaped and influenced by precisely what we claim to be non-neutral (legislation, constitutional law, etc.). No one can know in any non-controversial manner what today's common law would look like if we figuratively tried to subtract the effects of these other sources of law. Would we attempt to answer this question by trying to discern the common law before there was any legislation? Would we simply take what courts today label as "common law," even though it has been undeniably shaped, expanded, and contracted by the presence of legislation?

Dedifferentiation: This term implies a lack of distinction between two or more terms. The market is differentiated from regulation to the extent that we have the conceptual means to distinguish one from the other. It is, of course, always possible to write sentences that purport to distinguish A from B. But that does not suffice to show that A and B are in fact distinct or distinguishable. If we think about the terms in both the left-hand and right-hand columns, we will see that they are intermingled and that the move that would distinguish one from the other (i.e., a linguistic distinction or visual representation) only goes so far. When we think about it, the attempted distinctions do not hold. Thus, in contemporary society, the so-called free market is always infused with the allocative effects of various legal entitlements and disablements. Similarly, there is no common law apart from the designation of its scope, strength, and character by constitutional and statutory law. There is no status quo apart from one that is already infused with the institutions and practices of ongoing continuous change. To put it bluntly, the status quo is already a state of change. (This point will be developed below in the discussion of baseline collapse problems.)

Indeterminacy: Even apart from non-referentiality and dedifferentiation, each of the terms in the two columns is susceptible internally to differing interpretations and specifications. Thus, even if we were convinced that non-intervention is somehow distinguishable from intervention, or that the free market is distinguishable from government regulation, respectively, we would still have to choose and select among different interpretations of what counts as non-intervention (as distinct from intervention) and what counts as the free market (as distinct from regulation).[13]

If neutrality in the selection of baselines is indeed illusory, then this calls for some sort of account as to how it is we can nonetheless believe (as we often do) that some baselines are neutral, while others not. Just what explains this? There are many answers here, though none appear to be terribly satisfying. They are all at least a bit question-begging. Nonetheless, it is useful to take note of them in passing.

One answer is that the demand for neutrality in baselines is linked at a deep structural level to other legal notions, such as objectivity, the rule of law, and the like, that are believed to be crucial to our conception of law. To put it bluntly, neutrality is seen as a necessary aspect of a complex set of notions that are all deeply implicated in what we call law. To give up on neutrality in baselines thus seems to many legal professionals like the beginning of an unraveling of law itself (or at least what many legal professionals take law to be).

A second answer is that legal professionals, *having internalized* certain norms as baselines, tend to think of those norms as neutral. For instance, the famous rule of law virtues (notice, clarity, etc.) are sometimes treated this way—as aspects of regular and neutral order. They are not, of course, because as abstractions, they need to be elaborated before application. And the devil (or rather the lack of neutrality) emerges in the details. People tend to treat as neutral those legal or political norms they have themselves already internalized; they tend to think that there are clear examples of neutral baselines. This is not unique to the rule of law. We all have our own internalized baselines, and these will often not be apparent to us. And as they are ours, once they are pointed out, they may often seem to us to be neutral.

A third answer is that legal professionals of all kinds have powerful professionally reinforced motivations to distance themselves cognitively and psychologically from their own political choices. Judges who must render difficult decisions on questions that are intractable in milieus that are fraught develop a huge psychological dependence on the "binding character" of law. Judges quite understandably wish to be bound by law—rather than take personal, ethical, or epistemic responsibility for their decisions. They tend to project their own decisions or judgments onto the law itself and to accord law a determinacy and a force it might not have. Legal academics might be wary of this distorting judicial tendency in terms of teaching law to their students. At the same time, of course, legal academics should show a bit more empathy and realism vis-à-vis the tasks that judges confront. And legal academics are not free from distorting renditions of law either. Indeed, they have their own reasons for distancing themselves from political choice in law. As members of the university community, they would like law to be a knowledge or a discipline that they can then impart to their students. The introduction of politics into the picture seems to many of them to frustrate that desire. Meanwhile, a kind of automatic identification with judges, legal officials, their orientations and materials, can easily seem for many academics to resolve these issues. Law students meanwhile also have a cognitive interest that converges with that of judges and legal academics. Law students would like to believe that they are learning something of value—and if at all possible, something of enduring value, and at the very least something more than simply jural cosmetics for ungrounded political choices.

In sum, it may well be that neutrality often functions more as a laudatory label that legal professionals attach to their preferred baselines than as a perspicuous or decisive analytical criterion to help select among different baseline options.

B. DENIAL AND EVASION

Those legal professionals who acknowledge baseline neutrality problems (and many do) nonetheless strive to avoid the implications of these problems. Throughout much of the history of modern law, the evasion strategy of choice seems to involve the invocation of realpolitik, common sense, practicalities, pragmatism, institutional settlement, shared beliefs, political facts on the ground, or the like. This strategy is a kind of confession and avoidance. The confession involves an acknowledgment of the intellectual seriousness of the problem at the level of theory. The avoidance involves setting aside the theoretical difficulty in favor of an ostensibly practical effort to resolve "real" problems faced by "real" legal actors. The success of this strategy depends upon whether one experiences the confession as authorizing or foreclosing the avoidance.

The baseline neutrality problem (no neutral method to select or justify a baseline) is vexing for legal thinkers because it quite clearly makes explicit a moment of not fully grounded value choice about how our collective lives ought to be governed. This is experienced as a moment when law runs out, and legal professionals (at least judges, law professors, and law students—all for different reasons) generally find this moment unsettling and uncomfortable.

For the advocate, however, this is an opportunity! Consider the example of Colorado's 1992 Amendment 2, a statewide referendum that prohibited "Protected Status Based on Homosexual, Lesbian or Bisexual Orientation." The state framed its defense of the amendment to suggest a neutral baseline, arguing that the amendment put non-heterosexual people in the same position as all other persons. The Supreme Court explicitly rejected this framing, finding that the act was not preserving a neutral baseline, but in fact withdrew specific legal protections from only one class of people.[14]

Or consider Chief Justice Roberts's statement that "[t]he way to stop discrimination on the basis of race is to stop discriminating on the basis of race."[15] Choosing a particular point in time to "stop" preserves the status quo, which is of course a choice in itself. Recognizing the implicit baselines in an existing doctrine or an opponent's argument—who is being subsidized/ who is being penalized?—is critical.

III. Baseline Collapse Problems

The formula for a baseline collapse problem is easy to state in the abstract (though it is somewhat difficult to grasp). Tellingly, when we are dealing with baseline collapse problems we will be encountering distinctions that suffer from lack of conceptual intelligibility: they are simply incoherent. We will state the problem in the abstract succinctly and move quickly to a clarifying illustration.

> *The abstract formulation*: We have a baseline collapse problem when a law calls for the selection of a baseline, and it is evident that *the law itself already breaches any conceivable baseline*.
>
> *The illustration*: Take the famous or infamous maxim "Do not use your property in such a manner as to injure others."[16] On first impression, this seems like an eminently reasonable idea—one that might be of help in distinguishing permissible uses of private property from wrongful uses. But then a moment's thought: What precisely is the baseline here? How shall we know what counts as using private property in such a way as to injure (or not injure) others? As one ponders this question, a complication soon emerges: it turns out that private property and property usage are themselves, as *an economic and social matter*, permissions to injure others.[17] To say that A has a fee simple in X, for instance, generally means that B cannot use X, nor transfer X, without A saying so. It also means that A can use the object of this property—and lots of those uses will arguably be injuries to B. If A builds an ugly house or cuts down all the trees or, on the contrary, plants a whole bunch of new ones, B can be made to suffer. B is made worse off by A having property in X than if A did not and B could use it, take from it, or frustrate A's uses of it. Moreover, because it is A's property, B is under certain duties to avoid trespassing and destroying the property. The upshot is that, given the state of the law, A is already empowered by property law to injure B—economically, socially, aesthetically, and so on. Now, we might think that this permission to injure is all, or mostly, good and right—that the benefits to be derived from private property in this (or other instances) exceed the costs. True. But, as will be seen, this recognition is not the same as saying that private property does not injure B.

All of this creates a classic baseline collapse problem. To back up for a moment, we wanted to know what constitutes the use of property in a way that injures others. The problem we encountered is that property itself already injures others—by depriving them of resources, constraining their movements, enabling offending uses, and requiring them to heed legal obligations. That's what property is in part: the freedom to injure others without having to face legal redress.[18] So the principle that one should avoid the use of property to injure others is simply not coherent, not intelligible. It is even arguably a form of silliness akin to saying: "It's OK to engage in boxing, but not in a way that results in hurting people. We're going to keep a close eye to make sure no one hurts anyone. Now, go out there and box. No, not shadow-boxing. Real boxing. Be tough. But no hurting."

Accordingly, the attempt to limit the use of property or entitlements generally to non-injurious usages seems ill-fated. Instead we ought to be asking a different question—namely, which injurious uses should be permitted (and why)? Those, however, are much tougher, more perplexing (and more interesting) questions. How so? With these questions, our views are likely to be somewhat mixed, perhaps even conflicted: We all value freedoms that keep us safe from injury as well as freedoms that ineluctably involve injury to others. We simply differ (and this is, inter alia, a matter of politics, economics, culture, aesthetics, and morality) on where to draw the line: how much injury, when, to what degree, to whom, and so on. As law-trained professionals, we know fairly well what kinds of arguments to advance in support of our views. But we also know that these arguments run out—that at some level we are asserting as truths of law claims that we know run up against other non-negligible opposing arguments. We know that our judgments (whether widely shared or not) are contestable.[19]

This baseline collapse problem would not be so important were it not for the fact that it seems to crop up repeatedly. In other words, we are routinely called upon to apply some baseline to a state of affairs where the baseline has already collapsed. The classic article here is by Robert Hale, a legal realist, who in a few short pages showed that the classic jural strategies to draw a workable distinction between choice and coercion were ultimately question-begging or otherwise untenable.[20]

Here is another notorious example. Nearly all constitutional rights apply only when "state action" is present; the Constitution does not protect against private wrongs. "State action doctrine" requires that we search for a baseline to determine when the state is acting. In one sense, this is occurring all the time, since any sort of purportedly "private action" is traceable to a private right that is itself traceable to an entitlement created by the state. One might think, of course, that where the state neither prohibits nor requires action, there is no state action. But that is wrong, because in those instances, one frequently finds that the state permits or authorizes action. This is one of the most important reasons why state action doctrine is so confused. The state action doctrine is but a subset of what might be termed a broader distinction between public and private. As we know, this is an important distinction because different legal regimes and norms often apply depending upon whether some conduct or actor is deemed public or private. What then do we do if every form of conduct or actor is in some sense public?

We have powerful legal commitments that would lead us to resist this conclusion. And what's more, the conclusion can easily seem counterintuitive: the temptation here is to come up with counterexamples. The temptation is to say: "Look, here is my ring—it's private. There's nothing public about it." But that's not true: there are many aspects of ring ownership that are public in character. Thus, for instance, the state has enacted public norms that forbid you from doing all sorts of things with your ring (putting your neighbor's eye out, for instance). There are lots of things the state *requires* you to do if you want to retrieve your ring after it has been lost (better put some identifying mark on it).

Once baselines collapse, and cases are thought to fall, rather vexingly, on both sides of a distinction (public as well as private), the tendency of the courts is to use a variety of strategies to either *switch grounds* or to *deformalize the decision*. In other words, the courts will use some distinction other than public/private in order to decide (switch grounds) or they will start to hedge the decision through balancing or multifactor tests (deformalize the decision). Courts frequently turn to a context-driven, case-by-case approach (see, for example, the "fact-bound inquiry" of whether a private actor "could be described in all fairness as a state actor" under the state action doctrine,[21] or the importance of looking to "content, form, and context" to determine whether a public employee's speech addresses a matter of "public concern").[22]

In baseline collapse situations, we have two prevalent strategies for switching grounds.

> The first is to resort to *intent or motive.* If an action or an activity cannot easily be classified as either public or private, then legal decision-makers often resort to the motive or intent of those regulating the activity (e.g., the legislature) or the motive or intent of those regulated (the parties). In other words, recourse is made to intent or motive as rhetorical spaces that will allow characterization of the action or activity as either public or private. This is often more of a feint than a solution, however. The reason is simple: motives and intents are often highly speculative and conjectural. Often it seems that the legal decision-makers are simply creating

a relatively empty rhetorical space (motive or intent) that they can then characterize one way (i.e., public) or the other (i.e., private).

The second strategy is to look to *effects and consequences*. If a legal official cannot otherwise be sure, he or she looks to the likely effects or consequences to determine whether these are public or private. Again, this will often be unsatisfying. Again, we have the creation of a rhetorical space (effects and consequences) used to offer up speculative and conjectural solutions as if they were seriously grounded. How does a court determine whether a law violates the establishment clause (requiring a "religious" or "secular" baseline)? By asking, in part, whether its *effects* advance or inhibit religion.[23]

It bears noting that legal decision-makers will often use evidence of intent and motive to characterize and discern effects and consequences. Ironically, they will often use evidence of effects and consequences to characterize or discern motives and intents. (See "VISH" in chapter 8, "Cluster Logic.")

On occasion these *switching grounds* moves are compelling. Very often, however, they will not be. Very often as well, they will be combined with *deformalization* strategies. Thus, if a legal official is faced with the arduous task of determining whether an action or activity is public or private, we can expect the tests used to resort to quantitative terms (X is "primarily," "predominantly," "substantially," or "mostly" public or private) and/or to adopt a deformalized test (viewing X in terms of the "nexus of relations," "the totality of circumstances," "the multiple factors," etc.).

This is all somewhat vexing, and one might wonder whether we are not overstating the collapse of the public and the private. One wants to ask, "Aren't there certain things or matters—like my ring, for instance—that are clearly private?" The temptation is to say, "Enough of this! My ring is private! Leave my ring and me *alone!*" In law, however, leaving people alone is not an option. Why not? Because their "legal aloneness," so to speak (notice how this is actually an oxymoron), depends upon public legal entitlements or disablements—rules that enable or disallow various actors from engaging or not engaging in certain activities.

Consider the ring example again. Consider that when you say you want the law to leave you alone, you don't actually mean that. Consider that when *your ring* (assuming you meet the very public legal requirements to establish it as *yours*) is stolen, you will want the also very public agencies of the criminal law to become involved. And when the police tell you that they don't bother to investigate thefts of less than $2000 in value, you will likely be scandalized and come to consider their dereliction of duty a breach of the "public trust." So when you say, "I want to be left alone," that is not really true. It is not the gist of your claim. The gist of your claim regarding ring ownership is that you want (1) more rights and privileges for yourself, (2) less rights and privileges for others, and, accordingly, (3) more duties and disallowances on other people. In short, what you want is pretty much the usual, at least in the context of litigation: more entitlements for you/fewer entitlements for others. And if at all possible, all of it with the state on your side. There is nothing surprising or analytically flawed in making such claims. But to characterize the claims as wanting to "be left alone"—now that is neither a realistic option nor a fair representation of what you actually want.

Even those matters that the Supreme Court considers to be most private often turn out to have a non-negligible public aspect. Recognize the raw and painful irony in the fact that the right to privacy in choosing whether to have an abortion turns out to be one of the most intensely litigated, publicly regulated, excruciatingly gerrymandered constitutional issues—right down to a few feet of a mobile "bubble" pathway to the abortion provider's office.

So then what is the baseline for deciding whether an activity is or is not public? The problem is that we are already in a legal world where everything is arguably public. The notion then that, in such a world, we can find a baseline that effectively and analytically distinguishes the purely public from the purely private is illusory. It cannot be found.

In some ways, the prevalence of so many deformalized contemporary legal regimes seems to be a de facto (not fully self-conscious) recognition of this state of affairs. The fallback on quantitative images/metaphors ("primarily," "predominantly," "substantially," "mostly," etc.) discussed above is a de facto confession that the search for a baseline grounding the distinction at stake— here, public/private—has failed or is failing. There is a loosening of the joints in the legal architecture so that the distinction can be retained (there is a felt need to retain the distinction) and yet nonetheless manipulated to achieve ostensibly desirable ends (context-sensitive solutions, achievement of different goals, etc.). It is not the most candid or satisfying of juridical methods.

As suggested above, this loosening of the legal architecture is a justifiable response to the realizations that (1) the baseline categories (public/private) have lost their grip, and that (2) desired outcomes can be reached only through contextualization. This, however, is not the only story to be told here. This loosening could also be considered a kind of dissembling in the face of a collapsed baseline architecture. Either way, the loosening is a standing invitation to lawyers to argue and advocate for their preferred baselines.

That is perhaps the most practical point: when baseline collapse problems arise, it is time for legal decision-makers to worry and for lawyers to think hard about the creative arguments to make. When baseline collapse problems arise, that is when the advocate has the opportunity to shine.

There are lots of major distinctions where baseline collapse problems are likely to be encountered. Table 3.2 provides a list of a few of the more vulnerable *major distinctions*, along with an *argument pointer* signaling the kind of argument that would need to be made (with due attention to context, of course) to trigger the collapse of the distinction. An argument pointer is simply a more abstract (structural) variant of what Duncan Kennedy has called an "argument bite."[24]

We will return to these major distinctions in chapter 8, "Cluster Logic."

TABLE 3.2. Baseline Collapse Problems—Argument Pointers

Major Distinction	Argument Pointer
Public/Private	All public entitlements and disablements have distributional implications for private wealth and power/All private transactions are traceable to state establishment and enforcement of private law entitlements and disablements. In both cases, it is a question not of kind, but of degree.
Choice/Coercion	Every coerced action can be traced back to an anterior choice/Every choice can be traced back to an anterior context of coercion.
Process/Outcome	Every process yields influences and delimits possible outcomes/Every outcome is but an aspect of ongoing processes. Processes beget and delimit outcomes/Outcomes are embedded in greater ongoing processes.
Rules/Standards	Every rule is a standard to an even more "rule-like" rule/Every standard is a rule to an even more "standard-like" standard.
Form/Substance	Every legal form anticipates certain substantive requirements/Every substantive requirement institutes itself as a form demanding to be observed.
Free Market/Regulation	All markets depend upon regulation to define and enforce initial entitlements as well as transfer procedures, both of which unavoidably and by design limit the free market/All regulation of the market unavoidably internalizes the identities and relations of the free market in order to regulate it.

IV. Summary

The failure to understand and recognize baseline problems leads to serious deficits in legal analysis. For instance, consider the often heard argument that government is wasteful compared to the "free market." Notice how the argument typically proceeds: the claim is almost always that government has needlessly spent X dollars on various actions, persons, institutions, and processes. All right—fair enough: government waste does happen—in the sense that some costs might have been avoided or minimized (without undue loss elsewhere).

But if the claim is that the government is wasteful compared to the free market, shouldn't we look at the latter to see if there is any waste there? The answer is, of course, we should, and, of course, there is. Consider all those failed free market ventures, those bankruptcies, those businesses that go under. Consider all that duplication of effort by competitors trying independently to outsmart each other, or to undermine each other in ways that produce no consumer benefits. So here too it will be evident that there is waste—in the sense that some costs might have been avoided (without undue loss elsewhere). It is, of course, difficult to assess the fact and magnitude of such losses in an enlightened way. There is an awful tracing problem involved—the tracing of costs and benefits. But notice that, with a modicum of thought, the same difficulties emerge in identifying and eliminating government waste.

The point is that if we wish to be serious, we must try (however analytically challenging this may be) to be fair in our comparisons. Looking for needless incurrence of cost in one case (government) and neglecting it in the other (the market) is obviously wrong. How do we let this happen? The answer is both simple and vexing: we use an ideal model of the market to assess government waste and not surprisingly find that the government is a very poor approximation of what an idealized market would have produced. (Never mind that an idealized market could not have been actualized in the first instance.) Meanwhile, on the other side of the ledger, when we encounter an actual market, we tend to treat it almost automatically as if it were the actualization of an idealized market—as if the operation of the market were itself costless. Ronald H. Coase, the famous Nobel Prize winner, taught us not to make such mistakes, yet few of his many ardent followers seemed to have paid much attention.[25] These are mistakes that we should not be making.

Consider the popular argument that when the government raises income taxes, it is "taking your money." What is the implicit baseline in this argument? The answer is that "your money" is whatever you currently get after the government applies the tax rates currently in force. Relative to that amount (whatever it may be) a raise in taxes would be taking *your* money. But what makes it "your money" to begin with? It is only your money to the extent that it isn't taxed. If it were taxed (i.e., a tax raise) it wouldn't be *your* money.

Now you might say, "Well, that's just sophistry. The reason it is my money is not because the government lets me keep it. It is my money because I earned it." Well, no not really—that's not true, at least not as an economic matter. You are not the only *production factor* involved here. The fact is that the most significant productive factor is not you, but rather the accumulated collective educational level (technology, politics, know-how, culture, etc.) that you have internalized (much of it without paying for it). The economic fact of the matter is that if your income is $100,000 a year, very little of that is the result of *your own contribution*, and a great deal is due to millennia of learning, resource development, infrastructure, cultural know-how, and so on.

Moreover, if we look at things in terms of a shorter time span—say, your lifetime—it still isn't your money. After all, you are a beneficiary of all sorts of subsidies—many of which may have been doled out unequally in ways that have helped (or hurt) you. You are a beneficiary (or victim) of police protection, public education, public utilities, inheritance laws, property regimes, and so on. And most topically, you are also a beneficiary (and/or victim) of the tax laws. You earn what you get only in virtue of the legal system in place. And that means, in turn, that when people say it is *your* money, they are quite simply talking nonsense, economically speaking. Of course, in a *technical legal* sense, they may be right, but not in any way that helps their argument. It is true in the trivial sense that it is your money because the current (tax) laws say so. But that is a pretty trivial baseline, because as soon as we legally raise taxes, it is no longer your money.

Now you might think that it is your money in the sense that if the government doesn't tax it, the money goes to you as opposed to, say, your neighbor three blocks down the street. The neighbor down the street has no claim on it. True: if your neighbor tries to intervene and files with the IRS to redistribute your income *directly* to him, it will not work (and it could well precipitate fraud charges). But this is irrelevant to the point here. The fact that it is not your neighbor's money (that his political or moral entitlement claims are extremely weak to virtually non-existent) doesn't make it your money in terms of strengthening your claims to the money vis-à-vis the government or the community.

This is all an example of a baseline collapse problem. Much of popular political discussion about tax policy turns on who should be taxed and how much on *their* income. There is a more primordial issue at stake that is almost always buried in national political conversations—namely, what income should be considered (economically, politically, morally) *theirs* in the first place. That is a very tough economic, political, and moral issue—but that does not mean it can somehow be legitimately bypassed.

4

The Legal Distinction

Legal professionals are forever arguing over the terms of this or that legal distinction. Hence these familiar questions, among others:

"Should this distinction be used or that one?"
"Where should the line be drawn?"
"Will this distinction hold?"
"Can this distinction be easily understood, applied, and enforced?"
"Is this distinction sufficiently precise?"
"Is this distinction simply too easy for the parties to circumvent?"

Legal professionals traffic in legal distinctions day in and day out. In addition to identifying and using the distinctions already found in law, legal professionals must routinely offer up their own proposed distinctions and argue against those proposed by opposing counsel. Thus, legal professionals are often heard to say things like the following:

"The statute does not apply here because it governs only real property, not personal property." (real/personal property distinction)
"The defendant cannot be held liable because he was acting in his official capacity." (official/non-official distinction)
"This regulation does not violate freedom of speech because the regulation is not viewpoint-based." (viewpoint-based/subject matter–based distinction)

One obvious reason the legal distinction is so crucial to the expression and elaboration of law is that it is perhaps the preeminent legal artifact through which the limits of different legal regimes are established.[1] The legal distinction thus often serves as the linchpin on which determinations of liability/no liability, guilt/no guilt, right/no right, remedy/no remedy turn.

Not surprisingly, there is a great deal to be said about the legal distinction—how and when it works (and how and when it doesn't). In this chapter, we will address questions such as the following: What work do legal distinctions do? What kinds of criteria can be used to evaluate legal distinctions? What are the classic flaws that can afflict legal distinctions? Why do these flaws matter substantively? In reading this chapter, it will help considerably to think of the various sections as different perspectives on or entry points to the legal distinction—to wit, different ways of approaching the topic.

I. What Do Legal Distinctions Do?

Throughout law school, a law student will encounter hundreds, if not thousands, of legal distinctions. Some of these will be relatively local, obscure, perhaps even onetime occurrences, specific to a certain field, such as torts, contracts, or antitrust. Other distinctions, by contrast, will become extremely familiar—encountered repeatedly throughout the curriculum. Here are some examples of the latter:

Public/Private
Choice/Coercion
Substance/Form
Outcome/Process
Subjective/Objective
Absolute/Conditional
Determinate/Indeterminate

Given the importance of legal distinctions to law, it's something of a surprise that there isn't a straightforward contemporary treatment of the topic—a discussion of how legal distinctions work, what they do, how to craft them, and how they fall apart.

But if we think about it, we can bring together a lot of otherwise scattered learning on legal distinctions to provide a helpful overview. Many familiar topics (e.g., the slippery slope, indeterminacy, vagueness) are closely related to the way legal distinctions are crafted and criticized.

First, what legal work do legal distinctions perform? As a general matter, the distinction is one of the primary tools[2] through which a legal system creates *different legal regimes* that attach *different legal consequences* to behaviors, parties, statuses, and transactions.[3] Thus, the legal distinction serves to delineate the boundaries between one legal regime and another.

Example 1: If a murder is premeditated, it can be treated as first-degree murder. If it is not premeditated, it cannot be treated as first-degree murder. The pre-

meditated/non-premeditated distinction serves to distinguish different criminal offenses—first-degree murder and second-degree murder.

Example 2: If the defendant sold a product that caused the plaintiff's injury, the defendant may well be subject to a strict products liability regime. If, however, the defendant was merely providing a service, then the plaintiff will have to sue in negligence. Here the product/service distinction serves to delineate the scope of the strict liability vs. negligence regimes.

The common law distinctions used to categorize "found" property (unclaimed property that someone discovers and takes possession of) provide a classic example of how legal distinctions operate. The common law recognizes three basic categories of such property: (1) abandoned property, (2) lost property, and (3) mislaid property. The categories work to determine who has the superior right of ownership when property has been found. In simplest terms, a finder is entitled to keep abandoned property, is entitled to lost property against everyone except the true owner, and acquires no right in mislaid property.

Several important, if basic, points can be illustrated using this set of legal distinctions as an example. One point is that legal distinctions are rarely self-executing (and when they are, not surprisingly, no one argues about them). In other words, when disagreement arises, knowing the legal distinctions is not enough: the advocate needs to know how (and how not) to argue for a particular conception of the legal distinction. The three found property categories mentioned above make the intent of the original owner the fulcrum for the decision. Did the owner voluntarily relinquish the property (*abandoned*)? Involuntarily and inadvertently part with it (*lost*)? Place it somewhere and then forget to reclaim it (*mislaid*)? Because the original owner is typically not around in these disputes, a decision-maker must determine a possibly unknown person's intent with limited evidence. The advocate's job is, of course, to use the facts available to convince the decision-maker that they "fit" better in one category than another, a task that offers opportunity for creativity. Any effort to fit facts into a category involves manipulation of that category; any decision to apply or reject a distinction in particular circumstances changes the definition of that distinction, even if only in some small way.

Advocates can directly challenge a legal distinction as flawed and argue for a new distinction; similarly, decision-makers can reject distinctions or craft new ones. Below we address in detail the criteria for sound legal distinctions, and the classic flaws lawyers need to be aware of to either challenge or craft distinctions.

Most often, of course, advocates and decision-makers do not directly challenge legal distinctions but rather make arguments and reach decisions that presume the validity of the distinction. Lawyers frequently argue for a particular definition of a distinction, whether implicitly or explicitly, so that it includes or excludes the scenario posed in the lawsuit (for discussion on *how to interpret* legal distinctions, see chapter 7, "Interpretation"). Interpretation can lead in many directions, but three major interpretive moves involve arguing for (1) an expansive understanding of the distinction, (2) a narrow understanding, and (3) an exception to the distinction. Such an argument does not necessarily need to be framed in "legal distinction" terms, and in fact often is not.

For example, consider again the distinction between mislaid and abandoned property. An eccentric father was known to hide gold, cash, and other valuables in his home.[4] After he died, his daughters searched the house for valuables and found, among other things, ammunition cans containing gold or cash. Eventually the daughters sold the house "as is" to new owners. When the new owners renovated the home, they found an additional $500,000 in cash in ammunition cans. The new owners argued that the term "abandoned" should include this scenario—that the daughters abandoned the cash when they gave up searching for it and sold the home. The court disagreed, concluding that the daughters did not intend to abandon the money—to the contrary, as soon as they heard about it they filed a petition to recover it! The point, for our purposes, is that the decision required the court to determine how expansive the "abandoned" category ought to be. This court, thinking that no one ever voluntarily abandons money, decided the category should be read narrowly—so as to arguably exclude just about any property of value.

Another important role for legal distinctions is to provide the scaffolding for analogical reasoning. Consider the familiar idea of "distinguishing a case." This is the basic operation of showing that some case purportedly analogous to the one at hand is in some important way different from the case under consideration. The purpose of distinguishing a case is to support an argument that the current dispute belongs in a different category (created by a legal distinction) than the past case. Cash found in a cardboard box in the ceiling of a motel room is just like cash found in waterproof containers at the bottom of a pool: both are "mislaid" funds because they were intentionally hidden—the crux of that legal distinction. Distinguishing a case without reference to legal categories or concepts is rather pointless.

Legal distinctions also serve as the scaffolding for arguments based on principle, policy, or the like. Cases are often said to be distinguishable "on their facts," but this expression can be a bit misleading. If a case is distinguishable on its facts, then it is in part because those facts are associated with some other artifact (doctrine, principle, policy, etc.) that in turn supports making a distinction. When the facts seem to "fit" the wrong category, an advocate can argue for a policy- or principle-based exception to the distinction. For example, many landowners have successfully argued that even if property is deemed lost, the finder is not entitled to it because the finder was trespassing—he was a wrongdoer and not entitled to the property.

A quick look at any found property case makes the prevalence of policy- or principle-based arguments readily apparent—courts regularly consider whether an outcome would reward the undeserving. For example, one couple found $82,000 in the gas tank of a car they had just purchased from the government at auction. The court decided that the money had been "abandoned" because "drug traffickers know better" than to claim an interest in drug proceeds (according to the court, the currency thus "went back into a state of nature analogous to wild animals").[5] In deciding between the government and the car owners, the court noted that though the $82,000 was a windfall for the couple, the government should have been on notice ("[a]s early as the 1970's when 'Easy Rider' was aired") that drug dealers use gas tanks to hide contraband.[6] "[T]he equities" therefore, did not favor the government (or, of course, the drug traffickers).

Or consider the legal distinction created by the marital privilege. If two parties are married, they are not required to testify regarding communications made to each other. A lawyer prosecuting a defendant charged with murder desperately wanted to force the defendant's wife to testify that the defendant confessed the crime to her (which he had).[7] If the wife wasn't willing to testify, it seems pretty clear that the prosecutor would be out of luck: the parties were married and thus covered by the marital privilege. As it turned out, there was evidence that the defendant and his wife married only to prevent the wife from being deported. The prosecutor argued for a "fraudulent marriage exception" to the marital privilege law, for the sorts of policy reasons you can easily imagine. The court remained unconvinced (though the wife was in fact willing to testify voluntarily, which certainly may have swayed its decision). The legal distinction (all married people are entitled to the privilege) was challenged but held.

In short, as form, legal distinctions are crucial in all modes of legal argument: deductive reasoning relies on legal distinctions for its premises; inductive reasoning is used to create legal distinctions from individual rulings; analogical reasoning works in the framework of legal distinctions; arguments based on narrative theory are crafted to fit legal distinctions; arguments based on policy or principle expand, contract, or create exceptions to legal distinctions. Admittedly, this is all a bit oversimplified, but the point remains that an advocate or decision-maker who appreciates all the different work that legal distinctions do or enable has a clear advantage in crafting effective arguments.

II. Three Criteria for "Sound" Legal Distinctions

Legal distinctions are created and revised regularly—by statute or other enacted law, of course, but also by judges. Often, a lawyer or judge is called upon to criticize a legal distinction—to show that it is so deficient that it should be modified or replaced. That this happens often is not surprising: insofar as legal distinctions mark out the crucial dividing line or "break point" between one legal regime (e.g., negligence) and another (e.g., strict liability) or one set of consequences (e.g., plaintiff wins) and another (e.g., plaintiff loses) distinctions are stressed. That is to say, legal distinctions are often vigorously contested as the parties try variously to maintain or erode, contract or extend, reinforce or weaken them. When an advocate or decision-maker asks whether a particular set of facts falls on one side of a distinction or another, the conceptualization of the distinction is crucial to the answer. Thus, legal distinctions are in this limited sense challenged at every turn, even if the challenge is not express or clearly evident.

Because distinctions play such a crucial role in articulating the law, distinctions must be as convincing and effective as possible. Three aspects of legal distinctions are crucial in terms of deciding whether they are convincing and effective.

A. CONCEPTUAL INTELLIGIBILITY

For a legal distinction to work, it must appear that the two sides that define the distinction have some conceptual meaning that render them different. (Call this *conceptual intelligibility*.) It must be possible to know what each side means and to know how they differ relative to each other.[8] Occasionally, a legal distinction seems to lack conceptual intelligibility.

> *Example 1: In the early 1900s, the Supreme Court announced that the commerce clause authorized Congress to regulate some activities that were not commerce if they had a **direct effect** on commerce. Activities with **indirect effects**, however, remained beyond the reach of Congress under the commerce clause. The Court on several occasions invoked the direct/indirect test in its decisions, but it was never able to articulate an intelligible distinction. It wasn't just a question of fuzziness—there was no intelligible concept at work.*

Example 2: The distinction between civil and criminal contempt has often been criticized as unworkable—conceptually unintelligible. Whether contempt is civil or criminal is said to turn on the character of the sanction—civil if remedial and criminal if punitive, but "remedial" and "punitive" are hardly mutually exclusive.[9]

Whether a legal distinction is lacking in conceptual intelligibility is typically a matter of degree. Few distinctions are wholly unintelligible. Most legal distinctions seem to have some conceptual meaning (even if it is not entirely clear or fully determinate).

Three points are worth mentioning here.

First, when a legal distinction is originally announced, it is sometimes unclear in terms of conceptual intelligibility. Over time, however, as the court or other legal body applies the distinction in concrete instances, the distinction may gain in conceptual intelligibility. In other words, when first offered, a legal distinction will often seem abstract. But with time, the pattern of cases may well give the distinction some conceptual substance. Note that the reverse process is also possible. A legal distinction can start out as conceptually intelligible, but then, because of the odd or tendentious ways in which it is applied and elaborated in subsequent cases, the distinction can become increasingly less coherent.

Example: In 1945 the Supreme Court first used the phrase "minimum contacts" to determine whether a party has sufficient connections with a state so that the state's exercise of personal jurisdiction is constitutional.[10] *Each time the Court decides a personal jurisdiction case, that abstract phrase gains substantive meaning (even if inconsistently).*

Second, even where a legal distinction is somewhat lacking in conceptual intelligibility, it may not be entirely useless. A legal distinction somewhat deficient in conceptual intelligibility can nonetheless work as a shorthand that functions effectively as a "name" or a "label" for a conclusion.

Example: Consider the product/service distinction in the context of tort law. It lacks some degree of conceptual intelligibility. Not only do many transactions involve "hybrids" (an intermingling of product and service), but in many cases, it will not be clear whether something should be characterized in ways that render it a product (e.g., a widget) or a service (e.g., advice).

There is a general point here (to be elaborated later): legal distinctions, like any kind of legal term, serve an important dual purpose. In one sense, they are *tools of legal analysis*—the concepts or precepts that allow the legal professional to figure out "what the law is" or what it ought to be. (If legal distinctions lack conceptual intelligibility, they will not be of much help in this regard.) In a different sense, however, legal distinctions are *markers for declaring legal regimes*. (In this regard names or labels, even if analytically bereft, can nonetheless be functional as regime markers.)

> *Example: State action doctrine in constitutional law is, analytically speaking, a misnomer: there is no single state action doctrine and no amount of analytical reflection on the difference between state and non-state can yield one. Nor can the difference between action and non-action can be counted upon to yield much in the way of analytical insight into what the Supreme Court has in fact done with this topic. At the same time, state action doctrine, as a name or label for a set of varying and conflicting doctrines used by the Court, is useful to designate an element that must be established before due process, equal protection, and other such constitutional norms can be applied.*

Third, consider that many distinctions in law that often seem vague or unclear actually have a fair amount of conceptual meaning for legal professionals (even if not for the general public). Distinctions like reasonableness/ unreasonableness, substantial/insubstantial, and objective/subjective all have a lot of conceptual meaning for the legally trained. These distinctions come with baggage that immediately signals to the legal professional what is at stake, what to look for, what questions to ask, and so on. In part, of course, this is precisely because these distinctions form part of the structure and moves that traverse the law. For the legally trained, these otherwise vague terms immediately link up to various networks of legal associations that give them content.

Hence, for instance, a person trained in American law will immediately link up "reasonableness" to the following (and more):

The "reasonable person" standard
Cost-benefit analysis and the "Learned Hand test" from *United States v. Carroll Towing Co.*[11]
Different standards, such as good faith, strict liability, intentionality
Fact-based determinations appropriate for juries rather than courts
Objective tests as opposed to subjective tests
The need for examination of context: "all the circumstances"

B. PRACTICALITY

A well-functioning distinction must be capable of practical application. Conceptual intelligibility alone will not suffice. We must not only have a sense that the two sides are meaningfully distinct, but that the relevant stuff to be sorted can be relegated to one side or the other without too much difficulty or arbitrariness regardless of who does the sorting when.[12]

Example 1: At the beginning of the twentieth century, the US Supreme Court made a distinction (for purposes of the commerce clause) between manufacturing and commerce. This distinction might well have been conceptually intelligible: one might say that manufacturing is a kind of production and commerce is the exchange of goods. (Making things is arguably different from trading things.) But even if this distinction is conceptually intelligible, it lacks practicality. Why? Because, at least today, many businesses are integrated organizations that merge production and exchange in ways that render the two inextricably intertwined. This is a situation then where we have a legal distinction that is conceptually intelligible—one can imagine how manufacturing might be different from exchange, how production might differ from trade. But even though the distinction is conceptually intelligible, it turns out that in the world of actual economic activity, the two sides are generally intertwined. And so, in many instances (perhaps most?) the distinction does not track with economic activity as it actually occurs.

Example 2: One test proposed long ago for deciding what counts as speech under the First Amendment was the action/expression distinction. The idea was that if some sort of conduct was a kind of expression, then it would be protected. Conversely, if the conduct was deemed action, then it would be left unprotected. The distinction proved to be operationally intractable; think as much as you want about the distinction between action and expression, and then try to classify the following: flag burning, a cartel agreement, a defamatory statement, hate speech, and so on.

A distinction can be conceptually intelligible (as the examples above show) without being practical.

There are two major ways to craft legal distinctions so that they satisfy practicality. We will call them the *realist strategy* and the *formalist strategy*.

In the realist strategy, the law "tracks" an already existing division in the field of application. In other words, the law simply follows whatever distinctions are already marked out in the social, technological, or economic realm, *codifying* those distinctions into law.

Example: The motorized vehicle/non-motorized vehicle distinction seems relatively (not perfectly) secure. If one wanted, this distinction could be used to mark out different legal regimes (e.g., what kinds of vehicles are allowed in the park, different traffic rules, or different sales tax rates, etc.).

The move is thus to import an already existing seemingly non-legal distinction into the law.[13]

The formalist strategy strives to achieve practicality according to an altogether different logic. The formalist strategy is to create legal distinctions with the kinds of incentives (carrots) and/or deterrents (sticks) that will induce parties to conform their behavior to the distinction set forth. Formalities, as in contract law or in wills and trusts, for instance, are an obvious example.

> *Example: The requirements of signature, oath, witnesses, and the like serve as ways of establishing a clear demarcation between one legal status and another. Either the document has been signed or it hasn't. Either the party was under oath or not. These legal distinctions are easily applied.*

Realist and formalist strategies have much greater reach and significance than simply the discrete topic of legal distinctions. Much more will be said about this later. For now the important thing is to recognize that both of these strategies are in principle available for imposing legal distinctions and securing observance by parties. Of course, depending upon the context, the transactions at stake, the parties, and other considerations, one strategy may well be more successful or desirable than the other.

One last note: as with conceptual intelligibility above, practicality is mostly a question of degree. And quite obviously, the degree of practicality of a particular distinction may well depend upon the identity of the parties and their access (or lack of access) to professional legal services.

C. NORMATIVE APPEAL

For a legal distinction to work well, it must track closely with the reasons (i.e., the policies, principles, considerations, and values) that support drawing the distinction in the first place. This is where concerns such as justice, fairness, equality, efficiency, utility, and the like kick in. (We will call this aspect of the legal distinction *normative appeal.*) Legal distinctions conform to varying degrees to the reasons given for which they are drawn. When the distinction corresponds only poorly to the reasons given, then it suffers from a lack of normative appeal. Again, this is generally a question of degree.

> *Example 1: Assume the right to privacy is designed to protect consensual sexual intimacy. Until recently this right was extended by the Supreme Court to heterosexual but not homosexual activity. Obviously this distinction did not conform to the reasons given for the right. The heterosexual/homosexual distinction bore no obvious relation to the reasons given for the recognition of the right (at least as those reasons are articulated in this example).*

> *Example 2: Consider* Roe v. Wade's *trimester framework governing the regulation of abortions, and the Court's decision in* Planned Parenthood v. Casey[14] *to replace that framework with an undue burden analysis. For some (at least*

the authors of the Casey *opinion), the trimester framework was no longer an accurate proxy for viability of the fetus and needed to be changed. More to the point, for many others, neither decision has normative appeal because viability outside the womb does not correspond with their definition of life and thus does not adequately protect it.*

Note here an ambiguity in the notion of "reasons given." Some kinds of reason-giving in law can be seen as appealing to *intrinsic values*. An example of an intrinsic value might be "justice" or "fairness." If we are talking about these kinds of intrinsic values, then a legal distinction might itself be presented as an *actualization* of the value. For instance, recognizing that the murdering heir (who kills the testator) should not inherit might be seen to actualize the fairness principle that "persons should not profit from their own wrongs." The distinction here (murdering heir/non-murdering heir) is itself arguably *an instance* of what we mean by fairness. Now distinguish this last case from one in which we hold the use of explosives to a strict liability standard in order to enhance accident prevention. Framed this way, the normative appeal of the distinction (explosives/non-explosives) seems to be an *instrumental value*—namely, achieving a state of affairs where there are fewer accidents caused by the use of explosives.

Some legal thinkers would describe the murdering heir case as one animated by *principle* and describe the explosives case as one governed by *policy*.[15] Whether or not there is a fundamental difference between principles and policies (note that it is relatively easy to translate one into the form of the other), it is nonetheless crucial to appreciate that legal distinctions can have normative appeal in both of these ways—intrinsically and instrumentally. Sometimes a legal distinction is offered as a specification of a value. Sometimes a legal distinction is offered because it will ostensibly promote a state of affairs that is valued.

Emphasis is placed on this point because, in considering the normative appeal of any given distinction, it is important to pay attention to *both* intrinsic and instrumental aspects. The reason is simple. Some people are more easily convinced by one form of argument than the other. Moreover, weaknesses in one form of argument may well not exist when framed in the other. Back to our "found" property example as a way to make the point: a distinction that gives "mislaid" property to a landowner rather than a finder can be supported by an instrumental value—deterrence of trespassing—or an intrinsic value—it wouldn't be just to reward the wrongdoer (trespasser). Suppose now it comes out that no one is truly deterred from trespassing by the withholding of "mislaid" property. Even in that circumstance, one might still be convinced that it is wrong to reward the trespasser. The short of it is: instrumental and intrinsic value arguments are different modes—and each mode stands or falls in any given case with different kinds of supporting or critical arguments.

One further note: it could be argued that where legal distinctions are concerned, there is only one relevant consideration: normative appeal. On this view, conceptual intelligibility and practicality are mere subsets of normative appeal. One could view things this way, but for reasons of clarity we stick to a tripartite approach. There is a great deal more to be said about the different types of normative justifications available in law (but we limit our discussion here).[16]

III. The Trade-Offs among the Three Criteria

The three criteria for legal distinctions—conceptual intelligibility, practicality, and normative appeal—are not the only ones that can be applied to evaluate whether any given legal distinction is convincing or effective. But as *general* criteria for legal distinctions, they are among the most important. Imagine a legal distinction that was not conceptually intelligible. Then it could produce any result. Imagine a legal distinction with no practicality. Then no one would need (or be able) to follow it. Imagine a legal distinction that had no normative appeal. Then there would be no convincing reason to draw the distinction or to enforce it.

Optimally a legal distinction will satisfy each of the three criteria perfectly. That seldom (and quite possibly never) happens. Instead, the criteria usually stand in some tension. The party drawing the distinction will have to consider the trade-offs, perform some "triangulation," and come to some decision (one that likely will be imperfect).

Example: To illustrate these three criteria, consider laws pertaining to speeding. Colorado has a maximum speed limit of 75 mph. Now, that rule makes a distinction between those who drive at or below 75 mph (permissible behavior) and those who go above 75 mph (prohibited behavior). The "above 75/below 75" distinction displays a high degree of both conceptual intelligibility and practicality. With regard to conceptual intelligibility, no one has difficulty understanding what 75 mph means or making the above/below distinction. With regard to practicality, most people (if aided by a radar or a speedometer) will have a pretty easy time figuring out if a vehicle is going above or below 75 mph. With regard to normative appeal, however, the Colorado rule is less than entirely perfect. If we assume that the purpose here is to deter accidents, then it's obvious there are some problems with the rule. Some people, for instance, are such bad drivers that they shouldn't ever get close to 75 mph. Other people are such good drivers that if they were allowed to drive up to 80 mph, accidents would not increase measurably.

Then too consider that road conditions, weather, time of day, and more could all appreciably affect what constitutes a safe speed: in some cases (e.g., snow) cars should slow down to 40 mph. So the normative appeal of the 75 mph speed limit is less than perfect.

Now compare the Colorado rule to what used to be the Montana prima facie speeding law. This Montana speeding law (now defunct) prohibited driving at an unsafe speed in light of the conditions and the amount of traffic on the road. This law, in one sense, showed great normative appeal because it incorporated the ultimate function of speed regulation (i.e., safety) into the very wording of the law. By its terms, the law punished all those and only those who were driving at an unsafe speed. But the Montana speeding law posed significant practicality problems: How does one decide what is unsafe driving? And just what considerations go into making that determination? It's not at all clear.

In the best of all possible legal worlds, all legal distinctions would exhibit perfect conceptual intelligibility, perfect practicality, and perfect normative appeal. (Call a distinction that achieves this tripartite perfection an "ideal legal distinction.")

Ours is not the best of all possible legal worlds, and such ideal legal distinctions are hard to come by. Often it is necessary to draw a distinction that will exhibit some deficiency in terms of one, two, or perhaps even all three criteria. Very often, for instance, we will find that there is a trade-off to be made between normative appeal and practicality: a distinction that is perfect from the standpoint of normative appeal will be less than perfect from the standpoint of practicality (and vice versa), as the speeding law example above shows.

The art of the legal distinction lies in crafting distinctions that are as suitable as possible along all three aspects. We will get back to the task of crafting legal distinctions, but for now we want to look at some classic flaws in legal distinctions. These flaws all relate to the more general criteria described above, but it is important to master them as well because they are more targeted in the identification of the specific problem.

IV. The Classic Flaws and Why They Matter

A. THE CLASSIC FLAWS

Legal professionals must often criticize legal distinctions in order to advance their case. Sometimes they will attack a distinction for lack of conceptual intelligibility, practicality, or normative appeal (even if they don't use these terms). Frequently, they will frame their complaint or criticism more specifically. Here are some of the classic objections, any of which can be used by an advocate or a judge to challenge an existing or proposed distinction:[17]

1. *Overbreadth*: the distinction creates a set that includes more things than desirable or necessary.
2. *Underbreadth*: the distinction creates a set that includes fewer things than desirable or necessary.
3. *Overlap*: the distinction assumes that things are either X or Y, but it turns out that some things are both X and Y.
4. *Discontinuity*: the distinction is supposed to apply to a field in its entirety, but the two sets, X and Y, leave part of the field unclassified.
5. *False Dichotomy*: a distinction is an arbitrary line drawn through a spectrum.
6. *Incoherence*: In a distinction between X and Y, the presence of trait A means that something belongs in set X, while the presence of trait B means that something belongs in set Y. Meanwhile everything is both A and B.
7. *Vagueness*: The borders of a distinction are nebulous or unclear.

B. WHY THE CLASSIC FLAWS MATTER: FROM FORM TO SUBSTANCE

These objections describe ostensible flaws in a legal distinction. All the flaws relate in some way to *conceptual intelligibility, practicality,* or *normative appeal*. For instance, if a distinction is overbroad, then it lacks normative appeal and/or practicality. Some acts or persons are subjected to a legal regime when they shouldn't be, or the group is too diverse, too heterogeneous, to be subject to a single legal regime. If a distinction is vague, then it could lack conceptual intelligibility, practicality, normative appeal, or all three. Notice that a legal distinction can exhibit more than one classic flaw at a time. A distinction can be overbroad (we're *certain* that it applies to too much stuff) and vague as well (we're not sure exactly where the boundary lies).

Example: Consider the Supreme Court's decision to eliminate, for sales tax purposes, the distinction between businesses with a physical presence in the state and businesses without a physical presence.[18] States could require only those businesses with a physical presence in the state to collect and remit taxes. In overruling that distinction, the Court criticized it as an "arbitrary, formalistic distinction"[19] that treated economically identical actors differently for arbitrary reasons (false dichotomy and normative appeal), noting that it created market distortions (normative appeal); and was no longer easily applied (vague, incoherent, under-inclusive, conceptual intelligibility issues). It also forced states to try to collect taxes from individual purchasers (impracticable).

The classic flaws can easily seem highly conceptualist or technical in character. As such, they are ways of identifying good and bad legal form. There is more to them than that, however: they are linked to important "substantive" concerns. Here we will think about why we might care (value-wise) about whether a distinction exhibits the classic flaws or not.

Of course, most often in law, it will be impossible to avoid the classic flaws altogether. Very often, the relevant choice in law is not between adopting a flawed distinction and an unflawed one, but rather choosing among different kinds of flawed distinctions. For now, the important point is to recognize that the presence of classic flaws in a distinction will effectively raise important substantive concerns. Below, we look at the ways in which some of the classic flaws can frustrate or compromise important substantive values. These, of course, are only illustrative examples, not comprehensive by any means.

1. Waste

Much of legal decision-making involves crafting legal regimes that effectively allocate the relative scope and strength of two activities/considerations that are both valued but also conflict with each other, such as the following:

Fairness vs. Administrative Convenience
Freedom of Speech vs. Individual Privacy
Freedom of Contract vs. Security of Contracts
Liberty vs. Equality
Deterrence of Accidents vs. Minimization of Accident Avoidance Costs

The above are very high-level conflicts among valued concerns. Most often, of course, the conflicts between valued concerns arise in much more specific or technical legal contexts. The fact that valued concerns often conflict in law means that we have to worry about how we draw distinctions. If the distinction is poorly drawn, then waste will ensue. Waste occurs when at least one side of the value dispute is being sacrificed in a way that is not required to vindicate the other side. When can this occur? Well, precisely when the distinction is flawed in some way.

Example: Both the overbreadth doctrine and less restrictive means analysis in First Amendment case law provide wonderful illustrations of this phenomenon. Because the Supreme Court is so solicitous of speech (under the First and Fourteenth Amendments) it is very often in the position of striking down statutes by effectively saying to the states or the localities: "Yes, you have a valid governmental interest in . . . protecting the peace, avoiding civil disturbance, preventing crime . . . , but you (the state or the locality) could well have drafted a rule that vindicates that interest without impinging so much on speech activities (i.e., there are "less restrictive means"). You have unnecessarily impaired speech activities in a way that does not vindicate (i.e., this is waste!) your interest in protecting the peace, avoiding civil disturbance, and preventing crime."

These observations about waste are important because whenever we craft a legal distinction, we are often drawn at least a little bit toward the values or valued activities informing both sides of the distinction. If there is needless sacrifice on one side or the other (not to mention the possibility of sacrifices on both sides), then that is potentially waste that might have been avoided.

There's an important caveat to all this: just because a legal distinction creates *some* waste does not mean that we should reject or modify it. Why not? Well, it may be that the distinction is less wasteful than any of the other available distinctions. This is a point we have already encountered: where law is concerned we are seldom operating in an ideal world. We are almost always engaged in trade-offs—sacrificing a bit of this for a bit of that. The imperative "First, do no harm" is a principle of ethics in medicine. Even if it is readily applicable in that domain (a debatable matter), it is seldom an available option in law.

2. Fairness/Equality

Distinctions that are not appropriately fine-tuned can be seen to yield unfair or unequal results. *Vagueness* is a great example: if a distinction is vague, then chances are good that the parties applying the distinction (e.g., prosecutors, administrators, courts) may well apply the same distinction differently to similarly situated parties. In other words, two parties with exactly the same identity or conduct may well be treated differently simply because each decision-maker interprets the distinction differently.

Example: Consider the distinction between felonies and misdemeanors. Crimes categorized as felonies are often subject to more serious consequences (such as the loss of the right to vote or the right to hold public office). Meanwhile, the prosecution of crimes categorized as misdemeanors often has fewer procedural protections. Yet the differences between felonies and misdemeanors can be slight.

An *overlapping distinction* also exemplifies potential unfairness and inequality. Let's say we have an X/Y distinction. Those who engage in conduct X get four years in prison. Those who engage in conduct Y (which is not quite as bad as X) get only two years in prison. In an overlapping opposition there are some kinds of conduct that are both X and Y. Among cases that are both X and Y, decision-makers are likely to treat some of them as X and some of them as Y, even though there is no valid difference between the cases. Again, we would be treating similarly situated parties or concerns differently.

3. Subversion

Distinctions that exhibit the classic flaws will have unclear or uncertain application. One consequence is that the purposes for which the legal distinction is drawn will be subverted or frustrated. Not only will there be a lack of correspondence between the distinction and its ostensible normative appeal, but the uncertainty produced by the flaws will have other untoward effects. For instance, if a legal field is governed by flawed distinctions, the normal responses can involve any and all of the following: unproductive authority conflicts, parties escaping regulation, duplicative or redundant efforts by parties to protect their interests (and more).

4. Efficiency

Ideal distinctions (i.e., those that have high degrees of conceptual intelligibility, practicality, and normative appeal) are almost automatic in their application. They are perspicuous. They don't require a lot of thought or interpretation. By contrast, distinctions that are vague, overlapping, or otherwise flawed typically require further thought or interpretation. Either one invests effort in this further thought and interpretation, which is costly (these are known as *decision costs*), or one risks producing erroneous results, and that is costly as well (these are known as *error costs*). Similarly, in terms of the ex ante (i.e., the pre-dispute) context, flawed distinctions can yield enhanced transaction costs. When the legal regime is unclear, it is costly for the parties to bargain because it is unclear who has what and thus unclear how much they should be paid for giving it up. Such uncertainties about the law lead to greater uncertainties about bargaining positions and may make it difficult for parties to negotiate agreements or even to adapt their behavior to the law.

5. Rule of Law

Basic notions of the rule of law require that the law be both public and clear.[20] Flawed distinctions present challenges to both of these requirements. Indeed, flaws present the possibility that the legal distinction actually applied in a case is not the same as the one publicly announced. And the flawed distinctions also present the prospect that within the range of the flaw, decisions are rendered without reference to any distinction at all—that is to say, lawlessly.

It is important to understand how the classic flaws can be linked to these substantive concerns. The connections show that there is often a great deal at stake—more than simply "good legal form." Importantly, a lawyer or judge should always be prepared to articulate what substantive values are being sacrificed if a flawed distinction is asserted or proposed.

V. Crafting Legal Distinctions

Crafting a convincing legal distinction, of course, entails trying to minimize the classic flaws described above. Additionally, a well-crafted distinction will strive for the best possible trade-off among *conceptual intelligibility, practicality*, and *normative appeal.*

This much we know. But how is this accomplished? And what does the best possible trade-off mean?

Beginning with this latter question (the easier one), the best trade-off depends upon how one values each of the three aspects vis-à-vis each other. Some advocates and decision-makers will be particularly concerned with normative appeal, while others will be more concerned with practicality. They may also have different perspectives depending upon the legal context (e.g., torts or contracts, business dealings or individual rights?).

Now the tougher question—how to craft legal distinctions?

Ironically, there's not a lot to say here, though a few things might be noted. First and perhaps most important is that the choice of what distinction to draw is always a choice between various possible non-ideal distinctions. That is to say, all distinctions have flaws—that in some ways, they all fail to satisfy the three criteria perfectly.[21]

So how to choose?

Conceptual intelligibility and normative appeal are matters that, to a large degree, can be and generally are well addressed in law school classes. Making judgments about practicality, by contrast, is something best informed by experience with the actors and activities of the field. It requires immersion in the relevant factual or transactional context—and those are things generally not taught very well in law school (at least not through traditional methods). Perhaps the principal reason is, ironically, that student exposure to the relevant factual or transactional context is very often provided only by the reading of case law—to wit, judicial opinions. The latter, in turn, are generally written by people (i.e., judges) who believe they have done a pretty good job matching law to the facts. One way of doing that, of course, is to apprehend the facts through the conceptual architecture of the law.

To truly satisfy practicality, it is necessary to know something about the factual context in which the legal distinction is supposed to operate. Notice that, in one sense, this requirement holds even with regard to the "formalist strategy." Indeed, in order to use the formalist strategy well, one needs to know the relevant factual context well enough to recognize that a formalist strategy is likely to work—that the parties are likely to be induced to conform their behavior to a formalist conceptual architecture.

This point about knowing the factual and transactional context is sometimes slighted. A great many statutes and judicial opinions draw distinctions that seem truly excellent on paper (and perhaps even in class) but are nonetheless a complete mess when put into action. The explanation, very often, is that the judge or legislative staffer who crafted the distinctions did not know much about the social, technological, or economic institutions or practices to which the distinctions were supposed to apply. This actually happens a lot. Do not presume that merely by virtue of their status legal officials know what they are doing!

One easy way to satisfy practicality in articulating legal distinctions is to track with already existing social, economic, or technological practices and institutions. These will have their own "break points," and the law can be made to track with those. Language itself, of course, provides certain break points that are routinely tracked by law—in fact, so routinely, that many legal professionals don't even think about it. At other times, of course, normative considerations will prompt legal actors to create legal neologisms (new "legal conceptual boxes") to achieve desired objectives.

VI. Where Do You Draw the Line?

When a judge or a law professor asks, "Where do you draw the line?" this is often a clue that there is no perfect way to craft a legal distinction. When a judge asks the question, chances are good that she is looking for some help in fashioning a workable distinction. She will be concerned not just about the equities of the present case, but also about what a proposed distinction will mean by way of precedential authority for future cases and for parties not before the court. Judges are known to pose hypotheticals in oral argument in order to test proposed legal distinctions.

The question "Where do you draw the line?" implies that some distinction needs to be drawn between something like X and something like Y, but it's not clear how. Why should this be such a difficult question? After all, we are dealing here with a situation where everyone acknowledges that some distinction must be drawn. Why then the difficulties?

There are some answers. As discussed below there are different recurrent patterns that help explain why it may be hard to draw the line. It is important to understand all of them in their specificity because they call for different solutions.

A. THE NON-IDEAL WORLD AND THE INEVITABLE TRADE-OFFS

Choosing among non-ideal distinctions can be accomplished in several ways. One can ask a number of questions here. Which flaws are least (or most) troublesome, and when? Which criteria are most in need (or least in need) of satisfaction? And on what basis should such decisions be made? Obviously there are no easily generalizable answers to these questions.

> *Example: Suppose that if you draw the line at this point here, then maybe you avoid vagueness, but at the cost of some overbreadth. If, by contrast, you draw the line at that point there, then maybe you avoid overbreadth, but you get some discontinuity. And if you draw the line over there . . . then . . . (and so on). The idea here is that you have to make some trade-offs among the classic flaws. The question then becomes, How to choose? Is there even a good way to think about this? Do we just go with a gestalt sense?*

B. ARBITRARINESS

Often the specific problem is that the hypothetical cases presented to test a legal distinction (appellate judges and professors seem to be fond of this line of thought) all line up on a spectrum. Thus drawing the line at any given point will seem arbitrary.

> *Example 1: Many jurisdictions, for instance, set the number of jurors in criminal trials at twelve. But why twelve? Why not eleven? And if eleven, why not ten or nine or six or three? The point is that there is a range for setting the number of jurors that is irreducibly arbitrary . . . and yet no one disagrees that some minimum must be set.*

> *Example 2: How long should a defendant have to answer a complaint? Thirty days? Fifty days? Sixty days?*

The law must frequently impose distinctions (as the examples above reveal), even though there is no particular reason to favor one distinction over another. That is because nearly all points within the relevant spectrum seem equally valid. The choice, in these contexts, is arational. Notice that this is not a criticism: the law must often make choices (of this, we are sure) but without any clear justification for this choice as opposed to that one.

C. INDIVISIBILITIES

In economics, the concept of "indivisibility" refers to a production input unit—for instance, a printing press—that cannot be subdivided usefully for purposes of the business in question.[22] The idea of indivisibility is (despite the name) easy to understand. Some things are simply not helpfully divisible.

> *Example 1: A printing business might want to own one printing press or two printing presses, but purchasing one and a half printing presses is probably not advisable. A printing press is a valuable piece of machinery. One half of a printing press is merely a lot of metal.*
>
> *Example 2: A plane ticket from New York to Rome is valuable. A plane ticket to get you halfway to Rome will get you wet and likely will entail ocean rescue.*

So far as law is concerned we can generalize the concept of indivisibility to include not merely the economic, but the linguistic, economic, psychological, sociological, and so on. The idea is that each of these fields is marked out in terms of divisions that sometimes cannot be usefully subdivided any further.

One way of thinking about the indivisibility problem is to see it as the opposite of the spectrum problem. The spectrum problem presents an infinite number of possible distinctions—none more or less justifiable than the others. The indivisibility problem is the reverse: there are only a limited set of points (e.g., five) between the two poles where lines can be drawn, and we wish for normative reasons that there were more.

Here are some examples of conceptual indivisibility.

> *Example 1: In a typical torts class a student probably covers anywhere from seven to fifty-five different torts. Regardless whether the class covers seven or fifty-five, the likelihood is that only five different standards of care will be encountered:*
>
> *No liability*
> *Intentional tort*
> *Negligence*
> *Strict liability*
> *Absolute liability*
>
> *Admittedly, we could add "recklessness," "gross negligence," and "a high degree of vigilance," but beyond that it becomes more difficult. Consider: Would it be possible to come up with five or six distinct and meaningful standards of care that fall between intentional torts and negligence? Doubtful. Chances are they would collapse into each other and quite likely gravitate toward (and collapse into) one of the two poles: intentionality or negligence.*

Example 2: Mental states in criminal law exhibit the same sort of indivisibilities. Here are the classic options in American law:

Premeditation
Specific intent
General intent
Extreme indifference
Recklessness
Negligence
Strict liability

Here too, it seems difficult to come up with mental states that at once fall in between these classic options and yet do not "gravitate" toward and collapse into the options already listed. Presumably, we could add adjectives to the mental states. For instance, "reluctant premeditation" could be distinguished from "enthusiastic premeditation." But, while it is possible to imagine two different people displaying those affects, the question remains, Is the distinction itself meaningful?

These examples, taken from tort and criminal law, illustrate that if we care about conceptual intelligibility, the choice of plausible distinctions is far from infinite. On the contrary, the options may well be very limited.

Why does this matter practically speaking? It matters because legal professionals seem to think that they can draw distinctions wherever they choose. That is not so. And vexingly the attempt to draw distinctions while neglecting indivisibilities can yield nonsense.

Example: In law, it is very common to oppose the "bright line rule" and the "flexible standard." Now imagine trying to come up with distinctions between the two. Here's an easy one: the hybrid (which combines aspects of both ruleness and standardness). Here are two more: the rule-like hybrid and the standard-like hybrid . . . How about this possibility: the moderately rule-like hybrid? How far can we keep subdividing like this and still say something meaningful? Perhaps we've already gone too far. The point is that while it is possible to write sentences that seem to announce distinctions, the distinctions may amount to no more than words on the page.

Indivisibility concerns—and perhaps this is the more important problem—also arise when we turn to practicality. To display practicality, a legal distinction must track with the social, technological, or economic divisions already inscribed in the field of application (the realist strategy), or it must be sufficiently powerful to impose itself on the field (the formalist strategy).

Why does indivisibility create a problem for drawing legal distinctions? The answer has to do with normative appeal. Sometimes conceptual or operational indivisibilities *do not* track perfectly with the normative reasons we have for drawing a distinction. If that's the case, we will be drawing legal distinctions that perforce exhibit some of the classic flaws. We will be operating in a world of trade-offs.

Often appellate judges and law professors will pose a question about where to draw the line as if the field of application were static—as if the only thing affected by a rule change were the ostensibly targeted behavior (i.e., the nuisance, the breach, etc.). Such a static analysis is a simplification (and almost always wrongheaded). We have known for a long time that drawing a new distinction will yield effects on many activities in addition to the ostensibly targeted behavior.[23] This is so for several reasons.

First, a new distinction will, through stare decisis or analogical reasoning, have ripple effects throughout associated bodies of law or lines of authority. Moreover, despite what our legal training continually tells us, it seldom happens that a particular area of law can be isolated or segmented (in terms of consequences or implications) from the "seamless web" of law.[24] When we are not doing law we seem to understand and accept implicitly that everything affects everything (shades of the "butterfly effect"). When engaged in doing law (especially litigation) we seem to believe or at least pretend otherwise. This is a problem.

Second, a new distinction may well bring attitude changes and behavioral adjustments—not only in the parties engaged in the targeted behavior, *but among antagonists, competitors, allies, and even bystanders*. A new distinction can affect the demand for, or supply of, associated or substitute activities. The presence of a dynamic relations (and, offhand, all relations are dynamic) entails certain stereotyped patterns of behavioral adjustments. Among the most widely recognized in law are the following:

Opening the Floodgates of Litigation
Encouraging Resistance / Blowback Feedback Loop (Positive or Negative)
Tipping
Downstream and Upstream Effects
Chilling Effects
Unintended Consequences
Substitution
Exit

Anyone proposing a new legal distinction should think carefully about all these stereotyped patterns to test the viability and desirability of the distinction proposed. It is advisable to trace out all the effects and implications of both the existing and the proposed legal distinction.

E. PROBLEM FIELDS AND NON-FIELDS:
OF POLYCENTRICITY AND FLUX

Some dynamic relations pose particularly vexing challenges for the creation and application of legal distinctions. Below are two classic problems.

Polycentricity is a concept developed by Michael Polanyi and introduced into the legal vocabulary by Lon Fuller.[25] A polycentric dispute is one that has many interactive issues, parties, or considerations. Think here of a polycentric problem in the image of a spiderweb: there is no way to pull on one strand of the web without producing effects elsewhere; the nodes are all interconnected.[26] Adjudication with its characteristic part/whole framing (e.g., the breakdown of causes of action into discrete elements) is not well suited to deal with questions where the various issues, frames, and nodes have interactive effects on each other. Consider the following example given by Fuller:

> Some months ago a wealthy lady by the name of Timken died in New York leaving a valuable, but somewhat miscellaneous, collection of paintings to the Metropolitan Museum and the National Gallery "in equal shares," her will indicating no particular apportionment. When the will was probated the judge remarked something to the effect that the parties seemed to be confronted with a real problem. The attorney for one of the museums spoke up and said, "We are good friends. We will work it out somehow or other." What makes this problem of effecting an equal division of the paintings a polycentric task? It lies in the fact that the disposition of any single painting has implications for the proper disposition of every other painting. If it gets the Renoir, the Gallery may be less eager for the Cezanne but all the more eager for the Bellows, etc. If the proper apportionment were set for argument, there would be no clear issue to which either side could direct its proof and contentions. Any judge assigned to hear such an argument would be tempted to assume the role of mediator or to adopt the classical solution: Let the older brother (here the Metropolitan) divide the estate into what he regards as equal shares, let the younger brother (the National Gallery) take his pick.[27]

If the problem confronted is polycentric in this way, then the selection and enforcement of legal distinctions become a serious challenge.

Very often law does not confront polycentricity because the law's frameworks of distinctions have been already impressed on the social or economic relations such that they have already been cast in static part/whole terms. But when new relations emerge that are not already juridified in this way (think: cyberlaw, for example), polycentricity can be a huge problem. It is often thought that adjudication is inappropriate to deal with polycentric disputes—the reason being that adjudication is seldom (if ever?) in a position to comprehend the whole or the myriad ripple effects.

Flux is another instance in which crafting legal distinctions is extremely difficult. Heraclitus, the famous Greek philosopher, reportedly stated, "You cannot step in the same river twice." The idea is that the flow of water will have changed. Judge Andrews, in the famous case *Palsgraf v. Long Island Railroad*, repeatedly described causation in terms of water imagery. He invoked ripples in a lake and tributaries merging into a stream. With this liquidity metaphor, it was, of course, very difficult for him to set limits on causation. Indeed, consider at what point (can we really draw a line?) does a tributary merge with a stream? At what point do the ripples caused by a rock thrown into a lake cease? These questions are meant to indicate something rather obvious: if the field of application is to be apprehended not as a field at all, but rather as a flow, then any attempt to carve up this liquidity with distinctions is bound to seem arbitrary and perhaps even non-referential.

> *Example: In commerce clause jurisprudence, the "stream of commerce" test is often easy to apply. But there are circumstances where one can wonder, whether the stream of "commerce among the several states" has come to an end (and is thus beyond the purview of Congress) or whether the stream has even begun (and is also thus beyond the purview of Congress).[28]*

If the application of law is described in terms of "the field of application," then we are activating an image-metaphor of a stabilized two-dimensional space (the field). Such a static image-metaphor may well be appropriate in some circumstances, but not all. Family life, the internet, high finance, involve human relations or activities that might be better described, for instance, in terms of an image-metaphor of flux, or flow. But if liquidity seems more apt as image-metaphor (let's say it does), then the imposition of distinctions will be difficult or awkward or simply ineffective.

F. THE SLIPPERY SLOPE

The slippery slope is a commonplace argument in law. The basic idea is that if the court does not insist on a particular distinction in the present case, then later decision-makers will be unable, for a number of reasons, to draw a sound distinction at all.

> *Example 1: In* Lawrence v. Texas *(a homosexual sodomy case) Justice Scalia argued in dissent that if the state was not able to advance as a state interest a citi-*

zen's belief that certain kinds of sexual conduct are "immoral and unacceptable," then the state would be constitutionally unable to prohibit bigamy, adultery, incest, bestiality, and so on.

Example 2: In the famous First Amendment flag-burning case of Texas v. Johnson the Court asked rhetorically if states were allowed to ban flag burning, whether they would then be permitted to prohibit the burning of state flags, the presidential seal, or the Constitution, and so on.

The slippery slope argument is also known by other names: "the thin edge of the wedge," "the camel's nose under the tent," or "the parade of horribles."[29] While there may be some differences among these various arguments, they belong to the same argumentative neighborhood. The general idea is that if the court doesn't limit the reach of some principle, policy, value, or consideration in the present case, then that very same principle, policy, value, or consideration will deprive the court of establishing a viable distinction in later cases.

The interesting question is, Why would that happen? One answer is that there may be some kind of indivisibility (e.g., conceptualist, linguistic, social, economic) at work. The idea is that unless the court draws the line *here*, the next opportunity to draw the line is just too "far down" the slippery slope (perhaps even at "the bottom").

Example: Justice Scalia's dissent in Lawrence v. Texas (see above) offers this kind of argument. Justice Scalia could not see any moral difference (that the Court could take into account) between homosexual conduct, on the one hand, and bigamy, adultery, and incest, on the other. The implication for him is that unless the state is allowed to prohibit homosexual sodomy, the state is also precluded from prohibiting these other practices.

Slippery slope arguments can be countered in a variety of ways. One way to counter a slippery slope argument is simply to show that there are available distinctions to draw the line in future cases.

Example: Thus with regard to Justice Scalia's dissent in Lawrence v. Texas (see above) one could come up with reasons to distinguish homosexual sodomy from adultery, bigamy, incest, and so on. Adultery and bigamy, for instance, are breaches of the marital contract. Bigamy is, in practice, often a form of sex discrimination and arguably an exploitative relation. Incest brings about the risk of birth defects.

Another way to counter the slippery slope argument is to recharacterize the ostensibly noxious results as non-offensive.

Example: Maybe in fact the state ought not to be in the business of prohibiting bigamy or adultery?

Yet another kind of argument against the slippery slope is an assertion that there is no point on the slope that is not slippery.

> *Example: To continue with the image/metaphor of the slippery slope, a court shouldn't just look "downhill," but "uphill" as well. Maybe the entire slope is slippery—indeed, maybe it has always been slippery.*

VII. The Fetishism of the Legal Distinction

Legal professionals are often trained in law school to be as precise, clear, and accurate as possible. These qualities are often presented as highly appealing virtues in law. One imagines then that the best legal distinction to be drawn is what has been called here the *ideal legal distinction*—the one that satisfies *perfectly* the three criteria: *conceptual intelligibility*, *practicality*, and *normative appeal*.

The only doubts expressed so far about the ideal legal distinction are that, in our non-ideal world, such distinctions are seldom achievable. According to this view, there are generally (perhaps always) trade-offs to be made. From this non-ideal perspective it is important to remember that the choice is seldom (if ever) between an actual and an ideal legal distinction, but rather a choice among a set of legal distinctions—all of which are in various ways non-ideal. This is law. Nirvana is not an option.[30]

There are other reasons to be somewhat skeptical of overly insistent demands for ideal legal distinctions. It is certainly true that precision, clarity, and accuracy are important legal virtues. It is also true (though less seldom recognized) that sometimes they are not. To be sure, it's not clear that one ought to celebrate vagueness, ambiguity, or inaccuracy. But one might take note that precision, clarity, and accuracy sometimes create problems. Instead, one might give short shrift to precision, clarity, and accuracy in order to serve a number of different objectives, including the following:

Maintaining flexibility
Accommodating future change
Postponing decision-making
Deferring to other decision-makers
Delegating authority or power to decide to other decision-makers
Avoiding troublesome issues or decisions

Two other points seem worth raising here.

First, the attempt to articulate law in terms of ideal legal distinctions in effect supplants or encroaches upon the exercise of judgment, evaluation, perception, and reflection by others—citizens, professionals, scientists, and so on.[31] Indeed, there is a question to be faced about how much we want to leave undecided so that decision-making defers to or is shared with others not so closely associated with legal officials or the law.[32]

Second, an overly zealous commitment to ideal legal distinctions can easily lead to an unappealing "either/or-ism"—an almost compulsive binarism that ends up dividing the world into either this or that. In either/or-ism the legal professional posits that something (e.g., a property interest) can be X or Y. This invites (though it does not inevitably yield) certain mistakes. It leads away from recognizing that the thing in question might well be both X and Y as in XY . . . or that, given different contexts, time frames, or perspectives, and so on, the thing in question is sometimes X and sometimes Y . . . or the possibility that the thing in question is neither X nor Y but instead W or some unspecified and perhaps unspecifiable other entity . . . or that there are degrees of X-ness and Y-ness. In a particularly egregious display of either/or-ism, the legal professional will make the argument that since the thing in question is not X, it must be Y (neglecting the possibility that he or she might just as well have argued that since the something in question is not Y, it must be X).

Rules and Standards

Every law student has at some point encountered the "bright line rule" and the "flexible standard" as well as the arguments that can be advanced for or against each.[1] On the upside, rules are said to be certain and predictable. On the downside, they are said to be rigid and mechanical. Standards meanwhile are praised as flexible and adaptive. At the same time, they are criticized for being fuzzy and indeterminate.

In law school, this dispute is played out early and often—in fields as disparate as criminal procedure, the Uniform Commercial Code, constitutional law, and many more.

In one torts case, for instance, Justices Oliver Wendell Holmes and Benjamin Cardozo found themselves on opposite sides of a railroad crossing dispute.[2] They disagreed about what standard of conduct should define the obligations of a driver who comes to an unguarded railroad crossing. Holmes offered a rule: the driver must "stop and look." Cardozo rejected the rule and instead offered a standard: the driver must act with "reasonable caution." Which is the preferable approach? Holmes suggested that the requirements of due care at railroad crossings are clear, and, therefore, it is appropriate to crystallize these obligations into a simple rule of law. Cardozo countered with scenarios in which it would be neither wise nor prudent for a driver to stop and look. Holmes might well have answered that Cardozo's scenarios are exceptions and that exceptions prove the rule. Indeed, Holmes might have parried by suggesting that the definition of a standard of conduct by means of a legal rule is that it is predictable and certain, whereas standards and juries are not.

Much argument in modern legal systems (certainly in the American legal system) seems to be a manifestation of this stylized dispute about the relative virtues and vices of rules and standards. Indeed, the rules vs. standards disputes play an important role in fashioning legal directives. In this chapter we will consider the arguments for and against rules and standards.

The classic arguments for and against standards arise in two characteristic situations. One situation occurs when an advocate or decision-maker is faced with the question of whether to issue a directive in rule form or in standard form. Where such a choice is presented, the deployment of rules vs. standards arguments is very much to be expected. A second situation occurs where a directive is attacked by an advocate or decision-maker. In these circumstances, the advocate or decision-maker may well decide to characterize the directive as either a rule or a standard (and to urge the classic accompanying objections). The opposition may well respond accordingly.

This second situation brings up an interesting point. Whether a directive can be considered a rule or a standard is not merely a function of the directive itself, but of the context as well. Even a rule can seem standard-like when compared to an even more rule-like rule. Similarly, a standard can seem rule-like when compared to an even more standard-like standard. In this regard, it may sometimes be preferable to speak of ruleness and standardness as qualities (rather than as the essence of a directive).

I. Defining Rules and Standards

It is possible to look at positive law (constitutions, statutes, judicial opinions, and administrative orders) as a series of directives. The formula for a legal directive is "If this, then that." A directive thus has two parts: a "trigger," which identifies some phenomenon, and a "response," which requires or authorizes a legal consequence when that phenomenon is present.[3] Directives serve a number of *substantive* objectives, including the following:

Deterrence
Inducement
Allocation
Delegation
Correction
Structuration
Communication

Directives also have *formal* dimensions. For instance, directives can be the following:

General or specific[4]
Conditional or absolute

Narrow or broad[5]
Weak or strong[6]

And, most important here, they can also be rules or standards.[7] Thus, the opposition of rules and standards is one dimension of the form of a legal directive. Corresponding to the two parts of a directive, there are two sets of oppositions that constitute the rules vs. standards dichotomy: the trigger can be either empirical or evaluative, and the response can be either determined or guided. The paradigm example is a rule that has a hard empirical trigger and a hard determinate response. For instance, the directive that "sounds above seventy decibels shall be punished by a $10 fine" is an example of a rule. A standard, by contrast, has a soft evaluative trigger and a soft modulated response. The directive that "excessive loudness shall be enjoined upon a showing of irreparable harm" is an example of a standard.

Note that there are all sorts of difficulties with these definitions of rules and standards—not the least of which is the question of whether we should use a rule or a standard to decide what counts as a rule or a standard. The reason we care, of course, is that whether some directive is treated as a rule or instead as a standard immediately brings forth a whole series of different pro and con arguments. Another perplexing question is where we should look in deciding whether some directive is a rule or a standard: in the law books, in the way the directive is administered, or in the understandings of those subjected to the directive? More troubling still is the question of what counts as one complete directive. Note as well that, given the two-pronged aspects of legal directives (trigger and response), it is possible to have hybrids. (These complexities need not detain us here.)

II. The Rules vs. Standards Dialectic

The possibility of casting or construing directives as either rules or standards has given rise to patterned sets of "canned" pro and con arguments about the value of adopting either rules or standards in particular contexts. We call these stereotyped arguments the *dialectic*. It bears noting (as we shall see in the next section) that the rules vs. standards arguments comprise an arrested dialectic. The dialectic consists of ongoing, but inconclusive, arguments. The arguments do not lead anywhere—they simply go back and forth. It may be that a solution is found—but that is only because, at some point, the argument or the dispute is abandoned. One valorizes arguments on one side and disregards the rest.

TABLE 5.1. The Rules vs. Standards Dialectic

Pro Rules *You see, rules are good because they make the law . . .*	Con Rules *What nonsense! Rules are bad because they make the law . . .*	Pro Standards *In fact, it's really standards that are good because they make the law . . .*	Con Standards *What nonsense! Standards are bad because they make the law . . .*
determinate	mechanistic	flexible	vague
simple	crude	complex	muddy
sharp-edged	rigid	elastic	fuzzy
definitive	authoritarian	contextual	variable
elegant	reductionist	textured	messy
comprehensive	closed	open-ended	inchoate
autonomous	insular	connected	dependent

The pioneering work on rules vs. standards was done by Duncan Kennedy, who first described at some length the dialectical form of argument pitting the "bright line rule" against the "flexible standard." The arguments, as Kennedy pointed out, come in highly stereotyped forms. Hence they can be suggestively mapped out in tabular form—as in table 5.1, a slightly abridged and revised version of Kennedy's original chart.[8]

This is a relatively simple vices-and-virtues view of the rules vs. standards dispute, but it nonetheless summarizes accurately a great deal of the arguments commonly made for and against rules and standards.[9]

These arguments are ubiquitous—found in field after field. To give some sense of the ubiquity of the arguments, consider how easily one can deploy the canned pro and con arguments to argue for or against standard-like or rule-like versions of certain fundamental legal functions like deterrence, inducement, allocation, delegation, correction, structuration, or communication.

Here, for the sake of brevity, we will address only three of these functions: deterrence, delegation, and communication.

A. DETERRENCE

Many fields of law—including tort, criminal, and regulatory law—are ostensibly designed to deter selected activities or conduct. In any given situation, it is generally possible to argue both that deterrence is best served by rules and that it is best served by standards. The arguments are as shown in table 5.2.

TABLE 5.2. Deterrence: Pro and Con Arguments for Rules vs. Standards

	Rules
Pro	Rules draw a sharp line between forbidden and permissible conduct, allowing persons subject to the rule to determine whether their actual or contemplated conduct lies on one side of the line or the other. These persons are thus alerted to the nature of the prohibited conduct and can take steps to avoid it. The sharp line also ensures that no desirable or permissible conduct will be chilled. Furthermore, rules mete out a fixed quantum of predetermined deterrent, ensuring that a certain penalty will be imposed for engaging in the prohibited conduct.
Con	By specifying a sharp line between forbidden and permissible conduct, rules permit and encourage activity up to the boundary of permissible conduct. The application of the same deterrent force to forbidden conduct, regardless of how close or far it may be from permissible conduct, fails to distinguish between flagrant and technical violations. By predesignating and quantifying the magnitude of the penalty to be applied, rules allow Justice Holmes's proverbial "bad man" to treat the deterrent as a fixed cost of doing business.
	Standards
Pro	By describing the distinction between permissible and impermissible conduct in evaluative terms, standards allow the addressees to make individualized judgments about the substantive offensiveness or non-offensiveness of their own actual or contemplated conduct. Because the distinction between permissible and impermissible conduct is not fixed, but is case-specific, persons will be deterred from engaging in borderline conduct and encouraged to substitute less offensive types of conduct. Standards authorize application of a deterrent force proportional to the gravity of the evil, thus assuring that the strongest deterrent is reserved for and applied to the greatest social threats.
Con	Because standards do not draw a sharp line between permissible and impermissible conduct, some risk-averse people will be chilled from engaging in desirable or permissible activities, and some risk-preferring people will be encouraged to engage in antisocial conduct. Because the boundary between permissible and impermissible conduct is not preset, decision-makers in borderline cases are likely to reach erratic results, producing confusion about what is or is not permissible. The failure to announce in advance the magnitude of the penalty prevents persons subject to the standard from determining how much effort they should devote to avoiding violations.

B. DELEGATION

Many fields of law, such as agency, administrative, and constitutional law, are ostensibly designed to delegate functions, roles, or responsibilities to a variety of actors. As with deterrence, both pro and con arguments can be advanced to suggest that delegation is best effected by rules or by standards. See table 5.3 for these arguments.

C. COMMUNICATION/FORMALITIES/NOTICE

Much of contract, civil procedure, and property law is designed to establish systems through which various actors can communicate and thus give legal effect to their intentions. Again, there are pro and con arguments for the view that these formalities are best governed by rules and for the view that they are best governed by standards, as shown in table 5.4.

Once one becomes familiar with the rules vs. standards dialectic, one starts to recognize it and its analogous forms throughout law's empire. Indeed, given a bit of license, one might say:

Rules are to standards

as

formalism is to functionalism

as

hard law is to soft law

as

law is to equity.

TABLE 5.3. Delegation: Pro and Con Arguments for Rules vs. Standards

	Rules
Pro	Rules delegate by granting the subordinate complete authority and responsibility for the performance of certain factually defined tasks. By describing the subordinate's authority in empirical terms, the possibility of usurpation of authority by others or shirking of responsibility by the subordinate is minimized. The need for tests of authority between superior and subordinate is minimized, conflict is avoided, and time is saved. In granting complete authority over delegated matters, rules provide neat divisions of labor, thereby avoiding jurisdictional disputes and friction.
Con	Using rules to define the scope and nature of the subordinate's authority gives the subordinate ready-made safe havens that allow avoidance of responsibility or exercise of authority contrary to the objectives of the superior. Authority conflicts and wasted time are likely to be significant, as the delegation by rules results in exercise of authority or shirking of responsibility in ways and in contexts not expected by the superior. Because delegation by rules fails to discriminate in terms of the relative import or value of the matters that the subordinate performs, the likely result is that some significant matters will be handled by the subordinate, while some trivial matters are referred to the superior for action.
	Standards
Pro	Standards delegate by specifying the degree of authority the subordinate is to exercise in terms of the moral or aesthetic significance of the tasks. Standards ensure that the subordinate will exercise authority only over less significant matters and will refer more significant matters to the superior. Requiring that the subordinate make his own judgments as to the significance of various issues relieves the superior from a time-consuming screening function. By relating the subordinate's authority to the significance of the tasks, the superior minimizes the cost of fallout from the subordinate's erroneous decisions.
Con	Delegating by standards means that the subordinate will use whatever criteria he wants to decide whether or not he will exercise authority. The judgment of the subordinate about the significance of various issues simply cannot be trusted. Erroneous or subversive exercises of authority or shirking of responsibility will necessitate costly and time-consuming intervention by the superior. By requiring the subordinate to make difficult evaluative judgments, standards increase the likelihood of erroneous determinations.

TABLE 5.4. Communication: Pro and Con Arguments for Rules vs. Standards

	Rules
Pro	Rules describe permissible modes of communication in empirical terms by specifying terms of art, boilerplate messages, and acceptable methods of communication. By specifying routine means of communication, rules minimize the possibility of misunderstanding, making transactions more secure. Rules also make transactions more secure because parties know their intentions will be honored by the decisionmaker and because the costs of dispute resolutions are minimized. Rules reduce the cost of communicating intent or meaning by offering ready-made legal boxes signifying different meanings and intents. By attaching "either/or" consequences to communicative activity, rules encourage parties to learn and master the routine means of communication and thus facilitate most communications and transactions.
Con	The specification of routine means of communication by rules restricts and truncates communication, and thwarts understanding. Some transactions will be deterred because their substance cannot easily be communicated via the routinized means of communication and because failure to fit the transaction within an established legal box may result in nullity. Formalities cast in terms of rules can distort meaning and understanding and defeat authentic communication by favoring those most adept at manipulating legal boxes.

	Standards
Pro	Standards delineate the formal requirements of communications in evaluative terms designed to ascertain whether there has been effective communication. By allowing the parties to choose the most appropriate means of communication in light of their particular substantive intentions, standards minimize the possibility of distortion. Because standards are cast in evaluative terms, they place the onus on the parties to work out and communicate their intentions completely and thoroughly, thereby minimizing unexpected or unconsidered consequences of their transaction. Standards allow the parties to develop their own rituals. By tailoring the consequences of miscommunication to the gravity and the nature of the defect, standards serve to enforce the parties' expectations as to matters upon which communication was effective. In this way, standards give effect to the parties' intentions more accurately than the all-or-nothing consequences of complete effectuation or nullity.
Con	Standards encourage the proliferation of a multiplicity of communicative means and mediums, making communication more uncertain and transactions less secure. Even ritualized forms of communication established by the parties are insecure because there is a chance that the ritualized messages and meanings will not conform to the standard. Because the validity of the communication cannot be determined in advance by the parties, standards encourage parties who have the most to lose from adhering to the communication to seek invalidation of the communication by an official decisionmaker. Because standards provide a proportioned response to miscommunication rather than all-or-nothing response, the parties cannot gauge in advance what the consequences of miscommunication will be.

III. The Substantialized Versions of the Dialectic

The rules vs. standards dialectic appears all the more ubiquitous once one recognizes that the disputes are most often enacted in substantialized form and thus, on first impression, might not be immediately recognizable as rules vs. standards disputes. The rules vs. standards disputes are "substantialized" in the sense that the dialectic is *blended* in with the substantive transactional as well as normative aspects of the disputes. By way of example, table 5.5 provides some rule-like and standard-like versions of legal doctrine and legal values.

Once one recognizes that in any given dispute the sides can be characterized as rule-like and standard-like, it becomes possible to invoke the dialectic. Of course, often the arguments will be *substantialized*—dressed in the trappings of detail and the authority of the transactional and normative

TABLE 5.5. Legal Doctrine and Legal Values: Rule-Like and Standard-Like Approaches

	Doctrine	
	Rule-Like Approach	*Standard-Like Approach*
Possession (ferae naturae)	certain control	hot pursuit
Procedural Due Process	dignitary view	instrumental view
Evidence Law	admissible/inadmissible	unfairly prejudicial
Equal Protection	tiered review	sliding scale
Incorporation Controversy	total incorporation	fundamental rights
Contracts/Parol Evidence	four corners	intent of the parties
	Values	
	Rule-Like Approach	*Standard-Like Approach*
Fairness	uniform treatment[a]	just deserts[b]
Equality	formal equality[c]	substantive equality[d]
Neutrality	disinterestedness[e]	even-handedness
Freedom	negative[f]	positive[g]
Efficiency	Pareto efficiency[h]	Kaldor-Hicks efficiency[i]

[a]FREDERICK SCHAUER, PLAYING BY THE RULES: A PHILOSOPHICAL EXAMINATION OF RULE–BASED DECISION-MAKING IN LAW AND IN LIFE 149–53 (1991).

[b]Kathleen M. Sullivan, *The Justices of Rules and Standards*, 106 HARV. L. REV. 22, 66 (1992).

[c]FRIEDRICH A. HAYEK, THE CONSTITUTION OF LIBERTY 87 (1978).

[d]Martha Nussbaum, *Foreword: Constitutions and Capabilities; "Perception" against Lofty Formalism*, 121 HARV. L. REV. 4, 58 (2007).

[e]Scott Peppet, *Contractarian Economics and Mediation Ethics: The Case for Customizing Neutrality through Contingent Fee Mediation*, 82 TEX. L. REV. 227 (2003).

[f]Isaiah Berlin, *Two Concepts of Liberty, in* THE PROPER STUDY OF MANKIND 191, 203-06 (1997).

[g]Robin West, *Rights, Capabilities, and the Good Society*, 9 FORDHAM L. REV. 1901, 1906–07 (2001).

[h]Pareto optimality is achieved if there is no distribution that can make at least one person better off without making anyone worse off. (For obvious reasons, in the world of "forced exchanges" we generally know as law, we cannot have much use for this concept. Think of it this way: What are the chances that there is any change in legal doctrine (any change at all) that won't make at least one person worse off? *See generally* Guido Calabresi, *The Pointlessness of Pareto: Carrying Coase Further*, 100 YALE L.J. 1211 (1991).

[i]A legal or policy change is said to be Kaldor-Hicks efficient if the gainers gain sufficiently that they could compensate what the losers lose from the change. Kaldor-Hicks efficiency does not require that the compensation actually be made.

setting. But once the basic patterns of this rules vs. standards dialectic are mastered, the canned pro and con arguments can be marshaled in just about any context. Whether or not the arguments will be persuasive in any given context is, of course, a different question—one that depends largely on how the issues are framed, what values are held dear, the character of the audience, and other considerations that will be discussed later.

Many controversial issues in constitutional law (and elsewhere) are often cast as disputes over the relative appropriateness of rules and standards.

> *Example: Consider the power of police to search a vehicle incident to arrest. In Arizona v. Gant,[10] the Supreme Court considered the extent of this power in a rules vs. standards framework. Should the police have the power to search any vehicle when a recent occupant has been arrested (a rule)? Or only if the person arrested is within reach of the vehicle or it is reasonable for the police to believe the vehicle contains relevant evidence (a standard)?[11] Previous courts had interpreted Supreme Court precedent to create a bright line rule, and in Gant the Supreme Court changed that interpretation to what it considered a more appropriate standard.*

The ubiquity of the rules vs. standards arguments prompts a nagging and perhaps dispiriting question: Is there any substance to this heady and learned law-talk or is most of the argumentation simply a kind of rote repetition of the dialectic in different contexts? The next section defers this impertinent question and seeks instead to examine the rational accounts that might explain the dialectic.

IV. The Limitations of the Dialectic

The ubiquity of the rules vs. standards disputes has led to numerous efforts to try to rationalize the dispute—to render it intelligible in terms of various substantive normative concerns. As is frequent in legal thought, the attempt has been to try to generate general criteria to discern when to use a standard and when to use a rule. While we have not canvassed all the efforts in this regard—the rules vs. standards scholarship is now more than a cottage industry—our sense is that these efforts are likely to prove quixotic. The reason is simple: there is no place from which to adjudicate the rules vs. standards dispute that is itself outside of, or immune from, the rules vs. standards dialectic itself. As we will suggest in the section following this one, the dispute is irreducible.

Still, something might be learned by trying to canvass the kinds of explanations that have been given as to why we should choose rules or standards.

We will consider three of these here: the vices-and-virtues vision already encountered above, the polycentricity challenge, and the epistemological twist.

A. OF VICES AND VIRTUES

Perhaps the most common view of the rules vs. standards dialectic is the one we have just discussed: the vices-and-virtues vision that presents rules vs. standards disputes as a choice between competing formal values such as certainty or flexibility, uniformity or individualization. The idea, of course, is that one chooses a standard or a rule depending on which kind of virtue is most important to achieve (e.g., certainty or flexibility) or which vice is most important to avoid (e.g., rigidity or manipulability). There are, of course, many other accounts of the dialectic, but nearly all of them seem to accord integrity to the basic virtues and vices stereotypically associated with rules and standards.

There is something appealing about this explanation. First, it rings familiar: it confirms what we have known all along. Second, the explanation imports a meaningful normative coherence to the choice between rules and standards. A preference for either rules or standards can be seen as a coherent normative choice about which values ought to be preferred in a given context. This is all very comforting.

And it doesn't work.

One problem with the rules vs. standards dialectic is that it turns out that rules and standards exhibit their characteristic virtues only when they are ideally suited to the "substantive" context of application. This implies, among other things, that we can make no determination whether a rule or a standard will exhibit its characteristic virtues apart from an understanding of the substantive context of application. Whether a rule or a standard exhibits its characteristic virtues depends upon how well it fits the substantive context of application. Form does not, as a general matter, in and of itself determine the character of the field of application. Sometimes it will. Sometimes it won't. But the important point is that one cannot make that determination based purely on form. The relation of the form to the substantive context of application needs to be assessed.

> *Example 1: Imagine a well-settled custom or course of dealing among grain farmers with their suppliers. Imagine that this settled practice enables the various actors to apportion loss, compensate for delays, and so on in a very flexible, context-sensitive, standard-like way. Now imagine that the courts step in with all sorts of contract rules that effectively override the settled custom. Will that produce greater certainty or predictability? Doubtful. Sometimes, when standard-like*

social norms, habits, customs, or practices of a group of people are well settled, the best thing the law can do is to adopt a regime that incorporates or tracks those standard-like social norms, habits, and so on.

Example 2: Imagine that the US Supreme Court abandons the rule-like safe haven of the Miranda *warnings in favor of a coercion standard that frequently requires individualized judicial determinations as to whether a custodial interrogation is unconstitutionally coercive. As a result, there is a pervasive involvement by the courts in review of individual police actions. In what sense is this flexible or context-sensitive? Certainly the constancy of review is not flexible. As to whether the approach is context-sensitive, it is certainly not sensitive to the context of law enforcement procedures or personnel capabilities.*

The second big problem with the rules vs. standards dialectic is that when one actually inquires into the "substantive" context of application, it turns out that the context is itself capable of rule-like and standard-like descriptions. The upshot then is that one cannot confidently choose between rules and standards based upon a description of the "substantive" context of application without first choosing between the rule-like and the standard-like descriptions of that context.

The point is well illustrated by the railroad dispute between Justices Holmes and Cardozo discussed at the beginning of this chapter.[12] Recall that Holmes argued for a rule—requiring an automobile driver upon coming to an unguarded railroad crossing to stop, look, and listen. Recall that Cardozo opted for a standard—reasonable care under the circumstances. As one peruses their opinions, it turns out that Holmes and Cardozo have very different views of the substantive context of application—views that, not surprisingly, would predispose them to choosing a rule or a standard, respectively.

For Holmes, railroad crossings generally look alike, present the same dilemmas, and thus invite laying down a rule. Consider what Holmes says to justify his rule. He explains that when a man goes upon a railroad track, he knows he will be killed if a train comes. He knows—and now, this is the crucial part—that "he must stop for the train, not the train stop for him."[13] Here, Holmes is effectively characterizing the operative facts concerning drivers going through unguarded railroad crossings. What are these facts? They are generalized facts—imputed, apparently, to all drivers: the driver *knows that he must stop for the train, not the other way around.* Now, if those are the operative facts (not just in this case, but in *all* railroad crossing cases), then, of course, the responsibility rests on the driver, and, of course, it makes sense to impose a rule-like stop and look. Indeed, the appropriateness of the rule form has already been prefigured in Holmes's characterization of the operative facts, the relevant context—to wit: the knowledge of drivers *generally* upon coming to railroad crossings. (This is not to say, of course, that there aren't other ways to explain or interpret Holmes's decision.)

As for Cardozo's standard—it is already rhetorically anticipated in his recitation of the facts. For Cardozo, railroad crossing liabilities have nothing to do with what drivers know generally, and everything to do with the apparently variegated physical layout of railroad crossings and the widely varying risks and benefits of the possible precautions that drivers can take. The point is demonstrated in Cardozo's appropriately lengthy recitation of various railroad crossing scenarios:

> Standards of prudent conduct are declared at times by courts, but they are taken over from the facts of life. To get out of a vehicle and reconnoiter is an uncommon precaution, as everyday experience informs us. Besides being uncommon, it is very likely to be futile, and sometimes even dangerous. If the driver leaves his vehicle when he nears a cut or curve, he will learn nothing by getting out about the perils that lurk beyond. By the time he regains his seat and sets his car in motion, the hidden train may be upon him. Often the added safeguard will be dubious though the track happens to be straight, as it seems that this one was, at all events as far as the station, about five blocks to the north. A train traveling at a speed of thirty miles an hour will cover a quarter of a mile in the space of thirty seconds. It may thus emerge out of obscurity as the driver turns his back to regain the waiting car, and may then descend upon him suddenly when his car is on the track. Instead of helping himself by getting out, he might do better to press forward with all his faculties alert. So a train at a neighboring station, apparently at rest and harmless, may be transformed in a few seconds into an instrument of destruction. At times the course of safety may be different. One can figure to oneself a roadbed so level and unbroken that getting out will be a gain. Even then the balance of advantage depends on many circumstances and can be easily disturbed. Where was Pokora to leave his truck after getting out to reconnoiter? If he was to leave it on the switch, there was the possibility that the box cars would be shunted down upon him before he could regain his seat. The defendant did not show whether there was a locomotive at the forward end, or whether the cars were so few that a locomotive could be seen. If he was to leave his vehicle near the curb, there was even stronger reason to believe that the space to be covered in going back and forth would make his observations worthless. One must remember that while the traveler turns his eyes in one direction, a train or a loose engine may be approaching from the other.

Illustrations such as these bear witness to the need for caution in framing standards of behavior that amount to rules of law. Extraordinary situations may not wisely or fairly be subjected to tests or regulations that are fitting for the common-place or normal. In default of the guide of customary conduct, what is suitable for the traveler caught in a mesh where the ordinary safeguards fail him is for the judgment of a jury.[14]

Cardozo's view of railroad crossings is thus standard-like; he focuses on the particular, the specific, and the variegation (which is why his recital of the possible factual transactions is appropriately lengthy). His description effectively prepares the reader to conclude that reasonable precautions by a driver at railroad crossings will require a number of different behaviors depending on the disparate circumstances.

Notice what both Holmes and Cardozo have done. In both cases they have prefigured in their descriptions of railroad crossings the pro-rule and pro-standards positions that they will take as a matter of law. One might say that Holmes has a rule-like vision of railroad crossing accidents, while Cardozo has a standard-like vision.

All this is an extended illustration in the rules and standards context of what we will later call *recursivity*: the appropriateness of rules and standards at railroad crossings has already been prefigured in the description of the facts (the railroad crossing, the knowledge of the driver) and the transactional challenge (minimizing the harmful train/automobile encounter).

How does any of this matter practically? It matters in that the advocate must recall that the rules vs. standards dialectic is a patterned form of argument, the cogency of which depends upon how the "substantive" context of application is imagined. There can be no validation of the vices-and-virtues view of rules and standards absent an examination of the context of application. In turn, the context of application can almost always be described in a more rule-like or a more standard-like way.

None of this means that the rules vs. standards arguments are meaningless or without consequence. It does mean, however, that one cannot tell what those meanings or consequences will be absent an inquiry into the substantive transactional context. In turn, the substantive transactional context is itself susceptible to rule-like or standard-like descriptions. This, of course, creates something of a circle.

There are other problems with the vices-and-virtues vision—as described elsewhere.[15]

B. THE POLYCENTRICITY CHALLENGE

One possible account of the rules vs. standards dialectic is based on the notion that standards are more appropriate when a legal issue involves a multitude of interrelated and interactive variables (polycentricity). Lon Fuller, who introduced the concept of polycentricity to law, had something different in mind than the rules vs. standards dispute (namely, the effective limits of adjudication), but nonetheless the concept might be used as an argument for standards (and the gestalt judgment permitted by such). As Fuller noted,

> We may visualize this kind of [polycentric] situation by thinking of a spider web. A pull on one strand will distribute tensions after a complicated pattern throughout the web as a whole. Doubling the original pull will, in all likelihood, not simply double each of the resulting tensions but will rather create a different complicated pattern of tensions. This would certainly occur, for example, if the doubled pull caused one or more of the weaker strands to snap. This is a "polycentric" situation because it is "many centered"—each crossing of strands is a distinct center for distributing tensions.

Rules, in accordance with this line of reasoning, would be more appropriate when the legal issue involves merely drawing a line between two competing concerns.[16]

This explanation is weakened at the outset by the recognition that the rules vs. standards dialectic can arise even when there are only two competing concerns. Indeed, the standardized pro-con arguments about rules and standards were presented in the context of rigid dualities.

Still, there might be something to the claim that when a multitude of interrelated and interactive variables must be taken into account, standards are more appropriate than rules. The argument is that in these circumstances only a standard can allow for the trade-offs and balancing required. The appeal of this argument rests very much on the supposition that the choice is between one rule and one standard. This underlying imagery suggests that while one rule must perforce be simple, one standard can partake of infinite complexity.

But this underlying imagery must be questioned. If one rule means simply the attachment of an either/or consequence to the presence or absence of one empirical phenomenon, then indeed standards might be more appropriate than rules when the issue seems polycentric. This is a Pyrrhic conceptual victory, however, because there is no reason to suppose that one standard is more appropriate in dealing with a polycentric issue than a collection of rules is. Furthermore, even this point seems weak—what entitles us to call an issue polycentric? To suggest that an issue is polycentric bespeaks a standard-like way of framing the issue: the rule-like response is that the assertion of polycentricity in any given context stems from an improper amalgamation of conceptually distinct issues.

This approach based on a polycentric/bicentric distinction is also a variation on the vices-and-virtues vision. While it refuses to rationalize the dialectic by connecting it to normative values, this approach offers the minimal rationality of *formal coherence*. Thus, the notion that standards are appropriate when issues are polycentric, and rules appropriate when issues are not polycentric, can inform our choices about whether to adopt rules and standards by making a connection between the dialectic and another formal dimension of legal issues (polycentricity vs. bicentricity). While more modest than the vices-and-virtues vision, this approach allows judgments to be based on the view that there is a normative coherence among various formal dimensions. This, too, is a classic move: the idea is that while we can rarely say anything about how form relates to substance, we can, at least, say intelligent things about how one form relates to other forms.

One classic problem with this approach is deciding which form should be privileged. Which form should serve to explain the other? Initially we attempted to explain the dialectic in terms of the poly- or bi-centricity of the issue. But then it became apparent that this description was backward, and something like the reverse might be more accurate. We may be compelled to picture any given legal issue in rule-oriented or standard-oriented ways before we can decide whether the issue is polycentric or not.

This brings us to another problem with this "formal coherence" approach. It cannot spark our interest unless formal coherence has some ascertainable relation to substance. But by retreating to notions of formal coherence we have deprived ourselves of the ability to say anything about how form relates to substance. Why would we ever be interested in formal coherence for its own sake?

C. THE EPISTEMOLOGICAL TWIST

One last attempt to explain the rules vs. standards dialectic would be to suggest that standards are most appropriate when we lack knowledge or information about an issue. Thus we can picture the development of a particular legal standard, such as the reasonable person in tort law, leading to the development of specific rules. As the standard is applied to an increasing number of situations, more knowledge is gained concerning its meaning and slowly it is transformed into a collection of rules. This is the familiar process of synthesizing individual decisions into broader directives.

> *Example: Consider the exclusionary rule, which is (arguably) a standard: evidence improperly obtained should be excluded only if, under the circumstances, its exclusion would deter future bad behavior by police, and the deterrence value*

outweighs the cost of suppressing evidence (a cost to truth). A standard is (argu-
ably) the appropriate directive because a court can evaluate deterrence only on a
case-by-case basis. But the many decisions applying the exclusionary rule develop
what look much more like rules. When the police do X, the evidence should be
excluded, but when the police have done Y, it should not be.

Certainly we have seen examples of this transubstantiation of standards
into rules. But there are equally obvious counterexamples. Article 9 of the
Uniform Commercial Code, for instance, transformed a field of law once
governed by a meticulous architecture of rules into a domain of standards.
And in some instances, a field of rules can become littered with exceptions, so
that a rule loses its "bright line" quality. Quite obviously, the more counterexamples we develop, the more the epistemological twist seems inadequate.

The explanation fails for another reason. Upon closer inspection it turns
out that standards are most appropriate not when we lack knowledge generally, but when we lack *certain kinds* of knowledge. Specifically, when we have
difficulties evaluating the normative character of actions (but agree about
values) we are more likely to use standards. By contrast, when we lack knowledge (or consensus) about normative values we are more likely to cast directives in the form of rules. There is an intuitive appeal to this more refined
epistemological view—the economy of legal form it describes seems plausible. Sometimes the type of knowledge we possess on a given issue will allow
standards to work well and compel rules to fail, whereas with other issues the
situation might be reversed. With any given issue the appropriateness of rules
or standards depends upon the comparative status of our knowledge: Do we
know more about how to evaluate the facts, or do we know more about what
values to pursue?

There is, however, another way to restate the prongs of the distinction: Is
it the facts that we cannot evaluate? (If so, use a standard.) Or is our problem
a lack of knowledge about values? (If so, use a rule.) Restated in this manner,
the distinction collapses. There is no place outside the dialectic that would
allow us to decide this issue. Here too the dialectic seems primordial.

The epistemological twist is a specific illustration of a classic move to
reconcile oppositions in the face of imperfect knowledge: the *comparative
scheme.* The classic problem with using comparative schemes to reconcile
nonfungible oppositions, such as rules and standards, is that there is no single
language that can do justice to both of the oppositions. In the very process of
adopting a comparative scheme one is without a metaposition, and one must
necessarily prefer one conception to the other. The adoption of a comparative scheme is an attempt to temporize the irreconcilable oppositions. It fails

because the irreconcilability of the oppositions resurfaces in the attempt to develop a place from which to implement the comparative scheme.

We have surveyed a number of attempts to rationalize or understand the dialectic. There is power in each of the visions reviewed. There is also inadequacy in some crucial respects. The next section is an attempt to come to grips with the dialectic by explaining why it cannot be explained.

V. The Irreducibility of the Dialectic

The dialectic is irreducible. We cannot make sense of it in terms other than its own. Attempts to explain the dialectic founder in two ways.

First, attempts to explain the dialectic in terms of substantive legal values, or other dimensions of legal form, or in terms of political consciousness, succeed only in replicating the dialectic in these other domains. This yields the suspicion that these other domains, rather than explaining the dialectic, can themselves be understood in terms of the dialectic. There is a rather vexing reversal going on here. In trying to explain the dialectic by reference to substantive values or political schisms (and so on) we end up doing quite the opposite. It turns out that the dialectic seems primordial, and these other domains derivative.

But there is more—the second reason we cannot explain the dialectic is that the dialectic not only seems to replicate itself in any domain we choose to use as the basis for explanation, but also seems to mediate the very relation of the dialectic to these fields. In other words, the relation of the dialectic to these other fields is itself shaped by the dialectic.

Both of these problems can be restated in simpler and more abstract terms. We think it worthwhile to state the propositions in this more general and abstract manner, not only for the sake of clarity, but also because their application goes beyond the understanding of the dialectic. Indeed, the foregoing attempts to understand the dialectic illustrate the general problems inherent in the enterprise of explaining aspects of form by reference to substance.

The more abstract version goes like this: the dialectic is an aspect of form. Legal scholars and lawyers typically try to explain or understand form by relating it to substance. To varying degrees that is what the vices–and–virtues vision and its variations attempt to do. There are two problems with this approach.

The first problem is that every time we explain a form (the dialectic) in terms of substance we do not encounter substance but rather more form. In fact we encounter the very same form (the dialectic)—we are engaged in tautologies. Substance does not explain form; rather, it is more likely the other way around. Form appears primordial.

The second problem that we encounter in trying to explain form (the dialectic) by reference to substance is that the relation between form and substance seems to be itself colored by the form (the dialectic). The relation of form to substance appears to be a question of form.

Why should these problems recur in our attempts to understand the dialectic? Consider this speculative answer. First, all knowledges that might serve to explain the dialectic are themselves entrapped in a dialectic of their own. In other words, economics, psychology, sociology, and the other social or human sciences are each internally split along the lines of the dialectic. Second, very few people in law or in other disciplines are firmly committed to any position within the dialectic. In other words, virtually no one is committed to just the rule perspective or just the standard perspective.

Within any of the social or human sciences it is possible to see a more rule-like or a more standard-like vision of the theoretical base or crucial tenets of the science. A rule-like vision of the science uses a well-developed matrix of empirical categories to organize phenomena. The conclusions reached by means of these categories seem mechanistic, preordained. Vulgar Marxism, or popular understanding of Freud, for instance, might be examples of rule-like knowledges. The methodology of rule-like knowledges is conceptualist. It operates by defining and redefining categories and classifying phenomena into predetermined classifications. Standard-like knowledges, by contrast, do not have well-defined conceptual grids. Rather, these knowledges are heuristic and open-ended. The categories are not really categories at all. Instead, the structure of standard-like knowledges is based upon evaluative parameters or variables that overlap and seem fuzzy. Standard-like knowledges are self-consciously evaluative. The methodology of these knowledges operates by identifying relations, tendencies, and directions.

There are serious objections to both of these types of knowledges. Rule-like knowledges seem too simplistic. The grids are too rigid. One has the feeling that phenomena are crammed into the taxonomies whether they fit or not. Rule-like knowledges truncate much of what we would like explained by defining or classifying it away. Standard-like knowledges fare differently, but no better. These knowledges seem so tentative, so epistemologically insecure, that they furnish little in the way of learning. These knowledges place too much importance on context: everything becomes a question of context. The evaluative parameters are too many and too conflicting to be able to yield any predictions about human behavior.

So here we are: caught between the *inevitably crude naming* of rule-like knowledges and the *unavoidably vague evaluation* of standard-like knowledges. If this vision of the social or human sciences is correct, then these knowledges cannot help us explain the dialectic. For one thing, the dialectic is replicated in the very structure of these knowledges. For another, we are epistemologically dissatisfied with the ruleness or the standardness of these knowledges. We already know the objections.

Indeed, our dissatisfaction with both rule-oriented and standard-oriented approaches is reflected in the tendency of rules to evolve or degenerate, depending upon our perspective, into standards, and standards to evolve or degenerate into rules. This tendency toward refinement or entropy occurs via some routine patterns, as follows.

1. Standards tend to become concretized by means of specific rules. (The meaning of a general standard is found in its specific applications.)
2. Rules tend to yield specific exceptions that are generated by appeal to other standards. (The meaning of a general rule is found in the standards limiting its application.)
3. When discrete sets of rules and rule-like exceptions grow too large, they tend to be replaced by standards under the guise of rationalizing the law. (Excessive "ruleness" yields an attempt to rationalize by means of standards.)
4. When discrete sets of standards grow too large, they are ordered by means of overarching rules that prioritize the standards and define rigidly their jurisdictional application. (Standards must be ranked and prioritized.)
5. Terms that originally required standard-like thinking become frozen and are treated as rule-like names. (Even language that on its face smacks of evaluation may eventually have a naming function.)
6. Terms that originally served as names in rule-like constructs are redefined in terms of evaluative goals. (Even language that seems clearly to refer to empirical phenomena may become a term of art.)
7. Finally, of course, we get some radical breaks: a whole set of issues previously subject to rule-like directives is by fiat subject to a standard regime or vice versa.

6

Resolving Regime Conflicts

As mentioned earlier, modern legal systems can be seen as composed of various artifactual forms (or for the sake of simplicity, artifacts):

Concepts (e.g., "common carrier")
Directives (e.g., "A contract requires consideration")
Principles (e.g., "no liability without fault")
Policies (e.g., "Tort law aims to deter accidents")
Values (e.g., "fairness")
Considerations (e.g., "administrative convenience")
Interests (e.g., "privacy")

In any given area of law, these artifacts can be related to each other in a variety of ways. A directive (e.g., "no strict liability for product injuries without proof of a defect") might, for instance, *limit* the reach of a policy (e.g., cost spreading). A principle (e.g., "No persons should profit from their own wrongs") might *justify* a particular judicial directive (e.g., "The murdering heir cannot inherit from his victim"). A consideration (e.g., Who has the best access to evidence on this issue?) might be used to *extend* the reach of a doctrine (e.g., res ipsa loquitur). And so on.

The relations among the artifacts above are multiple and varying across different legal contexts. An artifact may perform any number of different actions on another—including *limit, extend, incorporate, justify, modify, strengthen, weaken,* and so on.

In this chapter, we focus on just one of these relations—namely, *opposition*. For our purposes, all of these artifacts *stand in opposition* to each other when they are made to yield conflicting outcomes. For ease of reference, we will call these oppositions *conflicts*.

Sometimes conflicts are stark—as in the case of a logical incompatibility: Rule 1 says that X is a common carrier, while Rule 2 says that X is not ever a common carrier. Sometimes incompatibility is of a more practical nature, albeit just as stark: Rule 3 requires A to do X, while Rule 4 prohibits A from doing X. Or to give an example in procedure, a binding decision requires a deferential standard of review in case Y, while another binding decision requires no deference in case Y.

At other times, the conflict is much more attenuated—as when two policies, principles, or values seem to "push" or "pull" in opposed directions. Thus, for instance, an interest in personal privacy will often conflict with the public's right to know. A policy of reducing accident costs will generally be in tension with a policy of limiting accident avoidance costs.

For the purposes of this chapter, *regime conflict* encompasses all forms of antagonism—logical incompatibility, practical impossibility, contradiction, competition, interference, tension, and divergence.

Judges and other legal officials have many different techniques available to avoid regime conflicts, including the following:

> The invocation of authority ("This precedent controls, and so this side prevails. Full stop.")
> The performance of legal interpretation ("Properly construed, this statute does not apply here, and so that other statute controls.")
> The deployment of legal or policy analysis ("To treat this interest to a property entitlement would yield untoward results, and so we decline to do so.")

What these techniques (invocation of authority, interpretation, and legal or policy analysis and some others) share in common is the *reframing of the issue*, so that what once may have appeared to be a "live conflict" is recast as not a conflict at all. Sometimes, such deployments of authority, interpretation, and legal or policy analysis will seem like perfectly legitimate methods to resolve conflict, while at other times, they will seem like artifice. Either way—good faith or artifice—we do not deal with these major forms of conflict avoidance in this chapter.

Instead, we address here those situations where the decision-maker recognizes the presence of some live conflict and undertakes to address and resolve it in some way by giving each side its due (so to speak). This is the difference in effect between making one side of the argument simply go away versus recognizing both sides but instituting something like a doctrinal truce between the two. It's the latter that we call a "regime conflict" and that we address here.

When confronting a regime conflict, there will always be at least one issue calling for some sort of choice (or selection) between two opposed sources of legal decision.[1] It is not at all uncommon, for example, for a state trial court to be faced with conflicting appellate decisions issued by different appellate panels, or for a statute's application to a new set of facts to conflict with a public policy.

Given that a regime conflict always involves at least two opposed sources of decision, the problem becomes, how does one decide which of the two sets of principles, policies, considerations, doctrines, and so on ought to prevail? The answer will likely be some version or combination of the techniques described below. The legal analyst has to ask: How do the two or more competing sources stand with regard to each other? Which prevails when—how and why?

It is here that things get interesting. It turns out that the set of conflict resolution techniques used by advocates and legal decision-makers generally falls within a small set of *formal* patterns:

Hierarchy (e.g., burdens, tiebreakers, default rules)
Sectorization (e.g., rule/exception, scope limitations, election of remedies)
Policy Judgment (e.g., principles, policies, values)
Balancing (e.g., ad hoc, categorical, comparative impairment)
Meta-quantification (e.g., utilitarianism, microeconomic analysis, cost-benefit analysis)
Conflict Prevention (e.g., safe harbors, safe havens, chilling effects)
Referral (e.g., delegation, institutional competence)
Channeling (e.g., process approaches)

Of course, courts may use more than one technique at a time. A court might, for example, use cost-benefit analysis to support a policy judgment, or an advocate might argue that key principles must be balanced to determine whether a dispute falls into a particular sector (more on these hybrid approaches later in this chapter).

One of the interesting aspects of the legal techniques mentioned above is that they can function in *at least three different capacities:*

Method: A given approach (e.g., balancing) can be used *as a method to arrive at* a legal regime. ("In formulating a test, the court should balance X against Y." The actual test the court devises, however, need not be a balancing test. It could be a per se rule, for instance.)

Justification: A given approach (e.g., balancing) can be used *as a justification of* a legal regime. ("The test announced by the court is justified because X is a weightier consideration than Y.")

Legal Regime: A given approach (e.g., balancing) can serve *as the legal regime itself.* ("What kind of test did the court announce? It was a balancing test.")

Courts and other legal decision-makers are not always clear in which of these three capacities the techniques are being used, though often it is possible to tell from the context.

I. Techniques

Here we describe the main techniques listed above in greater detail.

A. HIERARCHY

Hierarchy is a technique for rearranging conflicts so that one side trumps the other. The conflict is resolved because one set of artifacts (e.g., doctrines, policies) must give way to the opposed set of artifacts.

Example:

> *Constitutional law*
>   *(takes precedence over)*
>   *statutory law*
>   *(which takes precedence over)*
>   *common law*

A hierarchy can be *absolute* (*this* set of artifacts always prevails over *that* one). Or it can be a *modified* hierarchy (this set of artifacts prevails over that one "except when . . ." or "unless . . ." or "so long as . . ." etc.). Consider, for example, one of the hierarchies of First Amendment doctrine: when speech is deemed "public," freedom of speech as a value is elevated over privacy. Speech deemed "private" does not receive the same protection; it is lower in the "freedom of speech" hierarchy.

Perhaps the most salient examples of hierarchies in law are *burdens, tiebreakers,* and *default rules.*

> *Burdens:* Burdens of persuasion and proof can be seen as ways of ranking different legal regimes. Thus, the requirement that a plaintiff establish her claim of negligence by a "preponderance of the evidence" expresses a useful asymmetry in regimes. With this burden, the jury is effectively being told, Unless the plaintiff has established its case by a preponderance of the evidence, you must decide in favor of the defendant. Similar hierarchical orderings can be established through presumptions (rebuttable, shifting, etc.).

> *Example: In the torts context, consent is a defense to battery, and, accordingly, it would seem that the defendant would have the burden to establish consent. However, consent is also (at least sometimes) an issue pertaining to whether or*

not there was "a harmful or offensive touching," and so it would seem that the plaintiff would have the burden of showing the absence of consent. Deciding who has the burden of proof here arguably affects the policy or principle conflict: freedom from harm vs. freedom to act.

> *Tiebreakers:* Tiebreakers can be used where two conflicting legal regimes are applicable and otherwise valid, but impose conflicting requirements.

Example: In constitutional law, the mother of all tiebreakers is the supremacy clause, which effectively provides that in case of conflict between otherwise valid federal and state laws, the federal law takes precedence and displaces any conflicting state law. (Of course, this tie breaker often serves only to push the conflict to another analytical level—does the federal law actually conflict with the state law? If not, there is no regime conflict.)

> *Default Rules:* In transactional contexts (e.g., contracts, inheritance) default rules are those that apply when the parties have otherwise failed to make different arrangements.[2] Default rules are extremely important: they prescribe what happens when the relevant parties have reached no agreement on a particular question or matter. This can happen for any number of reasons: oversight (the parties failed to consider an issue), conflict avoidance (the parties wish to avoid a contentious question), a desire to use the default rules in place (the parties wish to rely upon the "off the shelf" applicable default rules), transaction cost avoidance (the parties wish to avoid the costs of negotiating and customizing specific provisions for themselves), and more.

The simplest hierarchies we call *absolute.*

Example: Some of the better-known, simple, rigid orderings are hierarchies of courts, such as trial, appellate, and appellate courts of last instance.[3]

One thing to be careful about here is that some hierarchies seem absolute as a *formal matter,* yet not when one examines *actual practice.* The hierarchy of sources of law is a great example. It's quite clear as noted above that, in a formal sense, the common law is subordinate to statutes, which in turn are subordinate to the Constitution. It is also true, however, as a practical matter that courts will often construe the Constitution to avoid finding statutes unconstitutional. Similarly, they will construe statutes to avoid displacing the common law. This is a familiar pattern: The corpus of the law establishes many hierarchies that appear to be absolute on paper and yet turn out not to be in action. Even the seemingly absolute hierarchies of trial and appellate courts are modified by standards of review—highly deferential standards serve to modify the hierarchy so that it is harder for an appellate court to overrule a lower one.

Generally speaking, "modified hierarchies" take the following forms:

This prevails over *that, unless X . . .*
This prevails over *that to the extent of Y . . .*
This prevails over *that so long as Z . . .*
This prevails over *that except where F . . .*

And, of course, it's the "*unless X*" or "*to the extent of Y*" or "*so long as Z*" or "*except where F*" that renders the hierarchy modified. There are many different kinds of modified hierarchies in American law.

> *Example 1: "Soft" stare decisis: a court at the top of a hierarchy should follow its own earlier precedent unless values, changed circumstances, new evidence, or other considerations dictate otherwise. For example, the Supreme Court of Washington recently held that the state's death penalty violated the state constitution, overruling earlier precedent.*[4] *"Newly available evidence" warranted revisiting the earlier decisions; the court was convinced that the death penalty was imposed in an arbitrary and racially biased manner and was thus unconstitutional. These considerations trumped stare decisis (interestingly, the court specifically noted that "we make this determination by way of legal analysis, not pure science").*[5]

> *Example 2: Consider the Supreme Court's decision that "[b]oth Religion Clauses bar the government from interfering with the decision of a religious group to fire one of its ministers."*[6] *This "ministerial exception" can operate as an affirmative defense against employment discrimination claims under established federal statutory regimes. In other words, the Americans with Disabilities Act protects employees unless that employee is covered by the ministerial exception.*

Tremendous complexity can be produced through serial modified hierarchies—that is to say, modified hierarchies conditioned on other modified hierarchies conditioned on other . . . and so on. The massive regulatory statutes in the US are often massive precisely because they have embedded within them elaborate modified hierarchies that will send the reader from one provision to another . . . and another . . . and another. The following are some relatively simple examples of modified hierarchies.

> *Example 1: Conditional Entitlements. You are entitled to do or have X unless you act with malice (e.g., qualified privileges in defamation).*

> *Example 2: Abuse Rules. Less common in the United States than in some other legal systems, abuse rules work in the following way: you are entitled to do or have X unless you abuse . . . (e.g., abuse of privilege in defamation law).*

> *Example 3: Defeasible Entitlements. You are entitled to do or have X unless some other person does Y (e.g., adverse possession, public necessity, etc.).*

B. SECTORIZATION

One way of resolving a conflict between legal regimes is simply to specify their relative scope so that their effects are confined to different fields of application. The idea is so obvious it tends to be overlooked: indeed, this technique is tantamount to drawing a distinction delineating when one regime applies as opposed to another (see chapter 4, "The Legal Distinction").

> *Example: A victim of rape sued a website owner for negligent failure to warn under state law. Her assailants had used the website (a networking site for people in the modeling industry) to lure her to a fake audition. The website owner argued that the claim was barred by federal law (the Communications Decency Act), and the trial court agreed. The appellate court, however, concluded that the plaintiff's failure to warn claim was not barred by the CDA; the immunity provided by the CDA was limited to liability only as a speaker or publisher—a different field of application. The plaintiff's claim was based on the website owner's alleged knowledge of criminal activity and failure to warn participants of that activity, thus it did not fit in the CDA "sector."*

Interestingly, as routine as this technique may be, it does have some built-in difficulties. The absolute or modified hierarchies always express a preference for *this* regime over *that* one. In case the decision-maker is ambivalent or undecided, the hierarchy yields a result. Sectorization, by contrast, expresses no such hierarchical preference and thus leaves the decision-maker uncertain as to what to do every time he or she doesn't know which regime applies.

C. POLICY JUDGMENTS

Hierarchy and sectorization are in some sense "old-school" strategies for reconciling regime conflicts. The grand era for these strategies of hierarchy and sectorization in American law was the period of "legal formalism" or "juristic science" in the late nineteenth century. It was very common in those days for law to be expressed in extended displays of classifications, and subclassifications and sub-subclassifications—all organized in impressively detailed hierarchical or sectorized grids of law. Indeed, it is no exaggeration to describe law in this era (and in this mode) as shaped by a *grid aesthetic* in which law is both apprehended and cast according to images and metaphors of territorialized spatial fields.[7]

Hierarchies and sectorization are no longer as crucial today (having been replaced by other aesthetics of law and other strategies). But they subsist nonetheless. Sometimes they work smoothly—drawing little objection. At the same time, however, today many of the specific hierarchies and sectors ensconced in the substantive law are experienced by legal professionals as infirm or even collapsed. They are felt to be less than completely cogent and insufficiently determinative. There are many reasons for this experience of infirmity and collapse, some of which will be explored later on. But for now it suffices to note that where the hierarchies are experienced as infirm or collapsed, judges and legal officials confront persistent and bedeviling problems in deciding which legal regimes or considerations prevail when.

> *Example 1: Consider the revival in the last few decades of federalism limits on congressional power. The doctrine on this issue in the last quarter of the twentieth century vacillated considerably. In part, of course, it is because the Court failed to address in any cogent way the apparent conflict between the supremacy clause of Article VI and the federalist structure that permeates the Constitution itself.*

> *Example 2: Consider the extent to which the establishment clause and the free exercise clause of the First Amendment are at war with each other. Candidly appraised, it would seem that each clause requires what the other forbids. (For obvious reasons, the Supreme Court strives mightily not to interpret things this way.)*

Throughout the twentieth century, judges and legal officials struggled amid various arrays of infirm and collapsed hierarchies. One predominant response was to recognize that existing hierarchies or sectors fail to resolve the regime conflict and that the decision-maker must somehow produce a novel and justifiable resolution in the very midst of the conflict he or she is trying to resolve. In this situation, recourse can be made to reasons (the various policies, principles, values, considerations, factors, and interests that ostensibly support the two sides to the conflict) to help resolve regime conflicts. We look to the justifications and try to decide on that basis which policy, principle, value, consideration, is:

> More important
> More in need of observance
> More intensely implicated
> More likely to be severely damaged if not honored

This approach can, but need not, involve balancing. It does, however, involve quantifying the effects (the term "more" in each case is a tip-off).

It can fairly be said that often we get a "battle of the hierarchies." A good example of courts grappling with regime conflicts is in the area of surrogacy contracts. In this context, courts have explicitly struggled to reconcile existing statutory family law schemes related to adoption and termination of parental rights with contract law and with public policy considerations. What trumps what among these various frames of law? The subject matter (family), the nature of the transaction (contracts), or public considerations (public policy)? In this battle of the hierarchies, courts have adopted a variety of approaches. Some courts have balanced the freedom to contract against policy interests that serve to protect the surrogate mother and the principle (among others) that "[t]here are, in a civilized society, some things that money cannot buy."[8] Some courts have exercised the general doctrinal principle that contracts contrary to public policy can be invalidated, while others have found that there are no state policies contrary to surrogacy agreements.[9] One, after concluding that the statutory scheme didn't provide a specific answer, turned to contract law and simply found the interests favoring enforcement "more compelling" than interests against it.[10]

D. BALANCING

In American law, balancing emerged as a *prominent conflict resolution technique* at the beginning of the twentieth century.[11] By the last quarter of that century, balancing had become the conflict resolution technique of choice. Faced with a conflict of policies, principles, values, considerations, factors, and interests, the decision-maker tries to balance the virtues and vices (or costs and benefits) on one side against those on the other. The point of the exercise lies in determining which considerations are "weightier." That last term, "weightier," is a bit vague. It implies quantification and measurement. But quantification and measurement of *what* precisely? And according to *what shared scale*? And with what kind of *metric*?

The short answer is that it is the conflicting policies, principles, values, considerations, factors, and/or interests that must be balanced. This is not a terribly satisfying answer—and the reasons are simple: In what *sense* and according to what *scale* and *metric* do any of these artifacts—the policies, principles, values, and consideration—have weight? And how much weight? And just how is their "weightiness" assessed or imputed? Within what frame or context? And just how does one perform the actual balancing (just what is the cognitive process here?) of these artifacts (e.g., a policy) against another (e.g., a principle)? The simplicity of the balancing metaphor (and its normative implication of even-handedness) in effect hides a great deal of the difficulties in the operation required of legal decision-makers.

There are other difficulties. How does one tell how much weight a policy, principle, value, consideration, factor, and/or interest has relative to another? The idea here is not that it cannot be done. In one sense, people do it all the time. But the question is, Just *what is it* that is being done? Does the decision-maker simply have a gestalt judgment or a gut sense, which is then labeled "balancing" to render an aura of rationality or legitimacy to the decision? Is there any reason to suppose that the decision-maker is doing anything more than simply choosing one side or the other in an intuitionist moment or through an ungrounded preference—in much the same way a toddler asked to choose between two toys might look to one and then the other before ultimately picking one? Does the toddler balance? Does the judge? Do we believe them because they say they are balancing?[12]

> *Example: The Federal Rules of Evidence require a judge to balance the probative value of evidence against its prejudicial effect. Only if the danger of unfair prejudice substantially outweighs the probative value should evidence be excluded. How do we know that a court has "balanced" these considerations (let alone, done so properly)? Perhaps because such balancing is difficult to judge, on appeal, courts apply a highly deferential abuse of discretion standard when reviewing the trial court's balance.[13] (One qualitative constraint: a court must actually review the evidence at issue in order to balance properly).[14]*

Now, as a counterpoint and in fairness to balancing, notice that even if the choice is intuitive or ungrounded, it is not wholly without method. On the contrary, balancing often involves the specification of the relevant considerations to be balanced. When courts or other legal officials announce a balancing test, they often indicate what it is that is to be balanced—the factors or considerations that matter (and, by omission, those that do not). In this regard, balancing has the virtues of providing a checklist (things that a decision-maker should consider).

There are a variety of well-known balancing techniques, as follows.[15]

> *Ad Hoc Balancing*: Cases arise in different contexts. It is up to the decision-maker to decide contextually in each case which policies, principles, values, considerations, factors, and interests are to be balanced.

> *Example 1: The constitutional right to speedy trial requires an ad hoc balancing test that considers factors such as the length of delay, the reason for the delay, the defendant's assertion of his right to a speedy trial, and prejudice to the defendant.[16]*

> *Example 2: The Supreme Court rejected the proposed "ad hoc balancing" of social costs and benefits in the First Amendment context, calling the suggestion "startling and dangerous,"[17] because ad hoc balancing did not incorporate the appropriate elevation of free speech over its costs.*

> *Categorical Balancing*: The policies, principles, values, considerations, factors, and interests to be balanced "cut across" the different individual cases, and thus the kinds of policies, principles, values, and considerations to be balanced are specified across contexts.

Example: Many courts balance consistent factors when determining the amount of spousal maintenance to be awarded in a divorce. While each award is individual, the underlying considerations are fairly consistent (financial circumstances of the parties, length of the marriage, the parties' earning capacity, the age and health of parties, and so forth).

Comparative Impairment: This balancing technique, from conflict of laws, decides not by examining which side outweighs the other, but rather which side would be most impaired, if a decision were rendered for the other side.

How does balancing yield results? Ultimately, balancing depends upon *quantification* and *measurement.* The idea is that one side on the scale is the following:

More significant
More important
More substantial
More weighty

Sometimes multifactor and totality of circumstances tests are treated as instances of balancing. They might be considered variations of balancing to the extent that the factors or circumstances are to be weighed against each other. But multifactor or totality of circumstances tests do not require balancing. Instead sometimes these tests operate simply as a checklist where a sufficient number of factors or circumstances have to be present to reach a particular conclusion.

E. META-QUANTIFICATION APPROACHES

During the course of the twentieth century, established hierarchies and sectorizations became increasingly impaired as methods to resolve legal conflict. Judges and other legal officials had to seek out or construct new techniques to resolve regime conflicts.

One of the most popular responses to this breakdown (in addition to the balancing described above) was to apprehend and frame regime conflicts in terms of quantification and commensuration. Balancing can be viewed as an unsophisticated variant of this approach, but insofar as balancing does not necessarily require precise quantification, we have treated it here separately.

The more sophisticated responses to the breakdown of hierarchies and sectorizations came in the form of utilitarianism and economic analysis of law. Cost-benefit analysis, as we use the expression here, was yet a third technique. As used here, cost-benefit analysis refers to an assessment of the costs

and benefits of a particular approach together with the prescription to minimize net loss or maximize net gain.

The great appeal of utilitarianism and microeconomics is that they promise to dissolve human values into universal metrics—utils and dollars, respectively. Utils are imaginary units of happiness or pleasure derived from
the enjoyment of a particular good, and dollars are . . . well, dollars. Both
utilitarianism and economic analysis of law claim to offer universal metrics in
the sense that they each claim that all value and values can be translated into
utils and dollars, respectively. If this is so (a questionable hypothesis), then it
becomes easier to assess the comparative value of various legal regimes.

> *Law & Economics (L&E)*: The well-known Chicago L&E reduces value (all
> value) to "willingness to pay" in dollars (or dollar equivalents).[18] This
> means that any value worthy of preservation or protection by the legal
> system can be quantified and translated into dollar amounts. Once one
> figures out the value of X in dollars to the *relevant* parties (and this is
> often a problematic exercise in guesswork and conjecture), it all becomes
> a question of comparing how much value in dollars various legal regimes
> will create.
>
> *Utilitarianism*: There are many kinds of utilitarianism (rule, act, total, av-
> erage, etc.), but the ones in vogue among judges and lawyers are fairly
> simple and relatively untheorized: What legal regime is likely to maximize
> the sum of happiness or pleasure over sadness or pain? On this view, what
> matters is which legal regime maximizes the surplus of happiness or plea-
> sure over sadness or pain (or when things are truly awful, minimizes the
> surplus of sadness or pain over happiness or pleasure).
>
> *Cost-Benefit Analysis*: Cost-benefit analysis (CBA), *as we use the term here*, re-
> fers to the relatively intuitionist approach often used by courts to weigh
> the costs and benefits of particular activities or regimes.[19] We will deal
> with CBA after a brief discussion of the more sophisticated approaches of
> utilitarianism and L&E.

Utilitarianism is distinguishable from Chicago L&E in two major (and
very important) ways: (1) Utilitarianism can authorize paternalistic decisions
where the state or the legal decision-maker can legitimately decide what is
best for other individuals—what they need or want. In sharp contrast to classic Chicago school L&E, utilitarianism does not presume that the individual
(the "rational utility maximizer") is always or generally the best judge of his
or her own welfare. Indeed, utilitarianism as a general tendency says nothing
about this issue. (2) Utilitarianism can be radically egalitarian, since, in sharp
contrast to L&E analysis, utilitarianism can accept the principle known as

the "declining marginal utility of the dollar"—to wit, the idea that the next dollar made by a millionaire is worth less to him than that same dollar would be worth to a pauper.

It is thus very important to distinguish utilitarianism from Chicago L&E because a faithful deployment of the two approaches will often yield different results. What they share in common (and this is why they are often confused) is (1) the presumption of a unitary metric (in one case utils, in the other dollars) in which all human values can be translated and commensurated, (2) a consequentialist approach to decision-making (a focus on the effects that the present decision will have on future actions), and (3) the use of quantification and measurement as the chief technique to resolve regime conflicts.

There are many problems with both utilitarianism and L&E analysis—of which we will mention only two.

First is the supposition that it is possible *conceptually* as well as *practically* to translate all political, social, and moral values into utils or dollars. Not all values (e.g., friendship, altruism, loyalty) will survive the translation required by utilitarianism and microeconomic analysis. Second, both utilitarianism and microeconomic analysis involve a great deal of ungrounded guesswork about the util or dollar values to be assigned to various goods. Indeed, contrary to first impressions, the quantification and measurement techniques turn out to be difficult and controversial.

As for cost-benefit analysis, it can mean many things to different people. (That is, as it turns out, one of its main problems.) Here we use the term in a specific sense to denote a kind of intuitionist approach used by judges or other legal officials. What renders this approach unsophisticated (as distinguished from utilitarianism and L&E) is that what counts as a cost or a benefit remains less than fully specified. That is to say, there is no technical definition. So what is a cost in cost-benefit analysis? Well, it might be market price, cost of production, opportunity cost, or some rough-and-ready sense of social cost, or . . . The same would also apply with the idea of a benefit.

By way of example, consider the Supreme Court's recognition of a good faith exception to the exclusionary rule.[20] Concluding that the exclusionary rule does not itself have a constitutional status, the Court framed the analysis as one that needed to be resolved by weighing the costs and benefits of suppressing evidence. Using words like "calculus,"[21] the Court weighed the competing goals of deterring official misconduct and protecting privacy against the truth-finding function of the jury. Finding no deterrence value when an officer acts in "objective good faith" on a warrant, the Court concluded that any benefits from exclusion were easily outweighed by its costs.

This sort of vagueness is not intrinsic to all forms of cost-benefit analysis,[22] but it is typical of the ad hoc approaches used by the courts (i.e., what we have called CBA). In many instances, courts consider economic considerations without a whole lot of precision. For example, a court might mention "transaction costs" without a rigorous law & economics analysis.

> *Example: A statute requires that the government make "reasonable efforts" to reunify a child with his parent; the court creates doctrine requiring that the "reasonable efforts" determination include "something resembling a cost-benefit analysis"[23] that considers the costs associated with services provided to the parent, and whether a parent and the family are likely to benefit from the services.*

F. CONFLICT PREVENTION APPROACHES

Conflict prevention approaches include legal notions such as "safe havens," "safe harbors," and "prophylactic approaches." The general idea is to define legal safety zones where, if parties comply with certain formalities or technical requirements, there will be no questioning of their actions or conduct.

Miranda warnings are a good example.[24] If law enforcement officials properly observe the warning requirements in custodial settings, then the court will not inquire (absent extreme circumstances) into whether a suspect's statements were coerced or not. Viewed in this way, the warnings serve to avoid (at least much of the time) what might otherwise be a very difficult, context-sensitive, fact-bound inquiry into whether or not law enforcement interrogations were unconstitutionally coercive.

In one sense, conflict prevention approaches differ from the other techniques described above: they do not so much "resolve" the conflict as strive to forestall its occurrence in the future. As a method of decision, the conflict prevention approach is tantamount to saying: "We do not know how to deal with this issue (or we do not want to deal with it), so we are going to construct a regime that will induce one (or both) parties to avoid presenting us with the issue in the future. If they meet the following number of conditions, we will not question their behavior, status, transaction, and so on."

Formalities such as having witnesses sign important documents are not generally considered conflict prevention approaches, but they could be seen as such. Consider that compliance with formalities such as signature requirements, consideration, delivery, summons, and the like helps avoid what might otherwise be fairly significant factual questions about the underlying transactions.

G. REFERRAL/DEFERENCE/DENIAL

Referral is our name for a technique through which regime conflicts are resolved by relegating the issue to some other institution. Common law courts, for instance, sometimes declare that a certain legal issue requires a "comprehensive" or "systematic" approach that can be adopted only by the legislature. The common law courts then decline to resolve the issue (which is, of course, a resolution of a sort). In constitutional law, one example of this referral technique is the Supreme Court's decision that the republican guaranty clause is addressed to the US Congress and is not justiciable. Similarly, the Supreme Court recently determined that "partisan gerrymandering claims present political questions beyond the reach of the federal courts" because of "the lack of legal standards to limit and direct their decisions."[25] These are all referral techniques insofar as they "resolve" the legal issue by in effect relegating ultimate resolution to some future decision by some other legal body.

Sometimes the referral is partial, not absolute—as when a court, for instance, retains jurisdiction to oversee a structural remedy to be implemented by the parties. In these contexts, a court may simply sketch out requirements to be followed, letting the parties negotiate their way to a more detailed resolution. Congress likewise can establish such procedures. For instance, in "cooperative federalism," Congress lays out a comprehensive statutory scheme enabling the states and federal agencies to cooperate in implementing legal solutions. Federal courts can certify a state law issue in a case to the highest state court, acknowledging the state court's authority over the issue.

Deference is our term for following a decision already made by some other institutional body. Here too examples abound. The courts will often defer to federal administrative agency interpretations of federal statutes. The Supreme Court will often show deference to the US Congress, to the president, and even to the states in reviewing the constitutionality of legislation. The old common law in its early incarnations was a display of deference toward customary practices in the community. The judges would effectively accord legal sanction to customary practice. The notion of "historical gloss" in constitutional law is similarly an example of deference to historical practice.

Example: The Supreme Court famously concluded that allowing Casey Martin to use a golf cart in a PGA competition would not fundamentally alter the nature of the tournament—analysis under the terms of the ADA. A Seventh Circuit panel had earlier concluded just the opposite—that allowing a golfer to use a cart in the competition would fundamentally alter the nature of the game. The Seventh Circuit considered the same sort of facts that the Supreme Court had—the physical and mental fatigue of the game—but ended by emphasizing its deference to

*golf's governing bodies. "[T]the decision on whether the rules of the game should
be adjusted to accommodate him is best left to those who hold the future of golf in
trust."²⁶ Perhaps that deference made the difference.*

Denial, as the term is used here, means simply a technique through which
judges and other officials basically decline to address the regime conflict. Perhaps there's no personal jurisdiction or no authority to decide the issue. Or
perhaps, in the constitutional context, there is no case or controversy.

In sum, *referral* relegates conflict resolution to some later decision by
some other institution. *Deference* resolves regime conflicts by deferring to
some decision already made by some other institutional body. And *denial*
is simply the brute (even if justifiable) refusal to resolve the regime conflict.

Perhaps the most elaborate expression of the referral/deference/denial
technique was elaborated by the mid-twentieth-century American school of
thought known as "legal process," and more specifically its master concept of
"institutional competence." The latter notion held that various institutions
(legislatures, courts, agencies, the market, etc.) had particular competen-
cies and comparative advantages vis-à-vis each other for addressing different
kinds of issues.²⁷

H. CHANNELING

All the techniques described above aim for some sort of resolution of regime
conflicts. A different approach aims at managing regime conflicts by "channeling" them through various processes.²⁸

Consider that struggles, disagreement, even antagonism, are not necessarily bad. It is not obvious that conflict should always be definitively resolved.
Nor is it obvious that if definitive resolution is required, the legal system
should take the leading role. In this regard, realize that there are many other
social conflict-processing mechanisms: social services, community organizations, the family, firms, technology, and so on. Each of these presumably has
comparative advantages and comparative deficits with respect to the others.

Sometimes law will decline to resolve conflict and instead institutionalize
it. The constitutional doctrine of separation of powers is a great example. The
various "swords" and "shields" accorded the three branches of the US government can be seen as ways to preserve and arguably create conflict.

*Example: The Supreme Court of the United States can review the acts of Congress
for constitutionality. The Congress can restrict the appellate jurisdiction of the US
Supreme Court. The US Supreme Court can review restrictions of its jurisdiction
for constitutionality. And so on.*

In constitutional theory, this fracturing of power aims at preserving some degree of conflict.

Institutionalization as a technique is an implicit recognition that some degree or some kinds of conflict cannot (or should not) be extinguished or resolved. The underlying assumption here is that it would be better (for any number of reasons) to channel and discipline the conflicts rather than try to resolve them. Perhaps such channeling and discipline can be justified on the grounds that the conflicts cannot themselves be resolved. Or perhaps such channeling can be justified on the grounds that there is some positive value in keeping the conflicts alive. Then too there is the (cynical or innocent) safety valve theory, according to which conflict is to be kept alive through channeling, so that the conflict can ultimately exhaust itself ("let off steam") without yielding undue harm.

> *Example: In* Whitney v. California, *Justice Brandeis formulated a safety valve theory of the First Amendment. As he put it, "Those who won our independence believed that . . . order cannot be secured merely through fear of punishment for its infraction; that it is hazardous to discourage thought, hope and imagination; that fear breeds repression; that repression breeds hate; that hate menaces stable government; that the path of safety lies in the opportunity to discuss freely supposed grievances and proposed remedies."[29]*

Whether the reasons for keeping conflict alive are innocent or cynical, consider that while the channeling and discipline go on, the parties are "engaged" by the system. Their actions and statements may be monitored, scripted, supervised, and restrained as they are compelled to restate and revise their narratives and claims to conform to those enabled by the system. In this way, they are compelled to deal with and to some degree take on the system's own agendas—its own protocols, goals, and objectives. In this way, law affords a ritualized diffusion and defusing of strife and antagonism.

II. Putting it Together

While these various techniques for resolving conflict can be used in isolation, they are often used in combination. Two kinds of combination—call them *hybrids* and *entailments*—are particularly important.

A. HYBRIDS

Hybrids are combinations of the techniques. For example, hierarchy is sometimes used in connection with referral/deference/denial. This occurs when an appellate court declines to reverse a trial court decision, noting that the trial court is in the better institutional position to resolve that particular issue. Sectorization can be combined with balancing. Imagine a judge deciding whether a statutory or doctrinal regime applies to new technology—she might balance the values at stake to determine whether the regime should apply. Justification can be combined with channeling. Thus, various justiciability concerns (e.g., standing, mootness, ripeness) can be justified on the grounds that they ensure a sufficiently sharp case or controversy to enable sound adjudication. This combination of techniques is commonplace.

> *Example: Government employers can restrict the speech of their employees under the* Pickering *balancing test. A court must balance the interests of the employee as a citizen with free speech rights and the interests of the State as an employer in providing public services.*[30] *But—for policy reasons and practical considerations (too burdensome for government employers, according to the Supreme Court)— the balancing test applies only if the speech is on a matter of public concern. Whether speech addresses a matter of public concern involves another set of considerations, including the context, content, and form of the speech—more of a totality of the circumstances technique.*[31]

Labeling the relevant artifacts does not mean the technique can be easily or confidently identified.

> *Example: Consider the test for joinder or severance in New York. This test includes a capacious set of concerns—according to one court: "considerations of public policy, legislative history and intent as to judicial efficiency, judicial economy and cost benefit analysis with proscribed due process constraints and limitations to ensure no denial of substantial rights to neither party."*[32] *So just what is this?*

B. ENTAILMENTS

Entailments occur when one technique leads to the adoption of another. Recall that each of the regime conflict resolution techniques can be used as a method, a justification, and a regime. There is no reason why the choice, for instance, of one technique as a *method* should lead to the same approach in formulating a *regime*. There need not be any consistency among the three (i.e., method, justification, and regime).

A balancing method or a utilitarian approach, for instance, could lead to the adoption of a hierarchy. A sectorization approach in turn could lead to a balancing approach. As one becomes more adept at recognizing these techniques it can increasingly seem that most legal regimes are composed of hybrids and entailments of these various techniques.

C. SUMMARY

For the advocate or decision-maker, this repertoire of conflict resolution mechanisms can be useful in a number of ways. Here, we describe two of the major ones.

First, where a choice is to be made about what conflict resolution technique to use, an awareness of the variety of legal options is surely a help. The repertoire described here is a helpful reminder that there are lots of options available (even if the basic set is in the end limited). Note, however, that the possibility of *hybrids* and *entailments* greatly increases the number of possibilities. Indeed, hybrids and entailments effectively act as multipliers— enabling the proliferation of complexity.

Second, the repertoire described here allows the advocate or decision-maker to identify (at least much of the time) the technique being proffered by someone else. In turn, that identification is the key predicate for advancing justifications and critiques of the technique—in short, for making arguments in favor or against the use of the technique in question in the given context. We have not elaborated these justifications and critiques here because they depend very much on which conflict resolution techniques are pitted against each other. (For instance, our sense is that the arguments for a channeling approach will differ depending upon whether channeling is pitted against hierarchy or instead balancing, or instead . . . and so on.[33])

7

Interpretation

In law, interpretation seems to be everywhere. Statutes, constitutional provisions, common law precedents, regulations, contracts, wills, trusts, documentary evidence—all frequently trigger interpretive efforts in order to discern their legal meaning. Indeed, it is only a small-to-middling exaggeration to say that almost any legal conflict can be turned into a question of interpretation.

As for doctrine, not only does doctrine sometimes require interpretation in order to discern its meaning, but indeed a lot of the topics of doctrine that we have covered—both issues and difficulties—are closely related to the work of interpretation. Thus, consider that whether or not a *legal distinction* suffers from a perceived flaw will often depend upon how that distinction is interpreted. Similarly, whether we encounter a *baseline* problem or not will often turn upon whether we interpret a legal text in such way as to render it determinate or indeterminate. Similarly, in close cases, whether a directive is taken to be a rule or a standard will often depend upon how the directive is construed. We could go on, but we won't. The point is clear: interpretation of legal texts can make the various doctrinal topics we have covered into live issues or to the contrary into non-problems.

What can we say about interpretation of legal texts in general? Well, it turns out that interpretation is very much a localized, context-sensitive, text-specific affair. Does this mean then that nothing of theoretical value can be said about legal interpretation? No. Not at all. What it does mean is that we need to develop a theoretical approach to legal interpretation that respects its local, contextual, text-specific character. We need to recognize that legal interpretation will not necessarily conform to high-order theoretical prescriptions.

Taking this caution to heart, we offer an approach here to legal interpretation that respects its local, contextual, and text-specific character. Hence, rather than trying to organize an understanding of legal interpretation in terms of systematic solutions or overarching prescriptions, we try to organize an understanding of legal interpretation in terms of stereotyped interpretive challenges and problems as these might be encountered or raised by a judge or lawyer.

In this chapter, we will deal with two predominant modes of legal interpretation—namely, textualism and purposivism. These two modes seem to recur frequently across many different national and international legal regimes. The inquiry here will focus on the stylized challenges and problems that arise *within* each mode of interpretation. Such an "intramodal" focus presumes the interpreter is already committed to a particular mode of interpretation rather than having to decide between different modes of interpretation (the "intermodal"). The focus on the intramodal allows the identification of the stereotyped decision points that a judge or lawyer confronts when practicing a particular mode of interpretation.[1]

Before turning specifically to the two modes of interpretation, however, a few general observations are warranted on what might be called "the interpretive situation"—namely, the contexts, conflicts, and tensions within which legal interpretation happens.

I. The Interpretive Situation: Recurrent Tensions and Conflicts

The two modes of interpretation—textualism and purposivism—share some common challenges. These challenges stem from recurrent tensions and conflicts that pervade the attempt to discern legal meaning. A thorough appreciation of these tensions and conflicts allows recognition of the many possibilities that are generally available in the interpretation of legal texts.

A. THE "LEGAL" IN THE LEGAL TEXT

Many jurists and legal theorists have infused their understandings of interpretation by borrowing from literary critics, linguists, and philosophers. Much of this has been helpful. Some of it has not. Be that as it may, there are certain aspects of legal interpretation that distinguish the endeavor relative to, for instance, literary or philosophical interpretation. One aspect of the interpretation of legal texts is that it is, and must be, shaped, guided, and directed by law itself. In this sense, jurisprudence and law impinge upon interpretation—in theory as well as in practice.[2]

Because law and laws provide prescriptive directives for the interpretation of legal texts, legal interpretation is *never just* a question of getting the semantic meaning of a legal text right. It is also a question of following jurisprudential and legal directives for how legal interpretation is to proceed. This is not to suggest, of course, that it is always or even often clear *which* directives must be followed in any given situation.[3] More vexing perhaps, this remains the case *even if*—(and here is the vexing part)—those jurisprudential and legal directives are in conflict with each other, or point to different conclusions, or even if, upon examination, they seem to miscast or misunderstand the nature of texts or interpretation.[4]

The practical issue thus arises, What is to be done when *the texts to be interpreted* seem to mean one thing, while the application of the *relevant interpretive directives* prescribed by law yields a different meaning? For an illustration we can think about the famous case *McCullough v. Maryland*, dealing with the constitutionality of the Second Bank of the United States.[5] Nowhere in the Constitution text was there any explicit mention of a power to create a bank. Chief Justice Marshall, however, made a great deal out of the fact that it is a constitution "we are expounding," and that therefore all sorts of interpretive implications followed, including a certain generosity in interpreting the powers of the national government.

This sort of conflict is ubiquitous: in fashioning an interpretation, how much does one heed the legal interpretive directives, and how much does one instead try to conform to the words of the text being interpreted? This practical question arises because law (*le droit*) is fundamentally unclear or perhaps more accurately ambivalent about the degree to which legal interpretation is a matter of *producing* legal meanings in accordance with interpretive directives as opposed to a matter of *finding* the meaning of the legal text at issue. Clearly, we have some of both going on. Discerning the appropriate ratio (or ratios) is a complicated problem. There is a great deal to be said about it—indeed far too much to pursue the question here.

B. THE INTERPRETIVE CONTEXTS

Among legal academics, the topic of legal interpretation is often approached in very abstract ways. Indeed, "legal interpretation" long ago became its own abstract stand-alone topic—frequently addressed outside any substantive issue or procedural context. This abstract perspective is very different from that of the judge or the lawyer who encounters an interpretive problem typically in a fact-rich and institutionally localized context where interpretive conclusions have discernible concrete consequences. In what follows, we elaborate on these various aspects of the judge's and the lawyer's situation.

1. Fact-Rich

Judges are not, as academics sometimes intimate, called upon to interpret legal texts in general—but rather to interpret a legal text (or usually a small part thereof) as it might bear on a particular case, a particular factual scenario. It may be that some degree of generality is required to resolve the particular interpretive question posed. This generality may be required by a judge's commitment to a certain kind of "principled" decision-making.[6] Or it may be required by a certain degree of pragmatism (e.g., the "Where do you draw the line?" kind of pragmatism). But either way, the *degree* and *direction* of this generality will be shaped by the legal issues and the factual scenario at hand.

> *Example 1: Consider the interpretation of the term "accident" in an insurance policy. A court determining whether multiple automobile collisions constitute a single "accident" has a very different task than a court determining whether a mosquito bite that led to death is an "accident,"[7] or whether sexual assault by an employee can be considered an "accident" covered by the employer's insurance.[8]*

> *Example 2: Consider "against the will of another" in a rape statute. The defendant pretended to be someone else, arranging the encounter on social media and asking the victim to blindfold herself before his arrival. The deception frames the task of interpreting "against the will of another" in an entirely different manner from a case concerning direct physical or verbal acts of coercion.[9]*

2. Institutionally Localized

The judge is constrained by a series of professional imperatives and restraints, including to heed the law, resolve disputes, preserve order, do justice, clear dockets, establish sensible regimes, respect litigants, and explain and justify decisions. These are fairly role-specific tasks, not common to legal academics or other mortals. The judge resolves an interpretive issue by working it through these institutional imperatives and restraints, as well as by working the institutional imperatives and restraints through his or her interpretations. It is important to note that the judge's professional role (how he or she views the mission at hand) is itself susceptible to (and perhaps demands) interpretation. Indeed, the insightful judge will learn to read legal texts not simply for the doctrines, policies, and principles they announce, but for what the legal texts reveal about his or her own roles, tasks, responsibilities, and limitations.

In this regard, the judge is positioned differently vis-à-vis a variety of legal institutions—the Constitution, the legislature, the administrative agencies, the executive branch, the appellate and the trial courts, the jury. The judge's relations to these institutions may well feature prominently in both the kind and scope of the interpretive work he or she undertakes. This would get us into very detailed discussions of substantive and procedural law (and so we will say no more).

> *Example: A judge might approach a procedural rule one way but a substantive criminal penalty another. Some statutes include explicit directives about a court's role: construe the statute to favor employees, for example. Some jurisdictions prefer to provide an all-inclusive directive: "In the construction of a statute, the office of the judge is simply to ascertain and declare what is in terms or in substance contained therein, not to insert what has been omitted or to omit what has been inserted."[10]*

3. Procedural Posture

Judges and lawyers are called upon to interpret legal texts at certain stages in the proceedings. The legal texts they must or are permitted to examine may well depend upon the specific identity of the court, its jurisdiction, and other institutional and procedural matters. While these are themselves subject to interpretation, it is nonetheless the case that judges will often have a much more localized focus than other kinds of interpreters, such as academics, journalists, and the like.

> *Example: The appellate structure and function might, for example, encourage the appellate court to take a long view, less focused on the immediate consequences for the parties. A federal court interpreting a state law might take a more deferential role than a state court interpreting the same state law. A lower court might be much more inclined to interpret a statute in a way that avoids a constitutional issue than an appellate court.*

4. Discernible Specific Consequences

When a judge rules on a question of legal interpretation (unlike, say, a journalist or an academic offering his or her views), discrete specific consequences ensue. Someone pays (or does not), goes to jail (or does not), ceases and desists (or does not), and so on. Judicial interpretation has consequences—some of them rather determinately laid out by the law itself. When the judge writes, he or she does so in the medium of law. His or her opinion registers automatically in the networks of law and has certain discrete automatic juridical effects.[11] It can be argued, of course, that such discrete specific effects ought not to be considered by the judge. But it can also be argued back that if the judge does not consider such effects, then he or she has a blinkered understanding of the identity and character of law and judgment. Again, one can find in the law a certain ambivalence about what must, can, and cannot be taken into consideration. Insofar as the polar extremes (one can *never take any* consequences into account/one *must take all* consequences into account) seem generally unacceptable, judges are left with what will sometimes be a difficult jurisprudential choice about just which consequences must, can, and cannot be taken into account. This, of course, will present not merely a conceptual challenge (specifying concepts), but a cognitive one as well (bending one's mind to conceptual demands).

> *Example 1: Interpretation is typically framed as a "question of law," but real people and particular facts shape the arguments on both sides. Imagine the task of a court interpreting the word "presence" in a statute defining criminal sexual conduct as including "lewd exhibition of the genitals in the presence of a minor"—does presence include exhibition via Facebook messenger (simultaneous electronic communications)? The decision is not simply a conceptual exercise about the meaning of "presence" or even the nature of modern communications, but one of very practical concerns.*

> *Example 2: Consider the interpretation of the term "neglect" in a child abuse and neglect statute—when deciding whether the term covers accidental behavior, a court had to face a father whose mistake led to his toddler son's death. How does a court evaluate the impact of its decision about the meaning of neglect on this father as against the impact on parents in future cases?*

C. THE TEXTUAL FEEDBACK LOOP

Every relatively complex text provides clues and even imperatives as to how it should be read. This is certainly true of legal texts. As we strive to interpret a text (however we may do it) the text acquires meaning for us. That meaning that we ascribe or derive in turn informs us as to how we are to read the text itself.[12] Interpretation begets meaning, and, in turn, meaning begets further interpretation.

While an integrated meaning is often what the judge or other legal officials seek, legal interpretation, if taken seriously, often leads in other directions. Some believe that this interpretive feedback loop can, in the image of an inward-running spiral, lead to a stable unitary, integrated meaning.[13] But there is no reason to suppose that this is invariably true.[14]

The important thing for the interpreter is to take notice of how her interpretation affects and sometimes changes the character of the text she is reading, thus requiring further efforts at interpretation. After a while, a legal text can begin to look less like a sharply delineated stable identity and more like an interactive constellation of meanings. The task and challenge of the judge and the lawyer will often be to morph the constellation into a manageable directive.

> *Example: A student's first encounter with the constitutional phrase "the power to regulate commerce among the several states" likely leads to a limited set of possibilities and a small number of issues. After marching through Supreme Court precedents on the commerce clause, however, the complexity and number of possibilities become much more significant. (Once the mind is opened, it's pretty hard to shut it down again.)*

D. THE PLURALITY OF CONTEXTS

It is commonplace that the meaning of a text is a function of context. This commonplace bears some elaboration, however, because the contexts that can potentially affect the meaning of the text are numerous and varied.

1. The Context of Application

The idea here is that the meaning of a law must be understood in light of the context of application—that is to say, the particular social or economic or historical context to which the law is to be applied. This might be conceptualized as a problem of interpretation as translation. That is to say, how does one translate a legal text that means X in context A to context B (where context B turns out to be significantly different)? Does X still mean X (i.e., literal transposition) or does X now need to be translated into Y because X in A means Y in B (analogical extrapolation)?[15]

> *Example: This occurs every time a court is asked to interpret text as it applies to new technology. How should the court "translate" the text so that it can be applied to a technology its authors never considered—in some cases, could not have known about?*

2. The Authorial Context

Even putting intentionalism aside, as we have here, the determination of authorship remains important. There are legal issues of competence, or scope of authority, that can arise. The purview of legitimate concerns, goals, or values served by a legal text can be ascertained in part by an examination of what agent or agency created a legal text.

3. The Addressee Context

A legal text is potentially addressed to many different kinds of addressees: states, parties, lawyers, courts, other governmental bodies, and more. The meaning of the text may well vary depending upon which parties are taken to be the (primary) addressees of the legal text.[16] Additionally, different addressees may be authorized or compelled to read the text differently or in some cases (i.e., non-justiciability) not to "read" parts of it at all.

4. The Functional Legal Context

The immediate legal entourage of a text may affect its meaning. Thus, it matters whether the object of interpretation is found in a legal text that has a prohibitory, delegative, permissive, distributive, and so on, effect. It also matters whether the text to be interpreted is understood to be embedded in a legal field rich with principles, policies, procedures, discretion (or not). In other words, even if one focuses on the interpretation of a discrete identified legal text, the interpretation cannot help but take into account the surrounding functional entourage.

> *Example: The interpretation of the term "neglect (of a child)" in a criminal statute is likely to be different than its interpretation in a family law statute that provides only civil remedies, such as termination of parental rights.*

5. Contexts Generally

As we have just seen, exploring the multiple contexts in which a legal text is embedded, it is possible to enhance the interpretive possibilities or, on the contrary, to bring them to closure.

There is one more twist to add. As the work of interpretation proceeds, the identity of the text can change. Here we provide a somewhat lengthy illustration of the point with the US Constitution.[17] Imagine a judge at once earnest and perceptive trying to figure out the meaning of the Constitution. She starts with a commitment to reading the Constitution in terms of the "plain meaning" of the text.

She reads through Article I (which seems to delineate the powers of a legislative branch) and Article II (which seems to establish the powers of an executive branch) and Article III (which seems to set forth the powers of a judicial branch).

Upon finishing Article III of the Constitution, the judge begins to recognize that she must revise her interpretive commitments. For one thing, her "plain meaning" approach has yielded what it was supposed to yield, that is, a plain meaning—one that reveals that there is a certain coherent structure to the Constitution that seems to describe three different branches of the federal government.

The judge must decide what importance to give to this structural feature. On the one hand, it is conceivable that this structural feature of the Constitution is simply a matter of presentation, of style—one that portends no more than a helpful and orderly presentation of the individual clauses. On the other hand, it might be said that this aspect of form has significance— that it reflects the primordial importance of the division of powers among a legislative, an executive, and a judicial branch.

Viewed in this latter way, the Constitution is no longer merely a continuous, homogeneous list of various powers, limitations, and entitlements, but also a hierarchically structured charter of government. In turn, identifying the Constitution as a charter has implications for the manner in which it will be read. Hence, if it is a charter, it must be interpreted in light of its structural organization. From this perspective, the "plain meaning" of the text is no longer the plain meaning of words or sentences but rather the plain meaning that the words and sentences must have in their capacity as discrete aspects of a government charter. This kind of structural interpretation is championed variously by such eminent constitutionalists as Charles Black, John Hart Ely, and, more recently, Akhil Amar.[18]

The judge decides to reread the document. This time she has abandoned a naive "plain meaning" approach in favor of reading the document as a charter of government. Again, she breezes through Article I and Article II. Article III is now of paramount interest—for indeed it is the article in the charter that most directly concerns her powers, her role, her function. What she notices is that the charter extends judicial power only so far as "cases and controversies"[19] are concerned. It is at this point that it dawns on the judge that her interest in the Constitution is not a generalizable interest in the Constitution's meaning, but rather a particular interest in what the Constitution means for the purposes of the judicial task of hearing "cases and controversies." The judge understands that she must now fashion some understanding of what her appropriate and legitimate role must be relative to the other branches of government and the states. Hers is an already contextualized interest in the meaning of the Constitution—an interest specified and established by Article III.

Notice that the identity of the Constitution has once again changed. Whereas at first it was a text and then a charter, now it appears that it is something else—something whose meaning and identity vary in accordance with the identity of the agents who are charged with its enforcement, interpretation, and elaboration (or whatever). For judges, the constitutional charter requires some sort of determination as to the appropriate scope and limits of the power that the judiciary can claim from the Constitution. What is required of judges when they "read" the Constitution is an appreciation and understanding of their role as interpreters and addressees of the Constitution. Their reading of the Constitution must be constrained by the limits of the judicial function. In a word, they are to read that part of the Constitution that is "law." This is the sort of insight that leads some legal thinkers to claim that the Constitution requires the development and articulation of a "theory" of adjudication—the sort of "theory" developed variously by such eminent legal thinkers as Herbert Wechsler, Robert Bork, and Ronald Dworkin.[20]

Once again the judge resumes her earnest reading—this time with meticulous attention to the limits and obligations of the judicial function. Things go well until the judge reaches the Bill of Rights and the Fourteenth Amendment. As she makes her way through these amendments, she trips up on phrases such as "due process of law," "liberty," "privileges and immunities," and "equal protection." These are grand but nebulous words. They are juridical in cast and seemingly addressed to the judiciary; yet they are vague, capacious, underspecified. Viewing these words from the perspective of the judicial function, the judge may feel a need to turn to various "external" sources—to history, to what is known of the framers' intent, to natural law, to political philosophy—in short, to anything that might serve to accord the words some delimited and suitably specific content.

But, in turning to such sources, the judge experiences a gestalt shift. Rather than seeing these external sources as vehicles by which to specify the meaning of constitutional rights, the judge comes to understand that the Constitution is itself an amalgamation of these various sources. The Constitution is not so much a text or a structure or a charter, but rather a combination of various modes of legal argument. What is to be interpreted and given effect is not words or clauses or even structures, but rather the self-referential practices of constitutional meaning. This is the kind of approach developed by Philip Bobbitt, who describes various modalities of constitutional argument, and Paul Kahn, who describes the Constitution as a tradition of dialogue that literally speaks (or writes) the Constitution into existence.[21]

Once again the Constitution has changed identities. Its identity is now quite difficult to describe, for the Constitution is now composed of historical practices, philosophical elaborations, directive intentions, sundry traditions, and so on. It is not just that the Constitution must be interpreted in light of or by reference to such sources. Rather, now the Constitution is itself a specific amalgamation of such sources. And indeed, at this point the identities of the Constitution multiply rapidly. It can be seen as a bridge to the past, a prophecy for the future, an iconic symbol, a sacred artifact. The identity of the Constitution becomes any number of things that have at various times been held to be the embodiment, the expression, of a political community.

Notice here that in reading the Constitution in all earnestness, we have begun with a plain meaning and ended up with a whole variety of ways of reading the Constitution. Which of these gets to the heart of the Constitution? What does "it" really mean?

This is a very difficult question. One difficulty is that "it" is always already presupposed prior to any argumentation. "It" is always already understood prior to any conscious or deliberate choice about how to read "it." Moreover, as we have just seen, any conscious or deliberate choice about how "it" is to be read is always at least potentially unstable. That is, any conscious or deliberate choice about how to read "it" (the Constitution) can very well prompt the adoption of a different mode of reading.

The point here is that the convenient presupposition that we all agree on what constitutes "the legal text"—that is in some sense fixed—is in fact nothing more than a presupposition, and one that upon reflection starts to fall apart fairly quickly (assuming there are stakes). Now there is something fixed in all this, of course: what is fixed are those markings on the parchment or the paper—the signifiers. Those do not change (absent error or fraud). But no one (absolutely no one) has yet explained, in any satisfying way, how mere markings can somehow produce a fixed and determinate meaning that is self-coinciding across time and iteration.

E. FIDELITY TO THE ORIGINAL MEANING

Here is the difficulty simply stated: What is one to do in transposing the meanings of a text crafted in a particular time and place (that of enactment or ratification) to another very different time and place (the facts of the case in issue)? This familiar difficulty arises in a variety of settings. It is particularly salient in those circumstances where the legal text was drafted in a historical, social, linguistic, and economic context different from our own. As technology yields ever more accelerating developments in social, economic, and cultural life (and as law fails to keep up) this difficulty will intensify. Indeed, the experience or sense of historical lag in law will occur across smaller time segments.[22]

When lag is significant, a thorny question arises: Is meaning best preserved and honored by a *literal transposition* that disregards changes in context, or is it best preserved and honored by *analogical extrapolation* in response to changes in context?[23] And if so, which changes, which contexts? Notice that this crucial question cannot be answered by saying that the interpreter is obliged to show fidelity to the original meaning. On the contrary, both approaches—literal transposition as well as analogical extrapolation—claim to be and, *in their own way*, are honoring the original meaning.

A more radical problem for fidelity to the original meaning is that there may not be an "original meaning" for the simple reason that a *legal* text, even as it might claim to be "original" or "constitutive," cannot possibly mean that in any strong sense. No legal text is ever a complete *rupture* with its antecedents. On the contrary, any *legal* text variously incorporates, depends upon, borrows, modifies, and disavows antecedent legal meanings and traditions in order to give effect to its own. This, of course, places on the interpreter the challenge of trying to discern and distinguish what has been carried over from what has not.

F. SUMMARY

These then are but a few of the stereotyped tensions and conflicts within which legal interpretation happens. Understanding and appreciating these tensions and conflicts allows the potential opening of a whole set of interpretive possibilities and attendant arguments. We turn now to textualism and purposivism to discuss their specific conflicts and tensions.

II. Textualism

In addition to the general conflicts and tensions articulated above, textualism presents certain stereotyped interpretive challenges that give rise to interpretive disputes. Here we describe some that are sufficiently stereotyped and recursive to warrant discussion.

One challenge lies in identifying the object of interpretation—is it a word, a phrase, a sentence, or just what precisely (the *individuation problem*)? A second challenge lies in respecting the meaning of the entire text (*intratextual integrity*). And a third challenge lies in respecting the meaning of texts related to the one interpreted (*intertextual integrity*).

A. INDIVIDUATION: WHAT IS THE
UNIT OF INTERPRETATION?

Treaties, constitutions, statutes, and regulations typically contain titles, which in turn contain sections, which contain subsections, which contain sentences, which contain phrases, which contain words. One might ask, in a given case, which unit is to serve as the unit of interpretation—the section, the subsection, the sentence, the phrase, or the word? This is a particular instance of what is sometimes called "the individuation problem."

In Anglo-American jurisprudence, the most famous example routinely used to illustrate this problem is H. L. A. Hart's famous hypothetical about an ordinance that "prohibits vehicles in the park."[24] The question is whether the ordinance covers tricycles, bicycles, the statue of a World War II tank, and so on. Hart believed that the key inquiry would have to turn on the semantic meaning of the term "vehicle." Fuller, taking a different stance, thought that one had to interpret the ordinance as a whole in terms of its ostensible purpose.

Among the several interpretive challenges raised by this hypothetical, one of the more interesting ones is the individuation problem: just what is the unit (in this case, a single word, the entire ordinance, or something even broader) that is to be the object of interpretation? On this question, the law and the learning are rather unhelpful. (The individuation problem has an interesting similarity to the generally intractable "level of abstraction" problem—which also tends to defy meaningful resolution.) What is clear, however, and this matters very much to the interpreter, is that a focus or emphasis on different units of interpretation may very well affect the outcome—or at least make one interpretation more plausible than another.

Example 1: Consider a rule prohibiting students from possessing weapons in school, providing that the term "weapon" "shall include but shall not be limited to any knife, cutting instrument, cutting tool, explosive, mace, nunchaku, firearm, shotgun, rifle and any other tool, instrument or implement capable of inflicting serious bodily injury."[25] One student stabbed another with a pencil. Can she be charged with violating the rule, because a pencil is "an instrument or implement capable of inflicting serious bodily injury"? The phrase just quoted suggests that a pencil is such an instrument or implement, but a more holistic reading of the rule and its purpose suggests that a pencil should not qualify.

Example 2: What about the words "tangible object" in the Sarbanes-Oxley Act (the act prompted by Enron's massive accounting fraud and the destruction of Enron documents)—do they include a fish? This was the dispute in a 2015

Supreme Court case where the defendant had been convicted of knowingly dis-
posing of fish with the intent of obstructing the government's investigation into
harvesting undersized fish.[26] *In a 5–4 decision, the Court determined that the*
words "tangible object" did not include fish, but only objects used to record or pre-
serve information. The relevant section of the law provides criminal sanctions for
a person who "knowingly alters, destroys, mutilates, conceals, covers up, falsifies,
or makes a false entry in any record, document, or tangible object with the intent
to impede, obstruct, or influence" a federal investigation. Justice Kagan wrote the
dissenting opinion (joined by Justices Scalia, Kennedy, and Thomas), pointing
out that fish "is a discrete thing that possesses physical form" (citing to Dr. Seuss).
While she "agree[d] with the plurality (really, who doesn't?) that context matters
in interpreting statutes," the context led her to a different conclusion.

B. INTRATEXTUAL INTEGRITY

Sophisticated textualists understand that the meaning of a text is not ex-
hausted simply by summing up the meanings of individual words. They
understand that texts are structured in all sorts of internal relations (hierarchies, cross-references, dependencies, encroachments, and so on and so
forth). Similarly, they understand that the meaning of a term might well turn
on its immediate syntactical entourage (e.g., the clause of which it is a part) or
instead on a technical use that remains constant throughout the text.[27] On the
whole, sophisticated textualists understand that terms mean in an interactive
way. In this interaction, the terms "do" things to each other (modify, qualify,
enhance, confirm, extend, and so on and so forth). Deciding what "impact"
words, clauses, sentences, paragraphs, and so on have on each other creates
many pathways for interpretive argument.

C. INTERTEXTUAL INTEGRITY

Law, as already suggested, is "layered" in multiple ways. The interpretation
of a given law has implications not just for that law, but also for other laws
to which it may be related. With just about any interpretation of a law, the
question arises: Must the interpretation offered conform to or accommodate
other associated laws (and, if so, how)? This is the paradigmatic question of
intertextual integrity. It is a question with both interpretive and jurisprudential aspects.[28]

III. Purposivism

Purposivism, as the term is used here, includes both principled interpretation and policy analysis when they are turned to the enterprise of interpretation. This is arguably an unusually encompassing use of the term. Indeed, some legal thinkers would greatly object (and for non-trivial reasons) to the conflation of principle and policy. Nonetheless, given a certain degree of abstraction, there are sufficient similarities in principle and policy interpretation that, for the limited purposes here, we can treat them together.[29]

Purposivism, as its name indicates, calls for an examination of the purpose or purposes of a particular law. In the "no vehicles in the park" hypothetical, a purposivist would try to figure out what sensible purpose might be served by prohibiting vehicles from the park.

Right away, the prohibition of vehicles from the park could be seen as serving a number of different purposes—among them, safety, noise abatement, aesthetic enjoyment, environmental concerns, wildlife preservation, landscape preservation, or indeed some combination of the foregoing. The wording of the ordinance itself provides few contextual cues. One significant cue is often the least noticed—the notion of park.[30] An inquiry into the kind of park we are talking about—a city park, a national preserve, a skateboarding arena, a botanical garden—might give an indication of the function of the park at stake, and thus what kind of purpose is to be served.[31]

But, as the hypothetical illustrates, the big challenge for purposivism lies in identifying and articulating the purposes ostensibly served by a law. Unfortunately, legal professionals tend to underestimate the difficulties in selecting purpose. As but one example, Henry Hart and Albert Sacks, the great US midcentury legal-process thinkers, advanced the notion that statutory meaning is to be derived by assuming that legislators are "reasonable men pursuing reasonable purposes reasonably, unless the contrary is made unmistakably to appear."[32] Whether or not making this assumption is itself reasonable (an interesting question) it seems clear that it is not altogether all that helpful.

Example 1: Consider the Supreme Court's interpretation of the Chemical Weapons Convention Implementation Act of 1998, making it a federal crime for a person to use or possess any chemical weapon and imposing harsh penalties.[33] The Court concluded that the term "chemical weapon" (defined broadly in the statute as any chemical that "can cause death, temporary incapacitation or permanent harm to humans or animals") did not include the toxic chemical used by the defendant to irritate her husband's girlfriend. The Court determined that the statute did not reach a "purely local crime"—"the global need to prevent chemical warfare does not require the Federal Government to reach into the kitchen cupboard."[34] *Is this conclusion reasonable? Would a contrary conclusion also be reasonable?*

Example 2: An Iowa statute defines a "farm tenancy" as an interest in "land held by a person who produces crops or provides for the care and feeding of livestock on the land."[35] *It defines "livestock" as "an animal" of a number of certain species, including the equine species. Yet the Supreme Court of Iowa, overruling a court of appeals decision, found that keeping a single thirty-eight-year-old horse on the property did not qualify the property as a farm tenancy. What would "reasonable men pursuing reasonable purposes reasonably," say?*

A. MULTIPLE PURPOSES

Any mildly complex decision generally involves multiple purposes. Imagine you are going on a vacation to the Alps. Whatever purposes might be served by such an action, it is unlikely to be singular. The purposes for taking a vacation are multiple: exercise, change of scenery, revitalization, challenge, time to think, and more. As a general matter, human beings and groups (e.g., institutions) do not generally act for singular or unitary purposes. The same is true of law. When one thinks about what the purpose for a particular provision might be, numerous possibilities come to mind. We have already seen this with regard to the "no vehicles in the park" hypothetical above.

How is one to select, then, among several different purposes? Should a judge interpreting a legal text simply assume that all "reasonable" purposes should be included in the interpretation of the ordinance? That is a possible strategy, but what happens when the purposes seem to indicate different conclusions? Moreover, consider that no one is ever willing to pursue any single legal objective endlessly. There is always a point at which one decides that pursuing a single objective (e.g., accident deterrence) has become too costly, unreasonable, or something of the sort. At some point, one encounters other objectives or values thought to be more compelling. Almost regardless of how we define the functions of a law (or the legal system generally) we will run up against a certain limit set forth in another law, or in the general policies, principles, values, or other considerations of the legal system. We should recognize that to do legal analysis or legal interpretation by deriving our conclusions from a single legal imperative is never the right way to proceed: all legal imperatives are always embedded in and circumscribed by other legal imperatives that pull or push in other directions.

Moreover, all reasonably complex laws, despite what may seem to be their singular form (e.g., a prohibition), will nonetheless effectuate multiple ends. Take a simple traffic code law that prohibits driving without proof of liability insurance. At first one thinks about what it is in form: a prohibition. But, de facto, it is not just a prohibition. For one thing, it is a subsidy to insurance companies. It is a delegation of authority to police officers to check for liability insurance. It is a tax or revenue-raising mechanism for the state. It is a measure to assure social confidence—namely, the possibility of corrective intervention by way of damages, risk spreading, and the like. Already then we see that the plausible purposes of a law are multiple—even if the form seems to be singular (e.g., a prohibition). Most laws will serve multiple purposes in exactly this way.

The difficulty from an interpretive standpoint lies in selecting which purposes are to be honored and which not, and how they are to be arranged in terms of their relative priority.

B. SELECTION

Confronted with many different purposes—as in the examples above—the immediate question becomes, Which of the several possible purposes are to be honored, and which are to be discounted? How much so? And on the basis of what criteria? These selection questions must be answered when indeed the purposes are in tension and point to different conclusions.

These are very tough questions. At one extreme one might say, as some legal thinkers have, that some coherent principles or criteria must be used to select which purposes are to be honored.[36] But formulating such principles or criteria is surely no easy task. On the one hand, one wants to avoid particularist situationism (along this line lies the descent of law into managerialism). On the other hand, one wants to avoid rigid monism (along this line lies mechanistic formalism). But if we reject these two polar extremes and opt for some "middle ground," just how much context-sensitivity should we demand of our coherence?

Applicable legal authorities tend to be ambivalent and vague on these problems. And understandably so: in law, we are interested in the kind of coherence that takes due account of differences and dissimilarities . . . which is to underscore the somewhat nebulous and elusive character of that which we seek.

C. THE STRUCTURE OF PURPOSE

Purpose is structured and organized in multiple ways—it can be seen as layered, conflicted, provisional, mutable, conditional, and so on. That is, once one turns to the interpretation of a particular law or provision, it becomes apparent that it has many conceivable purposes, some of which will be disjunctive or conflicting. This realization presents not just a selection question as described above, but an organizational one: How does one organize the various purposes identified? How do they relate to each other? Which, if any, are to be accorded primacy? What kind of structure can we give to the array of purposes? And from where are we to derive this structure?

IV. Summary

Just about any non-trivial legal issue can be presented as one involving interpretation. Once that framing of the issue is in place—that is, once the judge or other legal official recognizes that there is an interpretive dimension to the legal issue—all kinds of questions (namely, those described in this chapter) can be posed, and a wide array of arguments can be advanced to address the legal issues at stake. Whether any of the questions turn out to be salient, and whether the attendant arguments are deemed persuasive or not—these are altogether different matters. But at least it may help to have an index of possibilities to consider.

8

Cluster Logic

In this chapter, we return to the subject of legal distinctions. But not just any legal distinctions—rather those that play *fundamental roles* in the architecture of contemporary law and accordingly recur across many fields (e.g., property, contracts, securities). These we will call "structural distinctions." Here are a few examples (to be supplemented shortly):

Public/Private
Formalism/Realism
Choice/Coercion
Form/Substance
Is/Ought
Absolute/Conditional

These structural distinctions are extremely important because they comprise much of the basic framework of contemporary law.

The account provided here straddles structuralism and poststructuralism. It is very much influenced by the work of Duncan Kennedy, as well as Chaim Perelman and Lucie Olbrechts-Tyteca.[1]

Here, we imagine law as a series of floating structures and moves (some of which are more stylized, pervasive, and enduring than others). These are combined and recombined in various ways across time, field, and context. If this seems conceptually untidy or methodologically compromised, we can only answer that we are trying to show fidelity to our object: law.

I. A Cautionary Note

A great deal of the success of contemporary law (intellectually, practically, and politically) hangs on the conceptual, operational, and normative cogency of the structural distinctions yet to be described. This is not just because these structural distinctions are recursive (though they are). It is also because these structural distinctions are the movable pieces that shape the basic, even if mutable, architecture of contemporary law.

One might reasonably think that because these structural distinctions are so basic, articulating their meaning and roles would be an easy task. In actuality, it's more like the reverse: the very fact that they are basic or foundational makes understanding them much harder. Why? Two reasons.

First, as with any system (e.g., a religion, a language), as one approaches foundational levels, the system increasingly runs out of terms by which to define or articulate the basics. Indeed, efforts to do so very quickly run into circularity. A famous physicist, John Lighton Synge, illustrated this vicious circularity problem with a game known as VISH. The object of the game is to define a term in other terms (and so on and so forth) without using previously used terms. When a player screws up, another player can score by declaring "VISH" (for "vicious circle").[2]

Example 1: What is a foundation? Answer: The thing on which everything else rests. And what is the thing on which everything rests. Answer: It is the base. And what is a base? It is . . . a foundation?

Example 2: What is a right? Answer: A right is a certain kind of entitlement held by groups or individuals. And what is an entitlement? An entitlement is a grant of authority by the state enabling groups or individuals to do X legally free from certain restraints. And what is it to be legally free from certain restraints? It is to have . . . an entitlement?

Second, insofar as the structural distinctions play such an important and pervasive role in law, they are repeatedly subjected to contestation (e.g., litigation) *and* from all sides. It is not so much that they face direct or radical challenges: on the contrary, judges and officials are understandably loath to permit radical challenges to the fundamental distinctions that enable them to do their jobs. At the same time, however, because these structural distinctions are so basic there is a great deal to be gained by trying to tweak them this way or that. Even a small tweak can produce seismic ripple effects throughout the system.[3]

Because structural distinctions tend to be subjected to such stress, they are found, depending upon the field, context, and time, in various stages of impairment, or even collapse. It bears mentioning here that even if one believes that these structural distinctions are in various stages of collapse that in no way means that they go away or that legal professionals are reprieved from addressing them and operating with and within the fields that they mark out.

At the same time, most of these structural distinctions are in fact impaired—in the sense that there are well-recognized arguments (often arguments exploiting the "classic flaws" discussed in chapter 4, "The Legal Distinction") that effectively undermine the integrity of the structural distinctions and therefore, most importantly, undermine the arguments associated with the structural distinctions.[4]

II. The Structural Distinction Clusters

Each structural distinction appears throughout the corpus of the law in different guises. More accurately, we could say that there are groups of structural distinctions—we will call them structural distinction *clusters*—where each distinction can be seen as a variation on the others. Consider, for instance, the choice/coercion distinction. Another way of making *roughly* the same sort of distinction would be to talk about consent/necessity or, yet again, voluntary/involuntary or . . . and so on. We can thus talk about a "choice/coercion cluster" of structural distinctions arranged as shown in table 8.1.

TABLE 8.1. The Choice/Coercion Cluster

Choice	Coercion
freedom	slavery
contract	duress
consent	necessity
voluntary	involuntary
free will	determinism
permissive	mandatory
autonomy	heteronomy

Note that the various distinctions above *are not* the same. They have slightly different twists and implications: duress is not the same as necessity, which in turn is not the same as involuntariness. The terms are also encountered in different fields of law (e.g., property, antitrust). And the same terms can be accorded different meanings in different contexts. But despite these differences, these distinctions are homologous: they have *roughly* the same meaning and play *roughly* the same roles or functions in contemporary law.

Perhaps the easiest way to think of these clusters is in terms of Ludwig Wittgenstein's conception of "family resemblances."[5] Wittgenstein suggested that members of a family look alike not because they share traits common to all, but because each of the members shares some traits with several of the others. The same might be said of the structural distinction clusters: there is, in principle, no clear trait or set of traits constitutive of the cluster, but all the members go together, as in Wittgenstein's family resemblances. With perhaps this one modification: sometimes a distinction in one cluster could just as well be assigned to a different one.

In legal argument (e.g., a brief, an opinion, a law review article) it is, of course, important to pay attention to the specific doctrinal settings and meanings. It is important to get the nomenclature right. But, for the purposes of understanding law and making arguments, it is important as well to be able to attend to the more basic similarities across different doctrinal fields and contexts. Once one attends to these basic similarities it becomes much easier to navigate through the corpus of the law—to achieve a good understanding of how the parts do their work (or not).

Here we will try to do just that—namely, bracket (i.e., put aside and ignore) the fine variations in order to reveal the broader recurrent patterns. To this end, the more important structural distinctions are grouped together below with a *total disregard* for their appurtenance to specific doctrinal fields.[6] Each cluster represents distinctions that are roughly synonymous in meaning and that often serve similar roles and functions.[7] The point here is to recognize thematic similarities across doctrinal fields. It is *definitely not* to say that all doctrinal fields have the same structural distinctions (similar—yes; same—generally not). Nor is it to say that the recognized roles and functions are the same across doctrinal fields (again, similar but generally not the same).

Before elaborating the structural distinction clusters further, it may help to lay them out, as shown in table 8.2. This table, of course, hardly exhausts the important distinction clusters that form contemporary legal systems. But it does contain some of the more important and recurrent distinctions—those that are most basic to contemporary law viewed as a whole.

The meaning of this table may seem self-evident. But, it is not. There is more here than meets the eye. We need to tease out various aspects of this table to recognize that it offers a number of different implications. Or to put it more plainly, the table can be read in a number of ways. We will elaborate two of these right now under the headings *composition* and *pairing*. (A third, *dissociation*, we will leave for later.)

Composition. Notice two things about the clustering below. First, as mentioned earlier, the structural distinctions within a cluster are variations of each other. Thus under the "formalism/realism cluster," the entries rules/standards, categorical/balancing, absolute/relative are similar, but not exactly the same. What precisely then describes their differences? Our answer

TABLE 8.2. The Structural Distinction Clusters

Essential/Contingent Cluster		Choice/Coercion Cluster	
Essential	*Contingent*	*Choice*	*Coercion*
core	peripheral	freedom	slavery
rule	exception	contract	duress
necessary	accidental	consent	necessity
normal	aberrant	voluntary	involuntary
use	abuse	free will	determinism
Quantitative Cluster		permissive	mandatory
		autonomy	heteronomy
Substantial	*Minor*	**Public/Private Cluster**	
material	immaterial	*Public*	*Private*
direct	indirect		
primary	secondary	state	civil society
strong	weak	official	non-official
predominant	subsidiary	government	market
significant	de minimis	public sector	private sector
Figure/Ground Cluster		communal	individual
		public good	private good
Figure	*Ground*	other-regarding	self-regarding
construction	foundation	**Paternalism/Individualism Cluster**	
superstructure	base	*Paternalism*	*Individualism*
the constituted	the constituting		
the constituted	the constituent	altruism	egoism
form	power	interdependent	self-interested
Reality/Appearance Cluster		**Neutrality/Value-Laden Cluster**	
Reality	*Appearance*	*Neutral*	*Value-Laden*
true	false	impartial	committed
deep	shallow	disinterested	engaged
original	copy	principled	responsive
authentic	derivative	balanced	one-sided

is that, in the manner of Wittgenstein's family resemblances, each structural distinction varies relative to the others along different axes (in the same way that scarlet, crimson, maroon, burgundy all vary from each other along different axes).

We turn to some examples. So, what are the relations of formalism/realism to rules/standards? Well, first, formalism is roughly to rules as realism is to standards. How so? Well, we might say that formalism is the *projection* of the rule form to the *plane of theory* (or conversely, we might say that the rule form is the *projection* of formalism to the space of a *legal directive*). And we might say that realism is the projection of the standard form to the plane of theory

TABLE 8.2. *Continued*

Law/Politics Cluster		Theory/Practice Cluster	
Law	*Politics*	*Theory*	*Practice*
reason	discretion	law in the books	law in action
principle	fiat	logic of justification	logic of discovery
norm	judgment	Llewellyn's paper rules	Llewellyn's real rules

Subjective/Objective Cluster		Absolute/Conditional Cluster	
Subjective	*Objective*	*Conditional*	*Absolute*
appearance	reality	defeasible	indefeasible
mental	behavioral	presumptive	conclusive
mind	body	privilege	right
biased	neutral		
evaluative	factual	Is/Ought Cluster	
unreliable	reliable	*Is*	*Ought*
individual	collective	actual	ideal

Formalism/Realism Cluster			
Formalism	*Realism*	existing	aspirational
rules	standards	realistic	utopian
structure	function	Action/Omission Cluster	
absolute	relative	*Action*	*Omission*
categorical	balancing	misfeasance	nonfeasance
determinate	indeterminate	working a harm	withholding a benefit
distinction	spectrum		
per se	reasonable	Part/Whole Cluster	

Form/Substance Cluster		*Part*	*Whole*
Form	*Substance*	cause of action	element
style	content	division	subdivision
procedural	substantive	section	subsection
		micro micro-economics	macro macro-economics

Process/Outcome Cluster		Hierarchy/Equivalence Cluster	
Process	*Outcome*	*Hierarchy*	*Equivalence*
means	end	ranking	equality
path	goal		
methods	consequences		

(or conversely, we might say that the *standard form* is the reduction of realism to the space of a *legal directive*).

Another example: What are the relations of rules/standards to per se/reasonableness? Well, again rule is to per se roughly as standard is to reasonableness. How so? Well, a rule is the *projection* of the per se *approach to decision-making* to the articulation of a *legal directive* (or conversely, a per se approach is the *projection* of the rule form of the *legal directive* to the articulation of an *approach to decision-making*). And similarly, a standard is the *projection* of the reasonableness approach to the articulation of a legal directive (or conversely, a reasonableness approach is a *projection* of the standard form to the articulation of *an approach to decision-making*).

So much for examples. We could go on here. For quite some time. We won't. It is the basic idea that is important: all of these distinctions within clusters are related to each other via relations that can be articulated by reference to *principles of projection—for instance, extension, contraction, relocation*. The distinctions are roughly the same binary forms (with the same internal relations) projected onto different *fields, sectors, concerns, operations, tasks, and so on*. This, by the way, is why they are variations on each other and why they belong in the same cluster.

Now, because the distinctions that make up the clusters are variations on each other, the name of each cluster (e.g., the "formalism/realism cluster") is somewhat arbitrary. It could have been called the "rules/standards" cluster or the "structure/function" cluster. Interestingly, each distinction, when it occupies a superior "title" position arguably colors the entire cluster, gives the entire cluster a certain orientation, so to speak. (Try it.)

Pairing. In reading table 8.2, one can imagine the distinctions among the various clusters as stating a number of different relations. Among these are classificatory, oppositional, antithetical, and dissociative. Nearly all the clusters above can be used in all four ways. A distinction is *classificatory* if it merely divides stuff into sets (e.g., odd and even numbers). In law, however, classificatory distinctions almost always have attitude—that is to say, a classification brings about certain consequences: if in law we distinguish A from B, it is often because A and B are going to be submitted to different legal regimes. Accordingly, in law classificatory distinctions slide very quickly into oppositional distinctions. A distinction is *oppositional* if it is used as a pivot to trigger opposed treatment (e.g., guilty/not guilty, liable/not liable). Both classificatory and oppositional distinctions are used as splitters—as ways to separate out legal regimes. An oppositional distinction becomes an antithetical distinction when each pole is the negation of the other such that it is not possible that X could be both at once. The distinction between oppositional and antithetical matters quite a bit in law because it divides those legal professionals who think that some cluster is intact ("Whatever is private can never be public and vice versa"—an antithetical distinction) from those who think that a cluster might well be collapsed ("We might well have to decide ultimately whether to treat X as private or public, but let's be candid: X is both public and private"—an oppositional distinction).

Example: In law, the difference between oppositional and antithetical distinctions matters. Consider the choice/coercion cluster again. Many legal thinkers tend to view the pairing as antithetical. For them, this means that where there is coercion there is no choice, and where there is choice there is no coercion. The famous legal realist Robert Lee Hale pointed out that where law is concerned all choice is made in circumstances of (legal) coercion. The two are thus not antithetical, but can and, according to Hale, do coexist. The terms "choice" and "coercion" thus cease to be, if one follows Hale's thought, analytically antithetical. Effectively, they become oppositional in character and quite possibly mere labeling devices.

A third way of reading the distinctions above is as dissociative pairs. Again, we leave that complicated (but very useful) topic for later.

III. How the Clusters Matter

How does viewing law and its structural distinctions in terms of these clusters help? We have already noted that these clusters articulate the basic structure of contemporary law. Set forth below are descriptions of how the distinction clusters can be used in understanding and making legal arguments.

A. THE CLUSTERS AS CLASSIC OPTIONS

Grouping the structural distinctions into clusters allows us to see that a whole series of doctrinal distinctions that, on first impression, seem very different are in fact very much alike. These clusters lay out some classic options for making distinctions. Suppose, for instance, one believes that there was something vaguely coercive that led the defendant to act in the way she did (i.e., violate her employment contract). As one thinks about the case (in terms of the clusters) it turns out that *coercion* might not be exactly the thing: rather, it may be that she was compelled by an overriding need to help a coworker in some way (*necessity*). Or perhaps that she was trapped in a situation where great harm would befall her if she didn't do what she did (*duress*). Or perhaps she simply was not in control of the situation (*determinism*) or ... and so on. Recognizing that these are all similar notions allows the advocate to refine or choose among them (if the doctrine allows). There is a sense in which paying attention to the clusters (the broad picture) allows us to recognize the fine doctrinal gradations.

Example: The concepts labeled in table 8.2 as part of the quantitative cluster can be found everywhere. In civil procedure, courts may strike "immaterial" matters from a complaint, grant a motion for directed verdict if the evidence is "insubstantial," or deny jurisdiction under the federal question doctrine if the claim is

"insubstantial." In a patent law case, the accused activity and the patented in-
vention must be substantially the same (sometimes framed as the "insubstantial
differences" test). In criminal law, an attempt charge may require the prosecution
to show that the defendant took a "substantial step," and "insubstantial errors"
may not be reversible. In child custody cases in some jurisdictions, a biological
parent may be required to show that he or she had more than de minimis contact
with the child.

B. NUANCE: SUBSTITUTING ONE DISTINCTION OR ONE TERM FOR ANOTHER

Insofar as the distinctions are best understood as versions of each other, many
(not all) of the elements in one cluster can often be reconceptualized in terms
of the others. This will work much of the time, but not all of the time. It turns
out that structural distinctions are often defined in terms of their distinctions
drawn from the same cluster.

Thus, if one asks why some action X was *voluntary,* one might find an
opinion saying that action X was voluntary because the defendant *chose* to
carry it out or *consented* to carrying it out (and so on). In another case the
issue might well be whether the plaintiff's action Y constituted *consent* or
not. And one might find some opinion that states it was *consent* because the
defendant's action was *voluntary,* freely *chosen* (and so on).

Notice here that, as one looks at the whole, a certain (near) circularity
can become apparent. In case 1, X is deemed voluntary because choice and
consent are present. Meanwhile, in case 2, Y is consensual because it was voluntary and chosen. Meanwhile, in case 3 . . . and so on. We are back to VISH.
We are on the verge of a kind of (near) circularity here—which is precisely
the point: when we are dealing with structural distinctions it turns out that
each is often defined in terms of the others (assuming it is defined at all).

Note that, in terms of law, this (near) circularity is not necessarily objec-
tionable. At the same time, the inability or refusal to recognize this (near)
circularity is a problem. A failure to recognize this (near) circularity leads
legal professionals to believe that they are saying things that are clear and fully
secure, when instead they are simply failing to notice that their arguments
rest upon circularity (and accordingly may be undone once noticed).

Example: Consider the Tenth Circuit's analysis of whether an employee's testi-
mony in a child custody proceeding was a matter of public concern: the court
characterized a child custody hearing as "a purely personal dispute," and the
employee's motive for testifying as "personal," and so concluded the testimony

was not a matter of public concern.[8] *The dissenting judge focused instead on the "public interest" in child welfare, and the fact that the employee would have been required to testify by subpoena as evidence that his motive was not "personal," concluding that the testimony was a matter of public concern. The (somewhat unsatisfying) gist of these arguments: the speech is not public because it's personal or it is public because it's not personal.*

Another way of putting all this—one that avoids the image of circularity—is to say that the various cluster distinctions are linked together in accordance with a kind of associational logic. The terms on one side (e.g., choice, consent, free will) seem to "go together" and are often used to establish the presence of the others.

Example 1: "Because he had free will he had a choice in the matter and therefore his consent was freely given."

Example 2: "Of course, this is subjective. It's individualized and a matter of opinion."

C. CLUSTER FUNCTIONS

The cluster pairings are linked to important juridical, moral, or political functions. A great deal of the politics (symbolic and organizational) of American law (the basic juridical arrangement of social, economic, and political life) is articulated in these particular clusters. The term "articulated" is used here in two senses. In one sense, it means that the basic structure is expressed in terms of these clusters. In a second sense, it means that the articulations of the basic structure, *its major pivot points*, are enabled by these cluster pairings. The term "function" meanwhile is used in a non-technical sense to signify the role played by characterizing an action or activity as lying on one side of the distinction or the other.

Recognizing the similarities in the *functions* of the clusters helps us to recognize the juridical, moral, and political "logic" of the law. Below we will set forth what we take to be the basic functions for two illustrative clusters: choice/coercion and public/private. A caution here: precisely because these clusters are so basic, so fundamental, in contemporary law, it is difficult to describe their functions without yet again flirting with circularity.

The invocation of the clusters brings into play a stock set of stylized reasons, principles, policies, values, considerations, and justifications that resonate throughout American law. Correspondingly, because the movement works in both directions, a certain set of characteristic arguments will point to the desirability of invoking the use of a certain cluster. (The relations run both ways.)

We have already used the device of *argument tags* in the chapter 3 on baselines. Here we will resort to a similar idea—namely, *function tags*. The clusters often serve certain characteristic legal/political functions. We describe these functions as tags (in order to avoid an overly lengthy discussion). These function tags are stereotyped, and we will be describing the argument tags most frequently associated with a given cluster. But it is important to recognize that function tags are not exhaustive: clusters actually serve a lot more functions than the function tag lists below indicate.

Some cautionary notes before proceeding further. First, these function tags describe how the clusters *are in fact* still used in American law. Second, the functions are not necessarily coherent. Why might they not be coherent? Well, remember: these clusters have been severely stressed. They are impaired and in some cases even collapsed.

1. Function Tags for the Choice/Coercion Cluster

The choice/coercion cluster is comprised of the distinctions shown in table 8.3.

The characterization of an action as chosen, voluntary, intended, or the like by a party tends as a general matter to impose responsibility on that party.

TABLE 8.3. The Choice/Coercion Cluster

Choice[a]	Coercion[b]
freedom	slavery
contract	duress
consent	necessity
voluntary	involuntary
free will	determinism
permissive	mandatory
autonomy	heteronomy

[a]Consent notions appear in various doctrinal areas in a variety of different doctrinal formulations: contract, agreement, waiver, ratification, assumption of risk, estoppel, endorsement.

[b]Coercion notions appear in various doctrinal areas in a variety of different doctrinal formulations: coercion, necessity, duress, involuntariness, insanity, diminished capacity, intoxication, mandatory terms, compulsory terms.

We are using the term "responsibility" here in its broadest most encompassing senses.

Characterizing or classifying an action or activity as chosen implies the following.

a. *Attribution of responsibility for harm imposed on others.* X can be held responsible/liable for his action's consequences to others (e.g., criminal culpability).

    i. *Causal theory.* Choice serves as an "origin" in the causal chain (therefore action and harm are traceable back to X's choice, and responsibility/liability is appropriate). Choice, intent, and so on often serve as "origin points" in constructing relevant time or transactional frames.

    ii. *Ownership theory.* Choice shows that action and harm are X's.

    iii. *Agency theory.* X is responsible/liable because through the exercise of choice, consent, and so on, X shows he had the *power* to avoid action and harm and did not do so.

    iv. *Moral continuity theory.* Choice shows that this was X's action and harm, and thus X cannot now deny ownership.

    v. *Theory of the self.* Choice = exercise of agency = self.

    vi. *Self-selection theory.* Through his choice, consent, and so on he *distinguished* himself from all the other possible perpetrators and can thus be selected as the agent to be held liable/responsible.

b. *Attribution of responsibility for harm imposed on self.* Any adverse consequences of the action on X must be borne by X, who chose, intended (and so on) the action; see above (e.g., consent, waiver, ratification, assumption of risk . . .).

c. *Scope of responsibility.* Choice, intent, selection can serve to delimit scope of responsibility for others (e.g., undertaking theory in duty for torts). Similarly, the choice, or intent of others can sometimes "cut off" the liability of a party (e.g., proximate cause). Choice, intent, of another party often serves as a "termination point" in constructing relevant time or transactional frames.

The characterization of an action as the outgrowth of coercion, necessity, and so on tends, as a general matter, to have exculpatory effects. Characterizing or classifying an action or activity as coerced, mandated, driven by necessity, or the like implies the following.

a. *Disattribution of responsibility for harm to self.* Where X is coerced, X's action cannot be charged to X, and X cannot be held responsible/liable for the resulting harm to self.

b. *Disattribution of responsibility for harm to others.* Where X is coerced, X's action cannot be charged to X, and X cannot be held responsible/liable for the resulting harm to others.

c. *Scope of responsibility.* X's action cannot be used to define the scope or content of his or her obligations. If X is coerced, this can reduce the scope of X's obligations. Similarly, the coercive acts of another party may delimit the scope of X's obligations.

2. Function Tags for the Public/Private Cluster

The public/private cluster is comprised of the distinctions shown in table 8.4.

TABLE 8.4. The Public/Private Cluster

Public[a]	Private[b]
state	civil society
official	non-official
government	market
public sector	private sector
public good	private good
communal	individual
other-regarding	self-regarding

[a] Public notions appear in various doctrinal areas in a variety of different doctrinal formulations: public realm, public law, public rights, public interest, public policy, public figure, public utility, open to the public, public accommodation.

[b] Private notions appear in various doctrinal areas in a variety of different doctrinal formulations: private realm, private law, private rights, private property, private right of action, right of privacy, invasion of privacy, private information, private association, private place of business, private figure.

If an action or activity is characterized as public, then as a general matter it is subject to public deliberation, governance, and norms *except* (here comes the flip) when the public interest requires secrecy, non-disclosure, and so on. Still, generally, classifying an action or activity as public implies the following:[9]

a. *Authorization of state to rule and coerce.* One of the main functions of designating something as public (e.g., public good, of public interest) is to identify it as a proper subject for state coercion. Thus, once private law areas such as contracts, torts, or property become clothed with a public interest they become subject to public policy considerations and accordingly give way to protectionist measures (e.g., mandatory terms in contracts), welfarist distribution concerns (risk spreading in torts), and efficiency incentives (resource development in property). Public in this sense also means eligible for special obligations or burdens (as in public figures in defamation law).

b. *Democratic/collective decision-making.* Presumptively, the public realm ought to be subject to democratic, or administrative, decision-making procedures and norms. This decision-making presumptively should aim at achieving some generalized collective or communal good.

c. *Application of rule of law considerations.* The public realm is, or ought to be, kept free from undue influence of, and capture by, market actors, individual interests (*anti-bribery, anti-corruption, campaign financing, etc.*). Rule of law and neutral process considerations should be observed (notice, opportunity to be heard, impartial arbiter, etc.).

d. *Disclosure/transparency.* Public deliberation, norms, and governance are and should be subject to disclosure and transparency requirements (e.g., public notice, notice and comment, FOIA, open records, sunlight laws, etc.).

e. *State responsibility for welfare.* Public interests demand state recognition and protection. Public harms demand state intervention and correction.

If an action or activity is characterized as private, then as a general matter it is the domain of private consensual arrangements or individual choice and should be exempt from state interference *except* (here comes the flip) to protect the private realm from violation by third parties. Still, generally, classifying an action as private implies the following.

a. *Freedom from state interference.* One of the main reasons for designating something as private is to accord the individual some generalized realm of self-direction and autonomy (relatively) free of legal interference. This realm can, depending upon who is arguing, include anything from intimate behavior to market transactions.

b. *Governance by non-state institutions.* Often the term "private" is used to designate some sector of social or economic life that ought to be governed (if governed at all) by some purportedly non-state institutions such as religion, the market, morals, and so on.

c. *Individual discretion and preferences allowed (and protected).* If an action or activity is private, then individuals are free to pursue their own discretionary preferences.

d. *Protection from disclosure.* Closely related to the freedom from interference notion is the idea that certain kinds of activities or materials or information should (at the individual's option) remain exempt from publicity and disclosure requirements.

e. *Individual responsibility for welfare.* Individuals are, or should be, required to fend and provide for themselves.

IV. Operationalizing the Clusters: Interaction

Inasmuch as the clusters play such a crucial role in the organization of the basic structure of American law, it is important to understand the play that they afford the advocate. These clusters often underwrite a great deal of legal argument.

Thus, to take the choice/coercion cluster as an example, consider that just about any transaction can be, as an analytical matter, characterized as an instance of choice or of coercion. (Whether any given characterization turns out to be convincing or not is a different question—it is, for the speaker, a rhetorical matter.) If one wants to characterize an action as a choice, one fastens on those aspects that seem to reveal voluntariness, intent, and deliberation while underscoring the absence or inefficacy of constraint. If one wants to characterize an action as a form of coercion, one fastens on those circumstances and contexts that effectively restrain, limit, or otherwise shape and motivate the action taken while underemphasizing the moment of choice.

How is this accomplished?

A. COMBINING CLUSTERS

Notice that the various clusters can be combined in various ways to produce the structure of an argument. Thus to take the choice/coercion cluster as an example, consider how one might combine clusters to create the impression of choice or coercion on the part of the defendant. (See chapter 2, "Frames and Framing.")

To emphasize choice, one relegates all the matters that might influence or shape the defendant's action to the background. At the same time, agency and power are accorded to the defendant who ostensibly exercised the choice. That party is described as engaged in action. The action/omission distinction here could play a key role. Choice, free will, and intent are presented in the foreground as active.

If, by contrast, the objective is to emphasize coercion, one does the reverse: the circumstances, context, and actions of other parties are accorded agency and power. Choice, free will, and intent are presented as simply predictable or derivative effects of these antecedent causes and forces. The individual party is described as a passive conduit for actions originating elsewhere.

In making these kinds of descriptive claims ("This is an instance of *free will* because . . ." or "The party was *coerced* insofar as . . .") it's important to understand that in any human transaction there will be elements of both choice and coercion. Consider that even a person with a gun to his head has choices to make, and that even the billionaire choosing which car to buy is subject to social and psychological manipulation.

> *Example: In determining whether a defendant voluntarily confessed or voluntarily consented to a search, courts often have to grapple with the tension between coercion and consent. "Display of a weapon, shouting, and forcibly subduing or handcuffing a suspect does not per se vitiate a subsequent consent to search that the record otherwise shows to be un-coerced and freely given,"[10] reasoned one court. This is no doubt true, as far as it goes, though one could easily reverse the argument: "Even evidence that consent to search was un-coerced and freely given cannot per se vitiate the coercive effect that a prior display of a weapon, shouting, and forcibly subduing or handcuffing a suspect might have had." What about "threats to the defendant's ability to maintain contact with his infant daughter"? Are these sufficiently "psychologically coercive" to render a confession involuntary?[11]*

If all human transactions can be seen at the analytical level as a combination of both coercion and choice, then there are options in how to describe a given transaction. In other words, if all human transactions are both chosen and coerced, then the conclusion that a transaction is chosen as opposed to coerced is accomplished by highlighting the aspects of choice and backgrounding the aspects of coercion.

Already above we have seen that a number of frames or distinctions have been brought into play to effectuate both of these objectives. These frames include the following:

The Theatrical Metaphor (the Action/Scene Ratio)
The Action/Omission Frame

Given that human transactions are often recognized as composed of choice aspects as well as coercion aspects, advocates will very likely want to bring into play other clusters. In particular, they are likely to invoke the following to tip the characterization toward choice or instead toward coercion:

The Reality/Appearance Cluster
The Essential/Contingent Cluster
The Quantitative Cluster
The Figure/Ground Cluster

In other words, one side will want to make an argument whose tagline might be "The choice aspects here are *essential* to the transaction. The choice aspects are so *substantial* that they *predominate*." The other side can be counted upon to make an argument whose tagline might be "The *essential* cause that precipitated this action is external to any choice by the party. The conditions and context here made this action *necessary* and, in the *normal course* of events, it was simply unavoidable."

B. THE THEATRICAL METAPHOR

As previously discussed, Kenneth Burke's theater metaphor is composed of these key theatrical elements: action, scene, agent, agency, and purpose. In many of the clusters, many of the main terms are readily translatable into each of the five Burkean elements. To take the public/private cluster, for example, consider the ways in which public and private can be translated into these theatrical terms, as shown in table 8.5.

TABLE 8.5. Public/Private in Burke's Theatrical Terms

Theatrical Term	Public	Private
Act	other-regarding	self-regarding
	externalities	market exchange
Agent	state	person
	government	individual
	courts	parties
Agency	public goods	private goods
	coercion	choice
Scene	public sector	private sector
	public realm	private realm
	law	the market
Purpose	public interest	private interest
	policy	preference
	the public good	rent-seeking

The important practical point to be gleaned from table 8.5 is that when one wants to characterize an issue as public or private, one can look to each of the terms to see which ones tend to make the issue seem public or private in character. Depending upon one's aims, then one focuses on those terms (probably by using the essential/contingent cluster or the quantitative cluster).

> *Example: Consider the question of whether speech is of a "public or private concern" in the First Amendment context—public speech is entitled to special protection that private speech is not. The father of a soldier killed in the line of duty in Iraq filed suit against a fundamentalist church for picketing at his son's funeral.[12] The church members held signs that read "Thank God for Dead Soldiers," "You're Going to Hell," and "Fags Doom Nations," among others. The Supreme Court examined the "content, form, and context of the speech" to de-*

termine whether the speech was of a public nature. In concluding that the speech was public, the Court emphasized its "plainly" public content as highlighting important public issues ("the political and moral conduct of the United States and its citizens, the fate of the Nation, homosexuality in the military," and more) and downplayed the arguably private nature of a funeral. One can easily imagine alternate descriptions of the scene, the agents, the purpose, and so on.

V. The Logic of Dissociation

Almost entirely, up until this point, we have used the distinction as a *complete break* to separate incompatibilities. Presented with a conflict between X and Y, we have suggested that when the law deploys a distinction, it does so by making a clean break separating X and Y. (See chapter 4, "The Legal Distinction.") This technique is very simple and it works: X and Y conflict, but not if each is relegated to a different domain. Now, we need to qualify our answer to show that there is another dominant technique of the legal distinction that can be used to address incompatibilities and contradictions. This technique is brought to us by Chaim Perelman and Lucie Olbrechts-Tyteca in their pathbreaking work, *The New Rhetoric—A Treatise on Argumentation.*[13] There, they introduce dissociation as a different technique for dealing with incompatibilities and contradictions.

It is an extremely important technique. It will take a bit of time to lay out. It can easily be confused with the much more familiar application of the distinction as a complete break (described above). But that is to be resisted.

Perelman and Olbrechts-Tyteca introduce the idea of dissociation through the exposition of its use with the reality/appearance pair. In Western philosophy, this pair (as old as the ancient Greeks) is frequently used to reorient thought. Thus philosophers (of both the elite or garden variety) are prone to making statements such as "Yes, that's the appearance of the thing, but the reality is . . ." Or again: "Let us not be deceived by mere appearances; the reality is . . ." Or in a court of law: "Counsel urges that the issue before us is plain to see, but the reality is . . ." In these kinds of statements (and they are everywhere), there is sometimes something different from a mere effort to separate appearance and reality (the distinction as complete break). Sometimes, as Perelman and Olbrechts-Tyteca point out, *reality* is made to serve as the criterion and grounding for those aspects of *appearance* that are to be valued, credited, believed, and distinguished from those that are not. This is dissociation. As Chaim Perelman illustrates the idea,

> At first sight, appearance is nothing but a manifestation of reality: it is reality as it appears, as it presents itself to immediate experience. But when appear-

ances are incompatible—when, for example, the oar is plunged into the water and appears broken to our sight and straight when we touch it—they cannot represent reality as it is, since reality is governed by the principle of noncontradiction and cannot simultaneously, and in the same relationship, have and not have a given property. It is therefore essential to distinguish between appearances which correspond to reality and those which do not and are deceptive.[14]

The idea quite simply is that an appearance/reality relation is offered up that allows the reality term (it's called "Term II") to delineate and adjudicate the valued, credible, believable aspects of the appearance term (it's called "Term I") as opposed to those that are not valued, credible, or believable.

Now, of course, this is a conventional use of the appearance/reality relation. Note here that Perelman and Olbrechts-Tyteca are not trying to endorse this view (or its truth)—they are being descriptive. Instead, they are saying that this use of the appearance/reality pair is ubiquitous and that it does a lot of rhetorical work. It does this work by enabling Term II to *explain and justify* what is to be valued and not in Term I. It is important to note that in their view, nothing prevents a philosopher, an orator, a politician from working against the grain and inverting the relation (e.g., switching Term I and Term II). Perelman seems to treat Sartre in this way—as one who rejects the idea of a reality of "being" behind the concatenation or series of appearances of "existence."[15]

Perelman and Olbrechts-Tyteca's insight is by no means limited to the appearance/reality pairing. To the contrary, their point is a general one. They are merely using the appearance/reality pair as a helpful instance of the Term I/Term II relation applicable to all sorts of pairings common to Western thought (e.g., substance/form, practice/theory, outcome/process, etc.).

They suggest and we agree that many of the other pairings encountered in philosophy, politics, or law (think of table 8.2) also do work as dissociative pairs. That is to say that while the pairings are sometimes introduced onto the rhetorical scene as oppositional or antithetical pairs, they also often arrive to do work as dissociative pairs. As perhaps the most obvious example note how the *contingent/essential cluster*, the *quantitative cluster*, and the *figure/ground cluster* are ready-made substitutes for the dissociative work performed by the *reality/appearance* pair.

But Perelman and Olbrechts-Tyteca's point goes much further, however: they suggest that other pairs arguably deemed substantive (e.g., choice/coercion, private/public) are also often deployed on the rhetorical scene as dissociative pairs. That is, they arrive on the rhetorical scene with one side of the pairing (Term II) privileged vis-à-vis the other (Term I) (depending upon philosophy, discourse, context, or speaker).

For Perelman and Olbrechts-Tyteca this sort of conventionalized hierarchy between Term I and Term II is ubiquitous. Term I is the immediate, the apparent term—host to incompatibilities and contradictions. Term II is brought on the scene to explain and sort out what is and is not true, good, or otherwise valued by Term II. Relative to Term I, Term II is normative and explanatory. Philosophies, political tendencies, and legal theories distinguish themselves by how they arrange their various Term I / Term II pairings—*which terms* and *which pairings* they privilege and which ones they subordinate. Notice here that, in an appealing contrast to Jacques Derrida's oddly universalist hierarchization of pairs (e.g., speech / writing), Perelman and Olbrechts-Tyteca insist that Term I and Term II are sometimes reversed depending upon the philosophy, discourse, context, or speaker.

Recognizing their profound influence on our thinking, we now wish to elaborate on Perelman and Olbrechts-Tyteca to suggest how reading the clusters as dissociative pairs allows a particularly deep understanding of the ways in which jurists and scholars present and do law. Perelman and Olbrechts-Tyteca left no doubts about the relevance of their work for law:

> The effort to resolve incompatibilities is carried on at every level of legal activity. It is pursued by the legislator, the legal theorist, and the judge. When a judge encounters a juridical antinomy in a case he is hearing, he cannot entirely neglect one of the two rules at the expense of the other. He must justify his course of action by delimiting the sphere of application of each rule through interpretations that restore coherence to the juridical system. He will introduce distinctions for the purpose of reconciling what, without them, would be irreconcilable.[16]

A. CHAINING: RUNNING AN ARGUMENT THROUGH SUCCESSIVE CLUSTERS

In one sense, we have already seen a very simple example of *chaining* in the discussion of *combining clusters* above. There we showed how the reality / appearance, the essential / contingent, the quantitative, and the figure / ground cluster could be used to emphasize the coercive or choice aspects of a transaction. That sort of use of dissociative pairs is pretty simple in structure: it's basically a two-step argument.

A lot of doctrinal argument is more complex and involves a more protracted chaining, involving multiple succession of clusters—three, four, and so on. Thus to look at choice and coercion again, little is more common in the common law to decide whether choice or coercion is present than to frame the issue as one of form or substance. An advocate can concede that a transaction at the formal level is one of choice, but that its substance is coercion. The advocate can then use the essential/contingent cluster or the reality/appearance cluster to argue that it is form that matters or instead substance. The point is that the clusters delineate the structure of the argument.

In terms of the clusters, the law itself and the jurists and scholars are often in disagreement as to which is Term I and which is Term II. Does form, as they say, anticipate substance? If so, form would be Term II. Or, as they also say, does form simply follow function? If so, then form would be Term I. Is process to be designed to reach the right outcome? If so, process as a mere means is Term I. Or is sound process an end in itself, regardless of outcome? If so, process is Term II.

In a given philosophy, the author is likely to remain consistent throughout concerning the identities of Term I and Term II. Law, however, is a manifold developed by multitudes of authors, and thus consistency and coherence are only a sometime thing. What this disorder means practically speaking is that law provides much in the way of ample resources for argument.

B. CLUSTER ALLIANCES

Law may be attended by some disorder, as just mentioned, but it is, as we have been at pains to insist, nonetheless characterized by recursive patterns. One of these is what we call cluster alliances. That is to say, certain types of association among the pairings seem to recur throughout law (almost automatically, as it were). Thus, if something is said to be objective, it is almost always taken to be neutral. If something is taken to be formal, it is generally taken to be absolute and objective. If something is viewed as political, it is viewed as value laden, an ought, and subjective. These are loose associations, even as they are sometimes denied, dishonored, or rejected.

Notice that in speaking of cluster alliances one could also speak of cluster enmities. If something is political it is generally viewed as not neutral. As another example, while the "is" is generally viewed as "real," the "ought" is subject to attack as merely appearance.

It is important not to make too much of any of these alliances or enmities. What is interesting and renders them worthy of note is that they sometimes seem to do actual work.

VI. Cluster Logic

One interesting issue (and one crucial to the articulation of law) has to do with the ways in which the various structural distinctions themselves relate to each other. They are all frequently foundational in various doctrinal areas. But which are more foundational? Which are more basic? These are important questions.

One will find that in different subject matters of law (e.g., contracts) different clusters are accorded the privileged or fundamental roles. Thus in constitutional law, for instance, the public/private cluster plays a huge role (state action doctrine), whereas in antitrust law, the public/private cluster (a different state action doctrine) plays a role, but a less important one. In tort law, the action/omission cluster is huge—but in property law less so. One finds that while all the clusters seem to cut across the corpus of the law (they seem to be almost everywhere), nonetheless the clusters are accorded different degrees of importance in the various recognized doctrinal fields.

The same pattern is found at the theoretical level. Consider that different jurisprudential approaches will *privilege* (i.e., accord some sort of preferential hierarchical status to) a particular cluster or a small set of clusters. At the risk of oversimplification, various theories of law can be described in terms of their focus/fixation on one or some such privileged clusters. Thus, different theories of law give hierarchical preference to different pairings while subordinating the others or rendering them derivative, as follows:

> *Natural law* is acutely focused on the is/ought structural distinction. And, indeed, it strives mightily to *identify* and articulate the "oughts" of law so that these might effectively regulate the "is's" of law. Similarly, natural law struggles ardently to try to figure out how oughtness of law ought to be reconciled with what is. The focus of natural law on the is/ought distinction means that it is preeminently focused on the activity of justification.
>
> *Law & economics* is acutely focused on the government/free market distinction. And, indeed, many of its concepts, such as "externalities," "transaction costs," "public goods," "information costs," and so on serve as the *pivots* on which the government/free market distinction turns.
>
> *Critical legal studies* is acutely focused on the law/politics distinction. Indeed, many of its better-known critical efforts, such as critiques of objectivity, neutrality, and coherence, are aimed at *collapsing* the law/politics distinction.
>
> *Legal pragmatism* is acutely focused on the formalism/realism distinction— the ways and the degrees to which context shapes (and must shape) the articulation and application of law.

None of this should be taken to mean that individual work within any one of these schools will necessarily give pride of place to these particular pairings. But on the whole, the pattern is striking. And one could see the clash among these various jurisprudential approaches as traceable to differences as to which cluster or clusters they wish to privilege or subordinate.

One last, almost speculative, point merits mention. When they are viewed as dissociative pairs, one imagines that most theories or philosophies of law privilege only a few of the clusters. These are then used over and over again (both consciously and not) throughout the theories and philosophies in question to give shape to the other derivative or subordinate clusters deployed. In this way, a certain aura of coherence and consonance is achieved. Of course, a certain partiality as well.

Coda:
The Topics of Doctrine

Sharing this work with our students and colleagues has honed an insight into the character of doctrine. Toward the end of a seminar on this work, a law student burst out, "But . . . but . . . it's all the same!" This was a bit of an overstatement, and yet it displayed a profound insight. A couple years later, in presenting the work to our colleagues, one of them exclaimed, "Well, but now you're no longer talking about *baselines*—you're really talking about *interpretation!*"

Here, in this concluding section, we take these exclamations seriously to more fully articulate their insights, their truths. One of them is that our various chapter titles—from "The Legal Distinction" to "Interpretation" (and so on)—can be seen as "doctrinal topics" in the sense of the topoi as developed by Greek rhetoricians.

In Greek rhetoric, the topics divide into the common topics and the specific topics. It is the latter that are most comparable to the doctrinal topics we have elaborated (the legal distinction, rules vs. standards, decision regimes, etc.) What we have in mind is that our headings (and their elaboration) can serve as what E. P. I. Corbett described as "suggesters" or "prompters" that might help activate the argumentative spirit.[1]

In saying that our headings are *topics of doctrine*, we do not mean that they are germane *only* to legal doctrine. We do mean, however, to say that they are key to the practice of doctrinal argument—that they are the crucial levers and pivots used over and over again in the articulation, elaboration, and application of legal doctrine.

More strongly, in relation to a question we asked in chapter 1, "What is doctrine?," these doctrinal topics form part of the answer. Doctrine is, in important part, the legal regimes created *in the activation and as a result of* the deployment of these various doctrinal topics. To do doctrine is to engage with these doctrinal topics—to question distinctions, to form new ones, to look for missing baselines, to think about baseline options, to run arguments through cluster logic (and more). Excellent lawyers in past ages have developed this sort of know-how intuitively. Through experience, it has become second nature to them. Here we have tried to lay it all out in a systematic way so that it can be taught and learned. We have no wish (or capacity) to displace the school of experience, but we are trying to make it all a bit easier (and a bit more reflective). We feel confident that if the power of our doctrinal topics is not fully apparent during law school, it will become so through the ensuing years of practice.

Back now to what our student and our colleague said. The student said it was all the same. The colleague suggested that each topic melds into the others. Start with the latter—a move we want to develop here—call it "the blend."

This is not so much the idea that the doctrinal topics blend into some homogeneous mud (though, of course, they can and they sometimes do). Rather, it is blending in the sense that the one topic (e.g., baselines) flows and gives way to another topic (e.g., interpretation) and another topic (e.g., the legal distinction) . . . and another topic, and on and on. But this "giving way" is specific and relational. It is not some sort of catastrophic conceptual dam bursting (and laying total waste to the adjoining conceptual ecology). Rather, it is a partial melding discernible as limited in context.

We will give some examples of these relations between our doctrinal topics, though if we were to try to specify all of them (perish the thought!) this book would never end. So instead, here are a few spare examples to convey the general idea.

To start with an easy one—baselines and interpretation—consider that baseline problems can sometimes be avoided through efforts at interpretation. Indeed, if interpretive effort can transform some otherwise vague, ambiguous, or ambivalent bit of text into a law with determinate meaning, some baseline problems might well be made to disappear.

> *Example: In the baseline chapter, we discussed the example of "property" in the takings clause of the Fifth Amendment to the US Constitution. If it could be convincingly demonstrated that in the Fifth Amendment "property" means only property that was considered as such under the positive law of the state at the time of founding, then some baseline problems could be made to go away. (That is quite a supposition, of course, but the general idea at least is clear.)*

The converse might be true as well. A naive, overly confident interpretation of a legal text might well prompt the emergence of baseline problems.

Example: Famously, Justice Owen Roberts said, "When an act of Congress is appropriately challenged in the courts as not conforming to the constitutional mandate, the judicial branch of the government has only one duty; to lay the article of the Constitution which is invoked beside the statute which is challenged and to decide whether the latter squares with the former."[2] The metaphors for the judicial function of interpretation here invoke geometry—or more specifically, carpentry. That in turn makes one wonder, Just what is the appropriate baseline for the interpretation of legal meaning? Or more broadly, what is the appropriate frame? And thus it is that the very simplicity of Justice Owen Roberts's metaphor (the carpenter's square) can send the search for legal meaning spinning.

These are specific examples—and what matters is the general point: a legal doctrine can be approached by looking for baselines (which ones have been presumed?/which ones seem appropriate?) or deploying interpretation (what does this bit of legal doctrine mean or require?). Interpretation can be used to flush out hidden baselines, just as switching baselines can yield proliferating interpretations. The relations between baselines and interpretation are thus several and complex. Where one starts (and where one is willing to go) matters. Recall entry-framing and abandonment!

But the relations between baselines and interpretation are not unique to either.

Accordingly, baselines can be linked to the other topics. Thus, for instance, in thinking about the legal distinction trade-offs between *practicality* and *normative appeal,* one can try to identify a legal professional's baseline assumptions: what matters most to him or her—a hard and fast easy way to apply distinction (practicality) or one that seems closely linked to the values at stake (normative appeal)? From there, of course, it is but a small step to engage with the rules vs. standards dialectic to initiate the classic pro and con arguments that comprise the dispute.

Note, again, there is nothing special about these connections. We could make different connections. Baselines, for instance, could be viewed as an instance of framing. And the reverse is true as well: just as baselines are a kind of frame, so too can frames function as baselines. Deciding whether a legal distinction includes a particular fact or scenario can be seen as an act of interpretation; framing is a technique to avoid regime conflict; regime conflicts can be avoided by interpretation. And so on.

This may seem disappointing to the reader. At some point the reader may well think as our student did, "But . . . but, it's all the same!" Well, yes, it can sometimes seem that way—that these topics all have a striking, perhaps even disturbing, commonality, as if they had sprung from the same generative conceptual source (and achieved only a limited degree of differentiation).

TABLE C.1. Basic Roles/Functions of Topics of This Book

Topic	Basic Role or Function
The Legal Distinction	Separating things out from each other/Breaking wholes down into smaller parts
Rules vs. Standards	Attuning norms to the worlds of facts or the worlds of value
Decision Regimes	Formulating the ruling norms under which to calibrate, accommodate, and sacrifice conflicting values, legal considerations, etc.
Framing	Identifying, isolating, and locating the factual transaction or the law to be analyzed
Baselines	Selecting a supplementary norm to cure a given norm suffering from ambiguity, vagueness, incompleteness, incoherence, or other such infelicities
Interpretation	Discerning the meaning of a given bit of law
Cluster Logic	Laying out the relations among the fundamental binaries through which law is organized

But for all their similarities they are not all the same. What is true is that they are all crucial and that they all perform very basic (legal) roles or functions, shown in table C.1.

These are clearly not the only roles or functions that each of our doctrinal topics play. But one can see that, in law, these roles or functions seem basic to the doctrinal topics. Indeed, the doctrinal topics are so transparently basic, that one could easily say (of course, only to be contradicted almost immediately) that any of these topics is *first among equals.*

Consider the almost irresistible logic of the retort. Someone says that interpretation is the primary fundamental—the one that really rules. Almost right away someone retorts that before one can do legal *interpretation, framing* the issue is required (so as to know the point of the interpretation). Yet another then says that before one can *frame* the issue, it is necessary to offer relevant *legal distinctions* between the real issue at hand and those that are illusory or peripheral (lest one pursue useless paths of inquiry). Someone else intones that before one can offer relevant *legal distinctions,* one needs to know what the applicable *decision regime* is going to be (for otherwise there is nothing to guide the creation of appropriate legal distinctions).

All of these protagonists have a point. None is decisively wrong. The doctrinal topics are interdependent in this way—not quite *VISH* (but close). And depending upon where one starts (*entry-framing*), the various doctrinal topics bleed like colors into each other (or not). For the most part, none of this is a surprise[3]—these are all fundamental operations: each doctrinal topic in some sense merits being treated as first among equals. And in virtue of precisely that, the claims of each to superior status are inherently contestable.

Each can prevail in this context, in this moment, but never in any definitive way. Each lives in law's repertoire of plausible moves to be invoked (and *possibly* prevail) another day.

Notice that here we are encountering once again one of the general points of *cluster logic*—to wit, that when we get down to a contest of fundamentals, there is always very good reason to place any one of the fundamentals ahead of the others, and there is also very good reason to dethrone that fundamental in favor of any of the others.[4]

Is any doctrinal topic paramount? So no—not for the purposes of understanding legal doctrine as we see it. They are all interdependent—each calling upon the others to do work. One can try to subsume all the topics under a favored topic, but we suspect that artifice or bluster would have to attend the effort and that the resulting vision would be unconvincing—something like Hegel's "night in which all cows are black."

For purposes of *understanding* legal doctrine and law generally, it is probably best to resist the classic (theoretical) inclination to champion one doctrinal topic as chief among all the others. In other areas, this theoretical move has not fared well. For instance, in constitutional law, the effort of legal theorists to advance their favorite fundamental ahead of all the others has led to assertions of faith clothed somewhat uncomfortably in the trappings of reason. Once these theoretical efforts are brought together in terms of their predicate assumptions, they are less than persuasive. As stated elsewhere,[5]

> [I]t is staggering how many different credible endings can be attached to the phrase, "The first and paramount question for normative constitutional theory is . . ."
>
> 1. What is the appropriate role of the Supreme Court among the political branches? (a theory of judicial review)[6] or
> 2. What is the function of the Constitution or any of its parts? (a political theory)[7] or
> 3. What type of reasoning should the Court use in its decisions? (a theory of legal reasoning)[8] or
> 4. What types of questions are best suited to decisionmaking by adjudication rather than by legislation or management? (a theory of institutional competence)[9] or
> 5. What minimal entitlements must a just and legitimate state guarantee? (a political philosophy)[10] or
> 6. What does the Constitution mean? (a theory of interpretation).[11]

That was in the late 1980s. In this specific regard, at least, things apparently have not changed all that much in the intervening decades. Other examples of failed attempts to champion one fundamental over all others (the classic monotheistic strategy) would be easy to come by.[12]

Instead of asserting the primacy of one fundamental over all others, it is perhaps more useful for the student of law to take a cue from *cluster logic* and appreciate that while each doctrinal topic can be deployed as an organizing principle to subsume all the others, *this itself is a move.* And as no such move has yet produced any settlement, it can be made as well as unmade. As moves go, this one happens to be vulnerable precisely because it can also be made just as convincingly on behalf of all the other fundamental doctrinal topics. Indeed, the arguments against the primacy of each fundamental doctrinal topic are all so good that they become the philosophical equivalent of a circular firing squad.

So, to return to an earlier and somewhat vexing question: Are all the doctrinal topics the same? Well, no. But they are interdependent, and they are intermeshed: one no sooner invokes one doctrinal topic than another is called into play (and so on and so forth).

Why then are these doctrinal topics so ubiquitous? In part, as we have said, it is because they are fundamental. But there is more to it than that. Our view is that none of our topics (e.g., the legal distinction, baselines, etc.) has an a priori delimited domain—*a predetermined specific sphere of application.* On the contrary, as with the special topics of classical rhetoric, these doctrinal topics can be blended with specific legal issues and problems and thus made to yield insights, arguments, processes, and outcomes. The doctrinal topics are the ways we have, as legal professionals, of apprehending and creating legal doctrine as this or that. Sometimes (perhaps often) we do not recognize the choices available to us in our apprehension and creation of doctrine. But that is very likely because we have not become cognizant of our own entry-framing.

Acknowledgments

We are extremely grateful to the many people who have contributed to our work here, including University of Colorado Law School students in three seminars on legal reasoning, as well as many of our friends and colleagues. For their sustained comments, we wish to thank in particular Fred Bloom, David Eason, Sharon Jacobs, Chris Mueller, and Scott Skinner-Thompson. We are also grateful to Kelly Ilseng, our indefatigable faculty assistant, who worked hard editing and proofing the manuscript and getting it into shape for submission. We also wish to thank our colleagues who participated in a discussion of part of the work at the Colorado Law School Scholarship Retreat at the Stanley Hotel in Estes Park, Colorado, May 24, 2019. Thanks as well to Hugh Gottschalk and the Colorado Law School for graciously underwriting the faculty stay at this extraordinary venue.

Chapters 5 and 7 in this work, "Rules and Standards" and "Interpretation," have been published previously in substantially similar form. We thank the publishers for permission to republish here. The original articles are Pierre Schlag, *Rules and Standards*, 33 UCLA L. REV. 379 (1985), and Pierre Schlag, *On Textualist and Purposivist Interpretation (Challenges and Problems)*, in THE TRANSFORMATION OR RECONSTITUTION OF EUROPE: THE CRITICAL LEGAL STUDIES PERSPECTIVE ON THE ROLE OF THE COURTS IN THE EUROPEAN UNION (Tamara Persin & Sinisa Rodin, eds., 2018).

Small snippets, ranging from several paragraphs to a few pages each, have been taken by permission from Pierre Schlag, *Formalism and Realism in Ruins (Mapping the Logics of Collapse)*, 95 IOWA L. REV. 195 (2010); Pierre Schlag, *Hiding the Ball*, 71 N.Y.U. L. REV. 1681 (1996); and Pierre Schlag, *The Law Review Article*, 88 U. COLO. L. REV. 1043 (2018). We thank the publishers for permission.

Notes

Introduction

1. Alfred North Whitehead, Science and the Modern World 48 (1925).

2. Emerson H. Tiller & Frank B. Cross, *What Is Legal Doctrine?* 100 Nw. U. L. Rev. 517, 517 (2006) (emphasis added).

3. And as some of the champions of the "New Doctrinalism" point out, doctrine remains the key jural currency in the courts. Shyamkrishan Balganesh, *The Constraint of Legal Doctrine*, 163 U. Pa. L. Rev. 1843, 1845 (2015).

4. Here, by way of example, is one sophisticated account of the "New Doctrinalist" take on doctrine:

> Granular doctrinal analysis may provide the theoretical clarity that instrumental analysis has failed to produce. In recent years, there has been a renewed interest in the meaning and role of legal doctrine in the work of courts—a scholarly trend dubbed by some "the New Doctrinalism." This movement rejects the realists' depiction of doctrine as a set of mechanistic, self-referential rules that require specific outcomes, describing it instead as an analytical flowchart whose decision boxes are designed to carry normative considerations. The result is that "[d]octrine is . . . seen as important, not for its own sake, but because of its connection to normative criteria." Consequently, doctrinal "constraints"—far from limiting decision makers to a predetermined outcome—actually liberate them to draw from external bodies of information as they analyze particular elements of a cause of action. So instead of foreclosing external considerations, a New Doctrinal account of tort law may actually open windows through which instrumental concerns enter as analytical aids. In other words, the New Doctrinalism is not the antithesis of Legal Realism so much as it is the tool for "translation between social science and law" necessary to fulfill Legal Realism's early progressive promise.

Cristina Carmody Tilley, *Tort Law Inside Out*, 126 Yale L. J. 1320, 1336–37 (2017).

5. In the modern period, no article in the US has been more important in reviving this branch of jurisprudential study than Duncan Kennedy, *Form and Substance in Private Law Adjudication*, 85 Harv. L. Rev. 1685 (1976).

6. Typically, those who are not fond of doctrine do not so much examine or criticize its

identity, character, workings, and foibles as leave it behind for alternative forms—such as high theory, economic analysis, and the like.

Chapter One

1. BLACK'S LAW DICTIONARY 481 (6th ed. 1990). And in their article titled *What Is Legal Doctrine?*, the authors define doctrine as "the content of judicial opinions." Tiller & Cross, *What Is Legal Doctrine?*, at 525.

2. If we were concerned with analogical reasoning as the structure of law (also an important topic), we would, of course, delve into an exploration of the various aspects of the judicial opinion (e.g., holding, dicta, rationale).

3. We have no wish to slight legal pluralism (indeed in various places we have affirmed its import), but we are not concerned with legal pluralism in this work.

4. DUNCAN KENNEDY, THE RISE & FALL OF CLASSICAL LEGAL THOUGHT 256–61 (2006).

5. If any of these functions are not fulfilled, it would seem difficult for us to believe we are dealing with a modern legal system. Either it's not very modern or not very legal. And perhaps not much of a system.

6. In his famous account of the rule of law, Lon Fuller lists eight ways in which an effort to maintain a system of legal rules may go wrong:

> The first and most obvious lies in a failure to achieve rules at all, so that every issue must be decided on an ad hoc basis. The other routes are: (2) a failure to publicize, or at least to make available to the affected party, the rules he is expected to observe; (3) the abuse of retroactive legislation, which not only cannot itself guide action, but undercuts the integrity of rules prospective in effect, since it puts them under the threat of retrospective change; (4) a failure to make rules understandable; (5) the enactment of contradictory rules or (6) rules that require conduct beyond the powers of the affected party; (7) introducing such frequent changes in the rules that the subject cannot orient his action by them; and, finally, (8) a failure of congruence between the rules as announced and their actual administration.

LON L. FULLER, THE MORALITY OF LAW 39 (2d ed. 1969).

7. Ronald Dworkin's conception of "law as integrity" and the early Judge Posner's conception of law as a "wealth maximization" mechanism are also examples.

8. This helps us understand why so many judges and legal academics often place such a premium (wisely or not) on avoiding emotions and emotionalism in law and on juridical values such as "neutrality" and "objectivity."

9. Formal rationality might be likened to technocratic thought—it is instrumentalist, calculative, and pertains to the evaluation of means to the achievement of pre-given ends. MAX WEBER, ECONOMY AND SOCIETY 85–86 (1978).

10. In terms of historical evolution, the rise of law is more likely the reverse: from social norm to formal codification.

11. WILLIAM TWINING & DAVID MIERS, HOW TO DO THINGS WITH RULES 80 (Kindle ed. 2010) (Law in Context). H. L. A. Hart called this reflexivity "rules of recognition"—that is, rules addressed to and observed by legal officials. These rules specify "the criteria of validity" and "the rules of change and adjudication." H.L.A. HART, THE CONCEPT OF LAW 113 (1961). Accordingly, they enable legal officials to know when particular laws are indeed valid in the legal system and the ways in which, in compliance with the legal system, they can be changed.

The nomenclature "rules of recognition" is unfortunate because it's to be seriously doubted that such recognition generally takes the rule form. But the general idea (the law's reflexivity) is both sound and helpful.

12. This corresponds roughly to what H. L. A. Hart called somewhat infelicitously "secondary rules." HART, *supra* note 11, at 78–79.

13. Duncan Kennedy, *A Semiotics of Legal Argument*, 42 SYRACUSE L. REV. 75, 97–103 (1991).

14. Dred Scott v. Sanford, 60 U.S. (How. 19) 393 (1856).

15. Wesley Newcomb Hohfeld, *Some Fundamental Legal Conceptions as Applied in Judicial Reasoning*, 23 YALE L.J. 16 (1913). For a description of the Hohfeldian frameworks and its implications for contemporary legal thought, *see* Pierre Schlag, *How to Do Things with Hohfeld*, 78 LAW & CONTEMP. PROBS. 185 (2015).

16. 199 P.2d 1 (Cal. 1948).

17. TWINING & MIERS, *supra* note 11, at 80–92.

18. United States v. Calandara, 414 U.S. 338 (1974).

19. *See, e.g.*, Cox v. Evansville Police Dept, 107 N.E.3d 453 (Ind. 2018).

20. Thurman W. Arnold, *Criminal Attempts: The Rise and Fall of an Abstraction*, 40 YALE L.J. 53, 58 (1930) (quoting Thomas Reed Powell).

21. Black letter, n., OED online (December 2019).

22. Anne Fleming, *The Long Shadow of Doctrine*, 163 U. PA. L. REV. 337 (2014–15).

23. For an introduction to the conceptual character of metaphor, *see* Christopher Rideout, *Penumbral Thinking Revisited: Metaphor in Legal Argumentation*, 7 JOURNAL OF THE ASSOCIATION OF LEGAL WRITING DIRECTORS 155 (2010).

24. For an effort to develop an aesthetics of law—that is to say, the aesthetics expressed in law itself—*see* Pierre Schlag, *The Aesthetics of American Law*, 115 HARV. L. REV. 1047 (2002). For a thought-provoking discussion in the global context, see Mikhail Xifaras, *The Global Turn in Legal Theory*, 29 CAN. J. L & JUR. 215 (2016).

Chapter Two

1. These are all described in a pathbreaking article by Mark Kelman on which we rely extensively here. Mark Kelman, *Interpretive Construction in the Substantive Criminal Law*, 33 STAN. L. REV. 591, 593–94 (1981).

2. Much of this and the next paragraph is adapted from Pierre Schlag, *The Law Review Article*, 88 U. COLO. L. REV. 1043 (2018).

3. Louis Althusser, *Ideology and Ideological State Apparatuses*, *in* LENIN AND PHILOSOPHY AND OTHER ESSAYS (Ben Brewster trans., 1971).

4. For a brief discussion, *see* Pierre Schlag, *Pre-figuration and Evaluation*, 80 CALIF. L. REV. 965 (1992).

5. Kelman, *supra* note 1.

6. Michael McCann et al., *Java Jive: Genealogy of a Juridical Icon*, 56 U. MIAMI L. REV. 113, 119–20 (2001) (account of the facts).

7. 162 N.E. 99 (N.Y. 1928).

8. The arguments are from Kelman, *supra* note 1, at 594–95.

9. Joseph Singer, *The Reliance Interest in Property*, 40 STAN. L. REV. 611 (1988).

10. Richard A. Epstein, *A Theory of Strict Liability*, 2 J. LEGAL STUD. 151 (1973) (supporting the common law position that there is no duty to rescue).

11. 247 N.Y. 160 (1928).

12. 247 N.Y. 167.

13. 247 N.Y. 168 (emphasis added).

14. Hermann Oliphant, *A Return to Stare Decisis*, 6 AMERICAN LAW SCHOOL REVIEW 215, 217–18 (1928).

15. 347 U.S. 483 (1954).

16. 347 U.S. 495.

17. 381 U.S. 479 (1965)

18. U.S. v. Salgado, 250 F.3d 438 (6th Cir. 2000).

19. There are some helpful discussions, but (*and this is not meant as a criticism*) there is not a great deal to be said about the issue. Julius Stone, *The Ratio of the Ratio Decidendi*, 22 MOD. L. REV. 597 (1959); Laurence H. Tribe & Michael C. Dorf, *Levels of Generality in the Definition of Rights*, 57 U. CHI. L. REV. 1057 (1990); Gerard Conway, *Levels of Generality in the Legal Reasoning of the European Court of Justice*, 14 EUR. L.J. 787 (2008); MICHAEL FISCHL & JEREMY PAUL, GETTING TO MAYBE—HOW TO EXCEL ON LAW SCHOOL EXAMS 60–63 (1999) (broad and narrow case holdings).

20. Michael H. v. Gerald, 491 U.S. 110 (1989).

21. Mullenix v. Luna, 136 S. Ct. 305, 308 (2015) (quoting Ashcroft v. al-Kidd, 563 U.S. 731, 742 (2011)).

22. 28 U.S.C. § 2254(d) (1996).

23. Ruiz v. Victory Properties, LLC., 43 A.3d 186 (2012).

24. Tribe & Dorf, *supra* note 19.

25. KENNETH BURKE, ON SYMBOLS AND SOCIETY 135–38 (1989).

26. THOMAS CARLYLE, ON HEROES, HERO-WORSHIP, AND THE HEROIC IN HISTORY 2 (1888).

27. 192 N.Y.S.2d 913 (N.Y App. Div. 1959), *rev'd*, 168 N.E.2d 838 (N.Y. 1960).

Chapter Three

1. Elaboration: Robert Hale, *Coercion and Distribution in a Supposedly Noncoercive State*, 38 POL. SCI. Q. 470 (1923) (baselines in choice and coercion); Duncan Kennedy, *Cost-Benefit Analysis of Entitlement Problems: A Critique*, 33 STAN. L. REV. 387 (1981) (baselines in law & economics); Jack Beerman & Joseph W. Singer, *Baseline Questions in Legal Reasoning: The Example of Property in Jobs*, 23 GA. L. REV. 911 (1989) (baselines in property); WARD FARNSWORTH, THE LEGAL ANALYST: A TOOLKIT FOR THINKING ABOUT THE LAW, 198–206 (2007) (general discussion of baselines).

2. McCulloch v. Maryland, 17 U.S. (4 Wheat.) 316, 407 (1819).

3. *See* U.S. CONST. amend. V ("[N]or shall private property be taken for public use, without just compensation."); U.S. CONST. amend. XIV, § 1 ("[N]or shall any State deprive any person of life, liberty, or property, without due process of law.").

4. People v. Maya, 33 Cal. App. 5th 266 (2019).

5. Llorca v. Sheriff, Collier County, Florida, 893 F.3d 1319, 1325 (11th Cir. 2018).

6. Garner v. People, 436 P.3d 1107, 1111 (Colo. 2019).

7. Weida v. State, 94 N.E.2d 682, 690 (Ind. 2018).

8. Capitol Square Review and Advisory Bd. v. Pinette, 515 U.S. 753, 780 (1995) (O'Connor, J., concurring in part).

9. Capitol Square Review and Advisory Bd. v. Pinette, 515 U.S. 753, 800 fn. 5 (1995) (Stevens, J., dissenting).

10. Harry Surden, *Technological Costs Law in Intellectual Property*, 27 HARV. J. L. & TECH. 135 (2013).

11. Kennedy, *supra* note 1, at 413–14; Gary Peller, *The Metaphysics of American Law*, 73 CALIF. L. REV. 1151 (1985).

12. The canonical work elaborating and defending neutrality in American law is Herbert Wechsler, *Toward Neutral Principles in Constitutional Law*, 73 HARV. L. REV. 1 (1959). Google citations counts (July 13, 2019) reveal that it has been cited more than 4,000 times. In that sense, the article has withstood the test of time. But if one examines Wechsler's arguments in the piece, his conception of neutrality is remarkably weak. In the end, it does and can do almost no real work beyond matters of juridical etiquette unless, of course, the conception is misinterpreted or misapplied to have more bite than it actually does.

13. Kennedy, *supra* note 1, at 413–14.

14. *See* Romer v. Evans, 517 U.S. 629 (1996) and associated briefs.

15. Parents Involved in Community Schools v. Seattle School Dist. No. 1, 551 U.S. 701, 748 (2007).

16. *Sic utera tuo ut alienam non laedas.*

17. What follows in the text here is a simplified version of Hohfeldian analysis. Mastering Hohfeldian analysis (whether or not one agrees with Hohfeld's views) is well worth the effort of any serious law student. Hohfeld, *Fundamental Legal Conceptions*, 23 YALE L.J. 16 (1913). The article, however, is witheringly dry and almost impenetrable without assistance. For a more readable account of Hohfeld's article and a quick summary of many of its implications for contemporary forms of legal thought, *see* Pierre Schlag, *How to Do Things with Hohfeld*, 78 LAW & CONTEMP. PROBS. 185 (2015).

18. Hale, *supra* note 1.

19. DUNCAN KENNEDY, A CRITIQUE OF ADJUDICATION: FIN DE SIÈCLE 191–94 (1997).

20. Hale, *supra* note 1, at 474–77.

21. Edmonson v. Leesville Concrete Co., Inc., 500 U.S. 614, 620 (1991).

22. Connick v. Myers, 461 U.S. 138, 147–48 (1983).

23. Lemon v. Kurtzman, 403 U.S. 602, 613 (1971).

24. Duncan Kennedy, *A Semiotics of Legal Argument*, 42 SYRACUSE L. REV. 75 (1991).

25. Pierre Schlag, *Coase Minus the Coase Theorem—Some Problems with Chicago Transaction Cost Analysis*, 99 IOWA L. REV. 175 (2013).

Chapter Four

1. The obvious alternative for pride of place is the idea of the *legal concept*. The legal concept "lumps," and the legal distinction "splits." Both are key intellectual moves in law. Bradley C. Karkkainen, *New Governance in Legal Thought and in the World: Some Splitting as Antidote to Overzealous Lumping*, 89 MINN. L. REV. 471, 479 (2004). We have no wish to adjudicate the relative importance of the two—the legal distinction and the legal concept. Particularly in law, each is very much a function of the other. And both are key: as Linda Berger and Kathy Stanchi put it, "[L]egal persuasion results from making and breaking mental connections." LINDA L. BERGER & KATHY STANCHI, LEGAL PERSUASION xi (Kindle ed. 2018) (Law, Language and Communication). We give pride of place to the distinction here mostly because of our sense that its role and import have been *relatively under-recognized* in law. *See infra* note 3 .

2. Elaboration: The other main artifacts through which law is expressed include the following:

concepts (e.g., "common carrier")
directives (e.g., "If this, then that")
principles (e.g., "no liability without fault")
policies (e.g., "Law should encourage productivity")
values (e.g., "fairness")
considerations (e.g., "administrative convenience")
interests (e.g., privacy interest")

3. Elaboration: The topic of the legal distinction can be associated with an extensive and by no means uncontroversial literature in philosophy, computational logic, linguistics, and cognitive science about the identity, formation, and character of concepts and categories. For a useful collection of introductions to the topic, *see* FORMAL APPROACHES IN CATEGORIZATION (Emmanuel M. Pothos & Andy J. Wills eds., 2011) (cognitive science and psychology); GEORGE SPENCER-BROWN, LAWS OF FORM 1 (1972) (spatial logic). For elaboration of Spencer-Brown's work, *see George Spencer Brown and His Laws of Form: An Observer Web Focus File*, ENOLA GAIA (July 19, 2019), http://www.enolagaia.com/GSB.html (mathematics and philosophy). *See also* STEVEN WINTER, A CLEARING IN THE FOREST: LAW, LIFE, AND MIND (2001) (cognitive science, rhetoric, and law); BERGER & STANCHI, *supra* note 1 (same).

4. Grande v. Jennings, 278 P.3d 1287 (Ariz. App. Div. 1 2012).

5. *In re* Seizure of $82,000 More or Less, 119 F. Supp. 2d 1013, 1019 (W.D. Missouri 2000).

6. 119 F. Supp. 2d 1021.

7. Glover v. State, 836 N.E.2d 414 (Ind. 2005).

8. *See* Duncan Kennedy, *The Stages of the Decline of the Public/Private Distinction*, 130 U. PA. L. REV. 1349 (1982).

9. International Union, United Mine Workers of America v. Bagwell, 512 U.S. 819, 845 (1994).

10. International Shoe Co. v .Washington, 326 U.S. 310 (1945).

11. 159 F.2d 169 (2d Cir. 1947). The Judge Learned Hand test compares the burden (B) of avoiding the harm to the probability of harm (P) multiplied by the gravity of the injury (L): if B < PL, and the defendant did not take the precaution (B), then his conduct is deemed negligent.

12. Kennedy, *supra* note 8.

13. Elaboration: We hedge here with the expression "seemingly non-legal distinction" because in advanced societies there is very little left of the social, technological, or economic that is not already to some degree "legalicized." Consider that many of our everyday terms— "employee," "insurance," "corrupt," "HMO," "contract"—are already legalicized, are already in part products and functions of law (though not only). For a discussion of the pluralistic character of our legal-social-technological-economic-political conceptual architectures and the problems this creates for understanding, knowledge, and theory, *see* Pierre Schlag, *The Dedifferentiation Problem*, 42 CONTINENTAL PHIL. REV. 35 (2009) (special issue on continental philosophy of law).

14. Planned Parenthood of Se. Pennsylvania v. Casey, 505 U.S. 833, 878, 112 S. Ct. 2791, 2821, 120 L. Ed. 2d 674 (1992).

15. RONALD DWORKIN, TAKING RIGHTS SERIOUSLY 22 (1977).

16. Further reading: By way of an overarching introduction to normative argument, perhaps the best place to start is JOSEPH WILLIAM SINGER, PERSUASION GETTING TO THE OTHER SIDE (2020). For excellent articulations (and defenses) of specific kinds of normative arguments, see LLOYD WEINREB, LEGAL REASON: THE USE OF ANALOGY IN LEGAL ARGUMENT (2016) (analogical

reasoning); John C. P. Goldberg, *Introduction, Pragmatism and Private Law*, 125 HARV. L. REV. 1640 (2012) (pragmatism); RICHARD A. POSNER, ECONOMIC ANALYSIS OF LAW (9th ed. 2014); DUNCAN KENNEDY, A CRITIQUE OF ADJUDICATION (FIN DE SIÈCLE) (1998) (critical); Edward L. Rubin, *The New Legal Process, The Synthesis of Discourse and the Microanalysis of Institutions*, 109 HARV. L. REV. 1393 (1996) (legal process); Katharine Bartlett, *Feminist Legal Methods*, 123 HARV. L. REV. 829 (1990) (feminism).

17. Most of these come straight out of Duncan Kennedy's article. Kennedy, *supra* note 8.

18. South Dakota v. Wayfair, Inc., 138 S. Ct. 2080 (2018).

19. South Dakota v. Wayfair, Inc., 138 S. Ct. 2092.

20. Further reading: Joseph Raz, *The Rule of Law and Its Virtue, in* THE AUTHORITY OF LAW 210, 214 (1979) (on publicity); LON L. FULLER, THE MORALITY OF LAW 33–41, 49–51, 63–65 (1964) (on promulgation and clarity).

21. In terms of practice, the important thing here is to recognize right away that we are operating in a non-ideal world, and that, accordingly, no legal distinction will be perfect. Perfection in this context is almost never an option. Given this context, the discovery of a flaw in a given distinction is rarely a killer objection. It matters, of course, but it's not killer.

22. Further reading: Lee Anne Fennell, *Lumpy Property*, 160 U. PA. L. REV. 1955 (2012); Pierre Schlag, *The Problem of Transaction Costs*, 62 S. CAL. L. REV. 1661, 1669–71 (1989); William J. Baumol, *Indivisibilities, in* THE NEW PALGRAVE DICTIONARY OF ECONOMICS (September, 9, 2014), http://www.dictionaryofeconomics. com /article?id=pde2008_ I000069.

23. Ronald H. Coase, *The Problem of Social Cost*, 3 J.L. & ECON. 1, 38 (1960).

24. Pierre Schlag, *The Knowledge Bubble—Something Amiss in Expertopia, in* SEARCH FOR CONTEMPORARY LEGAL THOUGHT 428–53 (Justin Desautels-Stein and Christopher Tomlins eds., 2017).

25. *See* Lon L. Fuller, *The Forms and Limits of Adjudication*, 92 HARV. L. REV. 353, 394–404 (1978); MICHAEL POLANYI, THE LOGIC OF LIBERTY: REFLECTIONS AND REJOINDERS 171 (1951).

26. Fuller, *supra* note 25, at 394.

27. Fuller, *supra* note 25, at 395.

28. For a revealing encounter with arbitrariness, *compare* Stafford v. Wallace, 258 U.S. 495 (1922) (cattle are part of a stream of commerce proceeding from west to east), *with* A. L. A. Schechter Poultry Corp. v. United States, 295 U.S. 495 (1935) (the chicken had come to rest).

29. Further reading: Ruth E. Sternglantz, *Raining on the Parade of Horribles: Of Slippery Slopes, Faux Slopes, and Justice Scalia's Dissent in Lawrence v. Texas*, 153 U. PA. L. REV. 1097, 1101 (2005); Eugene Volokh, *The Mechanisms of the Slippery Slope*, 116 HARV. L. REV. 1026 (2003); Frederick Schauer, *Slippery Slopes*, 99 HARV. L. REV. 361 (1985).

30. *See* Harold Demsetz, *Information and Efficiency: Another Viewpoint*, 12 J.L. & ECON. 1 (1969).

31. Seana Valentine Shiffrin, *Inducing Moral Deliberation: On the Occasional Virtues of Fog*, 123 HARV. L. REV. 1214 (2010).

32. Further reading: Shiffrin, *supra* note 31.

Chapter Five

1. This chapter is an abridged and slightly revised version of Pierre Schlag, *Rules and Standards*, 33 UCLA L. REV. 379 (1985).

2. MARC A. FRANKLIN & ROBERT L. RABIN, Cases and Materials ON TORT LAW AND ALTERNATIVES 51–54 (3d ed. 1983). The dispute actually concerns two different railroads, but the issues

are essentially the same. *Compare* Baltimore & Ohio R.R. v. Goodman, 275 U.S. 66 (1927), *with* Pokora v. Wabash Ry., 292 U.S. 98 (1934).

3. This division of the directive into two component parts is rather conventional. *See, e.g.,* Lawrence M. Friedman, *Legal Rules and the Process of Social Change,* 19 Stan. L. Rev. 786, 786–87 (1967) (defining the two component parts of directives as a description of a state of affairs and a statement of consequences that attach if the specified state of affairs is present); *see also* Jean Dabin, The General Theory of Law § 42 (1944) (defining the "hypothesis" and the "solution" as the two components constitutive of every legal rule), *reprinted in* Kurt Wilk, The Legal Philosophies of Lask, Radbruch, and Dabin 267 (1950); R. Von Jhering, L'esprit du droit romain 52–53 (O. De Meulenaere trans., 1877).

4. Further reading: Colin Diver, *The Optimal Precision of Administrative Rules,* 93 Yale L.J. (1983): 65; Isaac Ehrlich & Richard A. Posner, *An Economic Analysis of Legal Rulemaking,* 3 J. Legal Stud. 257 (1974). For a discussion of the delegative function of generality, *see* Charles P. Curtis, *A Better Theory of Legal Interpretation,* 3 Vand. L. Rev. 407, 420–24 (1950). For the view that generality is an intrinsic aspect of systems for controlling and directing human activity, *see* Lon L. Fuller, The Morality of Law 48 (1964).

5. Further reading: Some commentators propose that the breadth of a legal directive is inversely proportional to its strength. *See, e.g.,* Ronald Dworkin, Taking Rights Seriously 260–61 (1977); Frederick Schauer, *Categories and the First Amendment: A Play in Three Acts,* 34 Vand. L. Rev. 265, 275–76 (1981).

6. Further reading: The strength or weight of a directive is a measure of its intensity. The more a directive demands to be followed in the face of potentially opposed values, concerns, or directives, the "stronger" or "heavier" it is said to be. *See* Joseph Raz, *Legal Principles and the Limits of Law,* 81 Yale L.J. 823, 832–33 (1972). Raz suggests that rules do have weight. But see Dworkin, Taking Rights Seriously, at 26 (arguing that rules, in contrast to "principles," do not have weight).

7. Roscoe Pound, *Hierarchy of Sources and Forms in Different Systems of Law,* 7 Tul. L. Rev. 475, 482–83, 485–86 (1933) (rules prescribe definite, detailed legal consequences to a definite set of detailed facts; standards, by contrast, specify a general limit of permissible conduct requiring application in view of the particular facts of the case). The definitions of rules and standards used in this article are borrowed from Hart and Sacks, and Kennedy. Henry M. Hart & Albert Sacks, The Legal Process 155–58 (unpublished manuscript) (tent. ed. 1958); Kennedy, *Form and Substance in Private Law Adjudication,* 89 Harv. L. Rev. 1685, at 1687–55 (1976).

8. Kennedy, *supra* note 7, at 1689–90.

9. Further reading: For some of the classic works, see Kathleen M. Sullivan, *The Justices of Rules and Standards,* 106 Harv. L. Rev. 22 (1992); Louis Kaplow, *Rules and Standards in Economic Analysis,* 42 Duke L.J. 557 (1992); Frederick Schauer, Playing by the Rules: A Philosophical Examination of Rule-Based Decisionmaking in Law and in Life 104, n.35 (1991); Schlag, *supra* note 1, at 379, 379–430; Kennedy, *supra* note 7, at 1687–1713.

10. Arizona v. Gant, 556 U.S. 332 (2009).

11. Arizona v. Gant, 556 U.S. 351.

12. Compare Baltimore & Ohio R.R. v. Goodman, 275 U.S. 66 (1927), *with* Pokora v. Wabash Ry., 292 U.S. 98 (1934).

13. Baltimore & Ohio R.R. v. Goodman, 275 U.S. 66, 70.

14. Pokora v. Wabash Ry. Co., 292 U.S. 98, 104–06 (citations omitted).

15. Schlag, *supra* note 1, at 410–18.

16. Further reading: On polycentricity in legal disputes, see Lon Fuller, *The Forms and Limits of Adjudication*, 92 HARV. L. REV. 353 (1978).

Chapter Six

1. Or, put differently, it could be one source, interpreted in two opposed ways.

2. Ian Ayres & Robert Gertner, *Filling Gaps in Incomplete Contracts: An Economic Theory of Default Rules*, 99 YALE L.J. 87 (1989). As Ayres and Gertner note, default rules are sometimes also called "background, backstop, enabling, fallback, gap-filling, off-the-rack, opt-in, opt-out, preformulated, preset, presumptive, standby, standard-form and suppletory rules" (at 91).

3. There are, in fact, very few simple, rigid orderings in law. It is almost always the case that a simple, rigid ordering turns out to be on further inspection not so simple and not so rigid. This, as it turns out, is even true of the hierarchies of the sources of law and the hierarchies of courts. *See* text accompanying notes in chapter 6.

4. State v. Gregory, 427 P.3d 621 (Wash. 2018).

5. State v. Gregory, 427 P.3d 634.

6. Hosanna-Tabor Evangelical Lutheran Church and School v. Equal Employment Opportunity Commission, 565 U.S. 171, 181 (2012).

7. Elaboration: Indeed, law in this era (and in this mode) can be described as shaped by a *grid aesthetic* in which law is both apprehended and cast according to images and metaphors of territorialized spatial fields. Pierre Schlag, *The Aesthetics of American Law*, 115 HARV. L. REV. 1047, 1055–70 (2002).

While this aesthetic of the grid has been displaced significantly by other aesthetics, hierarchies and sectorization nonetheless subsist today. Thus, for instance, the outline form and the decision tree—so familiar to legal professionals—still describe the schematic structure of key legal artifacts such as the legal brief, the law review article, and even the statutory scheme and the judicial opinion.

8. *In re* Baby M., 537 A.2d 1227 (N.J. 1988).

9. *See, e.g., In re* Baby, 447 S.W.3d 807, 823 (Tenn. 2014).

10. *In re* Paternity of F.T.R., 833 N.W.2d 634, 649 (Wis. 2013).

11. T. Alexander Aleinikoff, *Constitutional Law in the Age of Balancing*, 96 YALE L.J. 943 (1986) (on balancing); ROSCOE POUND, SOCIAL CONTROL THROUGH LAW (1996) (on balancing).

12. At least one of us (most likely both) would disbelieve a toddler announcing that he or she had engaged in balancing.

13. *See, e.g.*, U.S. v. Lopez, 649 F.3d 1222, 1247 (11th Cir. 2011) ("[W]e will find that the district court abused its discretion under Rule 403 in only the rarest of situations.").

14. U.S. v. Curtin, 489 F.3d 935, 956–57 (9th Cir. 2007) (en banc).

15. The tests known as "totality of circumstances" or "multifactor tests" (often used in the various ALI Restatements) are often lumped together with balancing approaches. A totality of circumstances test, however, is often used to determine whether a particular transaction fits into a particular category or not. In other words, the totality of circumstances test can be seen as a technique of classification.

16. Barker v. Wingo, 407 U.S. 514, 530 (1972).

17. U.S. v. Stevens, 559 U.S. 460, 470 (2010).

18. "The economic value of a good or service is how much someone is willing to pay for it

or, if he has it already, how much money he demands for parting with it." RICHARD A. POSNER, ECONOMIC ANALYSIS OF LAW 15 (8th ed. 2011 Kindle ed.).

19. For a helpful discussion and defense of more sophisticated conceptions of CBA, *see* Michael A. Livermore, *Can Cost-Benefit Analysis of Environmental Policy Go Global?* 19 N.Y.U. ENVTL. L.J. 146 (2011).

20. United States v. Leon, 468 U.S. 897 (1984).

21. United States v. Leon, 468 U.S. 911.

22. *See* Livermore, *supra* note 19.

23. Department of Human Services v. M.K., 306 P.3d 763, 767 (Or. App. 2013).

24. Miranda v. Arizona, 384 U.S. 436 (1966).

25. Rucho v. Common Cause, 139 S. Ct. 2484, 2506–07 (2019).

26. Olinger v. U.S. Golf Ass'n, 205 F.3d 1001, 1007 (7th Cir. 2000); *see also* PGA Tour, Inc. v. Martin, 532 U.S. 661 (2001).

27. *See, e.g.,* NEIL DUXBURY, PATTERNS OF AMERICAN JURISPRUDENCE 205–300 (1995) (legal process jurisprudence).

28. The "channeling" function here is a bit more intense than Lon Fuller's version. *See* Lon Fuller, *Consideration and Form,* 41 COLUM. L. REV. 799 (1941). The idea here is that channeling effectively domesticates conflict by running it through a set of ritualized legal language, operations, and institutions.

29. Whitney v. California, 274 U.S. 357, 375 (1927) (Brandeis, J. concurring).

30. Pickering v. Board of Ed. of Township High School Dist. 205, 391 U.S. 563, 568 (1968).

31. City of San Diego, Cal. v. Roe, 534 U.S. 77 (2004).

32. Clarke v. MVAIC, 63 Misc. 3d 1230 (Civil Court N.Y. 2019) (unreported).

33. In short, there are too many possibilities for us to deal with here in any useful manner.

Chapter Seven

1. One of us has done a fair amount of work on legal interpretation, but most of it has focused on the "intermodal." *See, e.g.,* Pierre Schlag, *Hiding the Ball,* 71 N.Y.U. L. REV. 1681 (1996).

2. For two opposed accounts of legal interpretation demonstrating this general point, *see* William Baude & Stephen E. Sachs, *The Law of Interpretation,* 130 HARV. L. REV. 1079 (2017); and Mark Greenberg, *What Makes a Method of Legal Interpretation Correct? Legal Standards vs Fundamental Determinants,* 130 HARV. L. REV. F. 105 (2017).

3. Compare the works cited in note 2 *supra.*

4. This is why even the work of Stanley Fish, Steven Knapp, and Walter Benn Michaels is instructive on the interpretation of texts; it nonetheless remains somewhat askew where the interpretation of *law* is concerned. The reason is simple: it is simply not clear that, where law is concerned, legal interpretation pertains merely to a text.

5. 17 U.S. (4 Wheat.) 316 (1819).

6. Some jurisprudential approaches, of course, explicitly demand a high degree of generality. *See, e.g.,* Herbert Wechsler, *Toward Neutral Principles of Constitutional Law,* 73 HARV. L. REV. 1 (1959).

7. Wells v. Minnesota Life Insurance Co., 885 F.3d 885 (5th Cir. 2018).

8. Liberty Surplus Insurance Cop. v. Ledesma & Meyer Construction Co., Inc., 418 P.3d 400 (2018).

9. State v. Kelso-Christy, 911 N.W.2d 663 (Iowa 2018).

10. Mont. Code Ann. § 1-2-101 (West).

11. Robert Cover, *Violence and the Word*, 95 YALE L.J. 1601 (1986).

12. HANS GEORG GADAMER, TRUTH AND METHOD 366–67 (2004).

13. RONALD DWORKIN, LAW'S EMPIRE (1986).

14. Schlag, *supra* note 1, at 1688–714.

15. Lawrence Lessig, *Fidelity in Translation*, 71 TEX. L. REV. 1165, 1189–92 (1993).

16. Meir Dan Cohen, *Decision Rules and Conduct Rules—Acoustic Separation in Criminal Law*, 97 HARV. L. REV. 625 (1984) (exploring the idea that criminal law rules communicate simultaneously different meanings to the public and to the courts).

17. This section on the "earnest judge" is taken from Schlag, *supra* note 1, at 1688–92.

18. *See generally* CHARLES L. BLACK, JR., STRUCTURE AND RELATIONSHIP IN CONSTITUTIONAL LAW (1969); JOHN HART ELY, DEMOCRACY AND DISTRUST: A THEORY OF JUDICIAL REVIEW (1980); Akhil Reed Amar & Neal K. Katyal, *Executive Privileges and Immunities: The Nixon and Clinton Cases*, 108 HARV. L. REV. 701 (1995).

19. U.S. CONST. art. III, § 2.

20. *See generally* Herbert Wechsler, *Toward Neutral Principles of Constitutional Law*, 73 HARV. L. REV. 1 (1959); Robert H. Bork, *Neutral Principles and Some First Amendment Problems*, 47 IND. L.J. 1 (1971); RONALD DWORKIN, LAW'S EMPIRE (1986).

21. *See generally* PHILIP BOBBITT, CONSTITUTIONAL INTERPRETATION (1991); PAUL W. KAHN, LEGITIMACY AND HISTORY: SELF-GOVERNMENT IN AMERICAN CONSTITUTIONAL THEORY (1992).

22. *Cf.* RAY KURZWEIL, THE SINGULARITY IS NEAR (2006).

23. *See* Lessig, *Fidelity in Translation*, 1170–76.

24. *See* H.L.A. Hart, *Positivism and the Separation of Law and Morals*, 71 HARV. L. REV. 593, 606–15 (1958). For Lon Fuller's response, *see* Lon L. Fuller, *Positivism and Fidelity to Law—A Reply to Professor Hart*, 71 HARV. L. REV. 630, 661–69 (1958). For an explanation of the jurisprudential context giving rise to the dispute between Hart and Fuller, *see* Frederick Schauer, *A Critical Guide to Vehicles in the Park*, 83 N.Y.U. L. REV. 1109 (2008). Since the original Hart-Fuller dispute, the hypothetical has taken on a life (several, actually) of its own. For discussion, *see* Pierre Schlag, *No Vehicles in the Park*, 23 SEATTLE U. L. REV. 381 (1999).

25. S.A. By H.O. v. Pittsburgh School Dist., 160 A.3d 940, 942 (Pa. Cmwlth. 2017).

26. Yates v. U.S., 574 U.S. 528, 1092 (2015) (Kagan, J., dissenting).

27. For one exploration, *see* Akhil Amar, *Intratextualism*, 112 HARV. L. REV. 747 (1999).

28. *See, e.g.*, Koen Lenaerts, *Discovering the Law of the EU: The European Court of Justice and the Comparative Law Method*, *in* THE TRANSFORMATION OR RECONSTITUTION OF EUROPE: THE CRITICAL LEGAL STUDIES PERSPECTIVE ON THE ROLE OF THE COURTS IN THE EUROPEAN UNION (Tamara Persin and Sinisa Rodin eds., 2018).

29. For an introduction to the analysis of purpose, *see* MICHAEL FISCHL & JEREMY PAUL, GETTING TO MAYBE—HOW TO EXCEL ON LAW SCHOOL EXAMS 40–47 (1999).

30. Steven Winter, *An Upside/Down View of the Countermajoritarian Difficulty*, 69 TEX. L. REV. 1881, 1886–88 (1991).

31. Winter, *supra* note 30.

32. Henry M. Hart & Albert Sacks, The Legal Process (unpublished manuscript) (tent. ed. 1958).

33. Bond v. U.S., 134 S.Ct. 2077 (2014).

34. Bond v. U.S., 134 S.Ct. 2083, 2093.

35. *See* Porter v. Harden, 891 N.W. 2d 420 (Iowa 2017).

36. Wechsler, *supra* note 6; DWORKIN, *supra* note 13.

Chapter Eight

1. Duncan Kennedy, *The Semiotics of Legal Argument*, 42 SYRACUSE L. REV. 79 (1991); CHAIM PERELMAN AND LUCIE OLBRECHTS-TYTECA, THE NEW RHETORIC 411–59 (1969).

2. JOHN LIGHTON SYNGE, SCIENCE: SENSE AND NONSENSE 23–24 (1951).

3. *Cf.* Duncan Kennedy, *The Stakes of Law or Hale and Foucault!* 15 LEGAL STUD. F. 327 (1991).

4. Hence, below, when the discussion turns to the classic stereotyped implications of describing A as chosen or coerced and B as public or private, and C as [. . .] or [. . .], it is extremely important to appreciate the dissonance of our legal condition: (1) the implications are classic stereotypes routinely used and affirmed by legal professionals in good standing, and nonetheless (2) those classic stereotyped implications frequently do not hold. They do not hold precisely because the distinctions (here, please refer to chapter 4) have in part collapsed. There is no way around this. Contemporary legal professionals have basically only two choices here: they can recognize the dissonance (as uncomfortable as it may be), or they can deny the collapse and stop thinking.

5. Wittgenstein's example was the concept of games. One thinks of games perhaps as being adversarial, but then there's solitaire. Or one thinks of games as involving winners/losers, but there are games where no one keeps score. Or one thinks of games as having pieces of equipment, but then there's charades. Or one thinks of . . . The point being, there is no unitary essence to the concept of game—no necessary and sufficient conditions. Instead, family resemblances allow us nonetheless to have a relatively clear idea of what is or is not a game. LUDWIG WITTGENSTEIN, PHILOSOPHICAL INVESTIGATIONS §§ 66, 67 (1954).

6. This was elaborated in Pierre Schlag, *Cannibal Moves—The Metamorphosis of the Legal Distinction*, 40 STAN. L. REV. 929 (1988).

7. There is, of course, an important caveat here: one cannot deploy these distinctions in legal arguments, briefs, scholarship, or indeed any formal legal forum *without paying attention to the specific doctrinal variations in the field!* For example, "assumption of risk" in tort law is a doctrinal defense to negligence. It is much like "consent" in its roles and functions. But it would be a serious mistake (indeed a serious, clear black letter law mistake) to say, for instance: "Assumption of risk is a defense to battery."

8. Butler v. Board of County Commissioners, 920 F.3d 651 (10th Cir. 2019).

9. Many of these function tags are distilled from Ruth Gavison, *Feminism and the Public/Private Distinction*, 45 STAN. L. REV. 1 (1992).

10. State v. Weisler, 35 A.3d 970, 986 (Vt. 2011).

11. Commonwealth v. Monroe, 35 N.E.3d 677, 684 (Mass. 2015).

12. Snyder v. Phelps, 562 U.S. 443 (2011).

13. PERELMAN & OLBRECHTS-TYTECA, *supra* note 1, at 411–50. For a useful explanation of their concept of dissociation, *see* ALAN D. GROSS & RAY D. DEARIN, CHAIM PERELMAN 81–97 (2010); JAMES JASINSKI, SOURCEBOOK ON RHETORIC 175–82 (2001).

14. CHAIM PERELMAN, THE REALM OF RHETORIC 126–27 (1982).

15. PERELMAN, *supra* note 14, at 132.

16. PERELMAN AND OLBRECHTS-TYTECA, *supra* note 1, at 414–15.

Coda

1. E.P.I. CORBETT, CLASSICAL RHETORIC FOR THE MODERN STUDENT 108–09 (2nd ed. 1971).

2. United States v. Butler, 297 U.S. 1, 62 (1936).

3. There is perhaps this bit of surprise: despite the obvious continuing debt of contemporary Western law to the monotheism of the Judeo-Christian tradition, it is also clear that this law has evolved quite a ways toward a polytheism of values. As it stands, contemporary law demands both the authority of a *unitary dogmatism* (the monotheism of *decision*) and the *pluralistic relativism of compromise* (the polytheism of *values*).

4. That point is implicit in Perelman and Olbrechts-Tyteca's work.

5. This is from Pierre Schlag, *Cannibal Moves— The Metamorphoses of the Legal Distinction*, 40 STAN. L. REV. 929 (1988). Notes 6–11 here appeared in the original article by Schlag.

6. *See, e.g.*, M. PERRY, THE CONSTITUTION, THE COURT, AND HUMAN RIGHTS (1982).

7. *See, e.g.*, JOHN HART ELY, DEMOCRACY AND DISTRUST: A THEORY OF JUDICIAL REVIEW (1980); Robert Bork, *Neutral Principles and Some First Amendment Problems*, 47 IND. L.J. 1 (1971).

8. *See, e.g.*, Ronald Dworkin, *The Forum of Principle*, 56 N.Y.U. L. REV. 469, 516–18 (1981); Dworkin, *Law as Interpretation*, 60 TEX. L. REV. 548–49 (1982).

9. *See, e.g.*, JESSE H. CHOPER, JUDICIAL REVIEW AND NATIONAL POLITICAL PROCESS: A FUNCTIONAL RECONSIDERATION OF THE ROLE OF THE SUPREME COURT (1983); Neil K. Komesar, *Taking Institutions Seriously: Introduction to a Strategy for Constitutional Analysis*, 51 U. Chi. L. Rev. 366 (1984).

10. *See, e.g.*, Frank I. Michelman, *The Supreme Court, 1968 Term: Foreword; On Protecting the Poor through the Fourteenth Amendment*, 83 HARV. L. REV. 7 (1969).

11. *See, e.g.*, William W. Van Alstyne, *Interpreting This Constitution: The Unhelpful Contributions of Special Theories of Judicial Review*, 35 U. FLA. L. REV. 209 (1983).

12. For instance, even when constitutional theory is narrowed to just one issue—say, for instance, the relations of the "is" and the "ought"—it is striking how many different positions are confidently advanced, as if they were attended with decisive or winning arguments. Again, as stated elsewhere (Schlag, *Hiding the Ball*, at 1681–82):

> If one examines the multitude of meanings ascribed to the authoritative legal sources, it becomes apparent just how capacious these sources can be. Indeed, they serve as hosts for a great number of (often conflicting) cognizable legal meanings. As an example, consider the Constitution. For some, the Constitution is fixed. For others, it is changing. For still others, it is both fixed and changing. For many people, the Constitution is a mythic symbol—a repository of hope and a statement of aspiration. For other people, it's just law—like other law. Then too, for some, the Constitution is what it is, whereas for others, it is what it ought to be. Indeed, there is a great deal of disagreement about how the "is" and the "ought" of the Constitution are related. Consider some of the professionally respectable possibilities:
>
> > What the Constitution ought to be is of no bearing on what it is. *See* Henry P. Monaghan, *Our Perfect Constitution*, 56 N.Y.U. L. REV. 353, 396 (1981).
> > What the Constitution ought to be ought to have no bearing on what it is. *See* ROBERT H. BORK, THE TEMPTING OF AMERICA: THE POLITICAL SEDUCTION OF THE LAW 176 (1989).
> > What the Constitution ought to be is of some bearing on what it is. *See* Richard H.

Fallon Jr., *A Constructivist Coherence Theory of Constitutional Interpretation*, 100 HARV. L. REV. 1189, 1231–37 (1987).

What the Constitution ought to be is determinative of what it is. *See* Lawrence G. Sager, *Justice in Plain Clothes: Reflections on the Thinness of Constitutional Law*, 88 Nw. U. L. REV. 410, 435 (1993).

The Constitution is always already becoming what it ought to be. *See* RONALD DWORKIN, LAW'S EMPIRE 413 (1986).

The Constitution is something that can never become what it ought to be. *See* Jacques Derrida, *Force of Law: The Mystical Foundations of Authority*, 11 CARDOZO L. REV. 919, 947 (1990).

One could go on like this for quite some time. What is more, one could repeat this exercise in the plurality of legal meaning with *just about* any interesting piece of common or statutory law.

Index

Page numbers followed by "f" or "t" refer to figures or tables, respectively.

abandoned vs. lost vs. mislaid property, 74–76
abortion, 68, 81–82
abstraction, level of, 40–47; baseline and, 57–59; defined, 40–41; and the individuation problem, 150; and the problem of individualization, 57
act (Burke's theatrical term), 47, 47t, 48, 172t
action/expression distinction, 80
action vs. omission, 37–40
"ad hoc balancing" of social costs and benefits, 128
addressee context (interpretation), 145
agency (Burke's theatrical term), 47, 47t, 48
agent (Burke's theatrical term), 47, 47t, 48, 172t
agreements, 21, 23, 24; vs. contracts, 21–24
alternative liability, 20
Althusser, Louis, 32
analogical extrapolation (interpretation), 144, 149
analogical reasoning, 2, 75, 76, 94
analogical transposition, 57
Andrews, William S., 36, 96
Antiterrorism and Effective Death Penalty Act of 1996 (AEDPA), 43
antithetical vs. oppositional distinctions, 162–63
appearance/reality cluster. See reality/appearance cluster
arbitrary decision-making, avoiding, 42–43
arbitrary distinctions, 85, 91, 96, 193n28
arbitration, 28
artifacts (of law), 10–12, 21, 119, 122, 127
artificial persons, 18
assumption of risk, 6, 198n7; primary and secondary, 49

attribution of responsibility, 48; for harm imposed on others and on self, 167
attribution rules, 19–20, 22
authorial context (interpretation), 144
authoritative, doctrine as, 23–25

balancing, ad hoc vs. categorical, 128
balancing techniques (conflict resolution), 121, 126–29, 136
base, defined, 157
baseline, variations within a single, 56; individualization, 57–58; level of abstraction, 57 (see also abstraction, level of); multiplicity, 58–59
baseline collapse problems, 64–69; abstract formulation, 64; argument pointers, 69, 69t; illustration, 64; strategies for switching grounds, 66–67
baseline neutrality problems, 59–60; denial and evasion, 63–64; failed neutrality, 60–63
baseline selection problems, 54–59
baselines, 52, 69–71, 179; classic, 55–56; deviations from, 52, 54–56, 59; ideal, 14; ostensibly neutral/political, 59–60, 60t; role/function of, 182t
battered woman defense, 33
binding character of law, 62
binding precedent and the use of binding authority, 27
black letter law, 10, 25–26
Brandeis, Louis, 135
breach of contract, 22. See also contract law
break points, 4, 29, 77, 90. See also decision points
bright line rule, 93, 100, 108, 115
Brown v. Board of Education I, 41
burdens, 122

Burke, Kenneth, 60; dramatistic theory, 50; theater metaphor of, 172 (*see also* theatrical metaphor); and theatrical elements/theatrical terms, 47, 47t, 49, 172t (*see also* theatrical elements/theatrical terms)
butterfly effect, 94

Cardozo, Benjamin, 35, 36, 40, 100, 110–12
case law analogies, 2. *See also* analogical reasoning
categorical balancing, 128
causal theory, 167
causation, 33, 47, 48; definitions, 22
causation requirements, 19–20
causes of action, 17
channeling, 13, 14, 121, 134–37, 196n28
Chemical Weapons Convention Implementation Act of 1998, 152–53
choice/coercion cluster, 158, 158t, 163, 165, 170–71, 175, 176, 198n4; function tags for, 166–68. *See also* voluntariness
choice/coercion dichotomy, 69t
circularity, 157, 164–65
cluster logic, 177–78, 180, 183, 184; cautionary note regarding, 156–58; role/function, 182t. *See also* structural distinction clusters
clusters, composition of, 159–60
Coase, Ronald H., 70
coerced vs. voluntary actions, 35. *See also* choice/ coercion cluster; voluntariness
coercion: authorization of state to coerce, 168; vs. consent, 171. *See also* choice/coercion cluster
coherence, 85, 154; formal, 114; normative, 109, 114
Colorado Amendment 2 (1992), 63
Commerce Clause, 77, 80, 96, 144
common law, 2, 12, 24; baselines and, 52, 53, 55, 57–61; on "found" property, 74; neutrality and, 59–61; referral, deference, and, 133; statutes and, 61, 123
common law rights, 55
common sense as baseline, 56
communication. *See under* rules vs. standards
Communications Decency Act (CDA), 125
comparative impairment, 129
comparative scheme, 115–16
concept (in law), defined, 11
conceptual indivisibility. *See* indivisibility
conceptual intelligibility, 77–79, 83, 84, 93; defined, 77; distinctions that suffer from lack of, 64, 77–79, 83–85; ideal legal distinction and, 84, 88, 98; normative appeal and, 83, 89; practicality and, 79–81, 89
conflict: defining, resolving, or extinguishing, 13–14. *See also* regime conflict resolution techniques
consent, 122–23, 141, 158, 164, 165, 166t, 167;

compared with assumption of risk, 6, 198n7; to search, 171. *See also* choice/coercion cluster
consequences, 22, 23, 67, 73; discernible specific, 140, 142–43
consequentialist approach to decision-making, 131
consideration, defined, 11
constitution, 2, 24
Constitution, U.S., 55, 97, 126, 140, 146–48, 199n12; articles, 145–46; as a charter, 146, 147; reading it in terms of the "plain meaning" of the text, 145–48; and the separation of powers, 134–35; statutes and, 123. *See also specific clauses*
constitutional amendments: First Amendment (*see* First Amendment); Fourth Amendment, 22, 42; Fifth Amendment, 29, 53, 55, 180; Eighth Amendment, 56, 57; Fourteenth Amendment, 18, 55, 147
constitutional charter, 147
constitutional law, 61, 133–34, 183; baselines and, 52–53, 55; controversial issues in, 108; state action doctrine in, 79; Supremacy Clause and, 123, 126. *See also* public/private cluster
constitutional rights, 43, 65, 128, 147; "state action" and, 55
constitutional standards, 43
constitutional theory, 184, 199n12
constitutionality, 24, 53, 124, 133, 134, 140
construct-a-person strategy, 18, 20
continuous vs. segmented transactions, 36–37
contract law, 21–24, 54, 104, 126–27
contracts vs. agreements, 21–24
conventions. *See* constitution
correction/rectification, 14, 16
cost-benefit analysis (CBA), 121, 129–32; definitions, 129–31
course of dealing, 56
critical legal studies, 177
custom/customary practice, 55–56. *See also* standards of care

dealing, course of: as baseline, 56
decision costs, 88. *See also* error costs
decision points, 4, 139. *See also* break points
decision regimes, 182; role/function, 182t
decision-making: approaches to, 161–62; democratic/collective, 169
dedifferentiation, 61; defined, 61
default rules, 122, 123
deference, 133–34; definition and nature of, 133, 134
deferential standards, 120, 123
deformalization strategies, 67
deformalized legal regimes, 68
deformalizing decisions, 66
delegation, 104, 105t

democratic/collective decision-making, 169
denial, 134
deviation, 52, 54–56, 59
directive aspect of doctrine, 23, 25
directives. *See* legal directives
disablements and entitlements, 17–19, 67, 69t. *See also* entitlements
disattribution of responsibility: for harm to others, 167–68; for harm to self, 167
disclosure, 169; protection from, 169
discontinuity between legal distinctions, 85
discrimination, 63, 96–97
dissociation, logic of, 173–75; chaining: running an argument through successive clusters, 175–76; cluster alliances, 176
distinguishing a case, 75–76
doctrinal argument(s), 2, 7, 29, 175–76; movement in, 51; nature of, 6; as stylized, 6; topics of doctrine and, 179; as transformative, 51; views regarding, 6
doctrinal distinctions and gradations, 163–64
doctrinal fields, 159, 177
doctrinal formulations, 166t, 168t
doctrinal structures and moves, 6–8
doctrine, legal, 1, 4, 21–22; characteristics, 23–25; defined, 1, 4, 10, 188n1; instruction in, 4, 6–7; nature of, 1, 4, 10, 21–22, 28, 179–80; rule-like and standard-like versions of, 107, 107t; sources of law for, 24; structured elasticity of, 25–28; as substance vs. form, 3, 4; the topics of, 179–84; understanding, 183. *See also* New Doctrinalism

economics, law and, 177
effects and consequences (as contrasted with intent and motive), 67. *See also* consequences
efficiency (of legal distinctions), 88
Eighth Amendment, 56, 57
elasticity. *See under* doctrine
entailments (regime conflict resolution techniques), 136–37
entitlements, 65, 68, 124; conditional, 124; defeasible, 124; defined, 157; disablements and, 17–19, 67, 69t; property, 74, 76, 120; rights and, 157
entry-framing, 32–33, 182, 184
equity, 24
error costs, 88. *See also* decision costs
essential/contingent cluster, 160t, 171–72, 174, 175
Establishment Clause, 58, 67, 126
exclusionary rule, 114–15, 131
exit-framing, 51
expectations as baseline, 55
extrapolation. *See* analogical extrapolation

facts, applying the law to, 31
fairness, 82

fairness/equity (of legal distinctions), 87
false dichotomy between legal distinctions, 85
family resemblances (Wittgenstein), 158–59
farm tenancy, 153
Fifth Amendment, 29, 53, 55, 180
figure/ground cluster, 160t, 174, 175
First Amendment, 86; action/expression distinction and, 80; "ad hoc balancing" of social costs and benefits in, 128; Establishment Clause, 58, 67, 126; public property, "public forum," and, 55; safety valve theory of, 135; and speech as a public vs. private concern, 122, 172. *See also* flag-burning cases
flag-burning cases, 45, 97
flag-burning scenario, values on both sides of the, 46
"flexible standard," 93, 100, 103
flux, 96
foreseeability analysis in negligence claims, 43–44
formal coherence. *See* coherence: formal
formal dimensions of legal issues, 114
formal matters, 123; vs. informal matters, 12
formal patterns, 121
formal rationality, 188n9
formalism, 125; nature of, 160; rules and, 159–61. *See also* deformalization strategies
formalism/realism cluster, 159–60, 161t
formalism/realism distinction, 80, 93, 177
formalist strategy, 80–81, 90
formalities, 38, 39, 81, 104–5, 106t, 132
form/substance dichotomy, 3, 4, 7, 69t
"found" property, 74
foundation, defined, 157
Fourteenth Amendment, 18, 55, 147
Fourth Amendment, 22, 42
framing, 31–32, 182; baselines and, 181; role/function, 182t; segmented vs. continuous, 36–37
framing options/framing choices, 31–32, 42, 45
Free Exercise Clause, 126
free market/regulation dichotomy, 69t
free will, 165, 170
freedom of speech values and considerations: in flag-burning scenario, 46. *See also* First Amendment
Fruit of the Poisonous Tree doctrine, 22
Fuller, Lon L., 95, 113, 150, 188n6
function/structure cluster. *See* structure/function cluster
function tags, 166–69
functional legal context, 145

Gant, Arizona v., 108
generality: of doctrine, 23, 25; level of (*see* abstraction, level of)
good faith as baseline, 56

governance: authorization of state to rule and coerce, 168–69; by non-state institutions, 169. *See also* regulation; state interference

Great Recession, 33

grid aesthetic, 125, 195n7

Griswold v. Connecticut, 41–42

gun control debate, 47–48

Hale, Robert Lee, 65, 163

harms, 20–21

Hart, H. L. A., 150, 188n11

Hart, Henry M., 152

hierarchies, 121–26, 129, 135–36; absolute vs. modified, 122–25; battle of the, 126–27; nature of, 122

"historical gloss" (constitutional law), 133–34

history as baseline, 55

Hohfeld, Wesley Newcomb, 19

Holmes, Oliver Wendell, Jr., 100, 110–12

homosexuality: and the right to privacy, 81. *See also* lesbian, gay, bisexual, and transgender (LGBT) legislation

hybrids (regime conflict resolution techniques), 135–37

ideal legal distinctions, 84, 88, 98–99; defined, 84, 88, 98; vs. non-ideal distinctions, 89, 91, 98

immunity for public officials, qualified, 43

imputed responsibility, 20

incoherence of legal distinctions, 85. *See also* coherence

indeterminacy, 61

individual discretion and preferences allowed (and protected), 169

individual responsibility for welfare, 169

individuation problem, 149, 150

indivisibility, 93–94, 97; defined, 92; examples, 92–93

institutional competence, 134

instrumental value, 82; vs. intrinsic value, 82–83

instrumentality (Burke's theatrical term), 48, 50, 172t

intent, 167, 170

intent and motive (as contrasted with effects and consequences), 66–67

intentional tort, 92

interests, 20–21; defined, 11

interlinking of doctrine, 24–25

interpellation, 32

interpretation, 140, 179, 182; modes of, 139 (*see also* purposivism; textualism); role/function, 182t; unit of, 150

interpretive challenges, 139, 149; fidelity to the original meaning, 148–49; "legal" in the legal text, 139–40; textual feedback loop, 143–44. *See also* interpretive contexts

interpretive contexts, 140; discernible specific consequences, 142–43; fat-rich, 141; institutionally localized, 141–42; the plurality of contexts, 144–48; procedural posture, 142

interpretive directives, 139–40

intertextual integrity, 149, 151–52

intratextual integrity, 149, 151

intrinsic value, 82; vs. instrumental value, 82–83

is/ought structural distinction, 177, 199n12

isolation (separation of parties/activities), 14

Johnson, Texas v., 97

judge-made law, doctrine as, 24, 25

jurisprudence of form, 4

jurisprudential and legal directives, 140

jurisprudential approaches (and cluster logic), 177, 178

juristic science, 125

justice, 82

justification of legal regimes, 121

Kagan, Elena, 151

Kennedy, Duncan, 69, 103, 201n5

knowledges, standard-like vs. rule-like, 117–18

law: anti-intellectual aspect, 5; classic options in American, 93; nature of, 1, 2, 7–8; sources of, 12

Lawrence v. Texas, 96–97

legal categories, 15

legal directives, 11–12, 119, 138–40, 161–62; decision-making and, 161–62; defined, 11; formal dimensions, 101–2; formalism/realism and, 160–61; formula for and parts of a directive, 101, 102; positive law as a series of, 101; rules/standards and, 11, 101, 102, 114–15, 118, 138, 160–62; strength, 194nn5–7; substantive objectives served by, 101; synthesizing individual decisions into broader, 114–15

legal distinction(s), 73; classic flaws in, 84–89; crafting, 89–90; criteria for "sound," 77–84; fetishism of the, 98–99; functions of, 73–77, 182t; and seemingly non-legal distinctions, 80, 192n13; where to draw the line, 90–98. *See also* ideal legal distinctions; *specific distinctions*

legal doctrine. *See* doctrine

legal elements, 17–21

legal formalism. *See* formalism

"legal" in the legal text, 139–40

legal interpretation. *See* interpretation

legal mind, 25

legal persons, 17–19; defined, 17

legal pluralism, 2, 188n3; defined, 2. *See also* pluralism

legal process (school of thought), 134

legal realism. *See* realism

legal regimes, 85, 86, 88, 121, 136, 139; assessing the

comparative value of various, 130; doctrine, doctrinal topics, and, 179–80; justification of, 121; legal distinctions as delineating boundaries between, 73, 77, 79, 80, 162; methods to arrive at, 121; problems in deciding which regimes prevail when, 125, 126; tiebreakers and, 123; ways of ranking different, 122

legal remedies. *See* remedies

legal rules. *See* rules

legal system, realization of the, 14–15

legal systems, modern: "artifacts" of (*see* artifacts); functions of, 12–17; stages of development of, 15

legal values. *See* values

legalicized terms, 192n13

legislation, 60–61

legitimation, 15

lesbian, gay, bisexual, and transgender (LGBT) legislation, 63, 96–97

less restrictive means, 86, 87

liability, 39; alternative, 20

Liebeck v. McDonald's Restaurants. See McDonald's coffee case

litigation, 25–26

marital privilege, 76

Marshall, John, 140

McCullough v. Maryland, 140

McDonald's coffee case, 34

mediation, 28

meta-quantification approaches (conflict resolution), 129–32

Miers, David, 21

Miranda warnings, 132

Moch Co. v. Rensselaer Water Co., 40

motive, 66–67

multifactor tests, 195n15

narratives, 2, 32, 34

natural law, 177

natural persons, 18

neglect, child, 143, 145

negligence, 92, 93; vs. intentionality, 92; liability and, 74; in *Palsgraf v. Long Island Railroad*, 34–36; vs. strict liability, 74, 77; in *Verduce v. Board of Education*, 49, 50

negligence claims, foreseeability analysis in, 43–44

negligence law, reasonable person test in, 57

nesting, 16

neutral baselines. *See* baseline neutrality problems

neutral/value-laden cluster, 160t; Herbert Wechsler on, 191n12

neutrality, 176; common law and, 59–61

New Doctrinalism, 3–4, 187nn3–4

non-referentiality, 60–61

normative appeal, 81–85, 88, 89; defined, 81; ideal legal distinction and, 84, 88, 98; indivisibility concerns and, 93–94; practicality and, 84, 89, 181

normative coherence. *See* coherence: normative

norms. *See* baselines

Olbrechts-Tyteca, Lucie, 173–75

Olinger v. U.S. Golf Ass'n, 133–34

Oliphant, Herman, 41

omission vs. action, 37–40

oppositional vs. antithetical distinctions, 162–63

oppositions: as conflicts, 119; irreconcilable, 115–16; reconciling, 115

"ordinary intelligence" baseline, 58

overbreadth doctrine, 86

overbreadth of legal distinctions, 85

overlapping legal distinctions, 85, 87–88

ownership theory, 167

pairing, 162–63

Palsgraf v. Long Island Railroad Co., 34–36, 96

paternalism/individualism cluster, 160t

Perelman, Chaim, 173–75

person/non-person distinction, 17, 18. *See also* legal persons

personhood, 18. *See also* legal persons

Pickering balancing test, 136

"plain meaning" of context, 145–48

Planned Parenthood v. Casey, 81–82

pluralism, 28. *See also* legal pluralism

policy, defined, 11

policy judgments (conflict resolution), 125–27

polycentric disputes, 95, 96

polycentricity, 95–96; vs. bicentricity of the rules vs. standards dialectic, 112–14

polytheism of values and monotheism of decision (in law), 199n3

positive law, 2, 15, 18, 101

Powell, Thomas Reed, 25

practicality, 79–81, 83–85, 89–90, 181; conceptual intelligibility and, 79–81, 89; ideal legal distinction and, 84, 88, 98; indivisibility concerns and, 93; normative appeal and, 84, 89, 181

pragmatism, legal, 177

prefiguration, 32–33; defined, 33

premeditation, 73–74, 93

principle, defined, 11

privacy, 42; right to, 42, 59, 68, 81

"private," implications of classifying an act as, 169

private action, 65. *See also* public/private dichotomy

private property, 53, 64. *See also* property

process/outcome dichotomy, 69t

projection, principles of, 162

property: abandoned vs. lost vs. mislaid, 74–76; "found," 74

property (Fifth Amendment), 29, 53, 55; defined, 180

"public": functions of designating something as, 168–69; meanings of the term, 169

public/private cluster, 160t, 162, 165, 168t, 172–73, 177; in Burke's theatrical terms, 172, 172t; function tags for the, 168–69

public/private dichotomy, 66–68, 69t, 122

public vs. private notions, 168t. *See also* public/private cluster

punishment, 57

purpose (Burke's theatrical term), 47, 47t, 50, 172t

purposivism, 139, 152–53; the big challenge for, 152; meaning and scope of the term, 152; multiple purposes, 153–54; selection, 154; the structure of purpose, 154–55

quantitative cluster, 160t, 163, 174, 175

realism: nature of, 160–61; New Doctrinalism and, 3, 187n4; standards and, 159–61

realist strategy, 80, 93

reality/appearance cluster, 160t, 173–76

reasonable observer, 58

reasonable person, 57, 79

reasonableness, 55, 56, 79, 152, 153, 161–62

reasoning, analogical. *See* analogical reasoning

recognition, rules of, 188n11

rectification/correction, 14, 16

recursivity, 112

referral (technique), 133, 134; defined, 133

reflexivity, 15–17, 188n11

reframing, 120

regime conflict, 120–21, 123, 129, 134; avoiding, 120, 132, 181; definition and scope of the term, 120; managing conflicts by channeling, 134–35 (*see also* channeling); resolution of, 123, 125, 126, 129, 131, 133, 134, 136 (*see also* regime conflict resolution techniques)

regime conflict resolution techniques, 121, 136; combining (hybrids and entailments), 135–37; hierarchy, 122–24; meta-quantification approaches, 129–32; policy judgments, 125–27; referral/deference/denial, 133–34; sectorization, 125. *See also* balancing techniques

regulation, 2, 14, 59, 61. *See also* governance

remedies, 21

responsibility, 47, 167; individual, 169; scope of, 167, 168. *See also* attribution of responsibility

rights, 157; common law, 55; defined, 157. *See also* constitutional rights; privacy

risk. *See* assumption of risk

Roberts, Owen, 63, 181

Roe v. Wade, 81–82

Romer v. Evans. See Colorado Amendment 2

rule of law, 13, 62, 88–89; application of rule of law considerations, 169; defined, 13; ways an effort to maintain a system of legal rules may go wrong, 188n6

rule-like knowledges, 117–18

rules: defined, 102, 194n7; nature of, 102; transubstantiation of standards into, 114–15

rules and "ruleness," 118

rules/standards cluster, 69t, 159–60; formalism/realism cluster and, 159–61; per se/reasonableness and, 161–62

rules vs. standards, 100–101, 182t, 194n7; arguments, 106t, 112; communication/formalities/notice and, 104–5, 106t; delegation and, 104, 105t; deterrence and, 103, 104t; directives and, 138, 160–62; oppositions that constitute the dichotomy of, 102; role/function, 182t; rule-like and standard-like approaches to legal doctrine and legal values, 107, 107t. *See also* bright line rule; "flexible standard"

rules vs. standards dialectic, 102–5, 103t, 181; bicentricity vs. polycentricity of the, 112–14; irreducibility of the, 116–18; limitations of the, 108–16; substantialized versions of the, 106–8; virtues-and-vices vision of the, 100–101, 109, 112–14, 116

Sacks, Albert, 152

safety valve theory of the First Amendment, 135

Sarbanes–Oxley Act, 150

Scalia, Antonin, 42–43, 96–97

scene (Burke's theatrical term), 47, 47t, 172t

science, standard-like vs. rule-like vision of, 117

sectorization (conflict resolution), 125

segmented vs. continuous transactions, 36–37

self, theory of the, 167

self-defense, 33, 48

self-selection theory, 167

separation of powers, 134–35

sexual intimacy: privacy and, 81. *See also* lesbian, gay, bisexual, and transgender (LGBT) legislation

slippery slope, 96–98

sociological success of modern legal systems, 16

standardization, 5

standard-like knowledges, 117, 118; unavoidably vague evaluation of, 118

standards: defined, 102, 194n7; delegating by, 105t; nature of, 102, 162. *See also* rules vs. standards

standards of care, 55–56, 92

standards of review, 120, 123

state action doctrine, 65–66, 79, 177

state interference, freedom from, 169. *See also* governance

state responsibility for welfare, 169

status quo as baseline, 56
statutes, 2, 24
"stream of commerce" test, 96
structural distinction clusters, 158–59, 160t; as classic options, 163–64; composition, 159–62; functions, 165–69; how the clusters matter, 163–73; nuance: substituting one distinction or term for another, 164–65; pairing, 162–63
structural distinctions, 156–58, 164, 177; defined, 156; importance, 156
structuration, 13, 16; defined, 13
structure/function cluster, 162
substance. *See* form/substance dichotomy
subversion (legal distinctions), 88
Summers v. Tice, 20
Supremacy Clause, 123, 126
Supreme Court, U.S., 25
surrogacy contracts, 126
switching grounds, strategies for, 66–67
Synge, John Lighton, 157

Takings Clause (Fifth Amendment), 180
taxation, 70–71, 85
textualism, 139, 149–51
theatrical elements/theatrical terms, 47–49, 47t, 172, 172t
theatrical metaphor, 38, 47, 48, 172
theory: law expressed in terms of, 2; plane of, 161
tiebreakers, 122, 123
Tilley, Cristina Carmody, 187n4
time frames, broad vs. narrow, 33–36
topics of doctrine. *See* doctrine: the topics of
tort law, 49. *See also specific topics*
tort reform, 34
totality of circumstances, 195n15
tradition/history as baseline, 55
transactions, segmented vs. continuous, 36–37

transfer mechanisms (transfer of interests), 20
transparency, 169
transposing analogically, 57
trigger and response aspects of legal directives, 11, 21–22, 24, 101, 102
Twining, William, 21

underbreadth of legal distinctions, 85
Uniform Commercial Code, 100, 115
utilitarianism, 129–31

vagueness of legal distinctions, 85, 87
validity, criteria of, 188n11
value and willingness to pay, 130
valued concerns, conflicts among, 86
values: defined, 11; rule-like and standard-like versions of, 107, 107t. *See also* neutral/value-laden cluster
Verduce v. Board of Education, 48–50
vicarious liability, 22
virtues-and-vices view of rules vs. standards dispute, 100–101, 109, 112–14, 116
VISH, 157, 164, 182
voluntariness: coercion, consent, choice, and, 35, 158, 164, 168, 170, 171; necessity and, 158. *See also* choice/coercion cluster

waste (legal distinctions), 86–87
Wayfair, South Dakota v., 85
Wechsler, Herbert, 191n12
Whitehead, Alfred North, 1
Whitney v. California, 135
willingness to pay, 130
Wittgenstein, Ludwig, 158–60, 198n5

zone of danger rationale, 35

www.ingramcontent.com/pod-product-compliance
Lightning Source LLC
Chambersburg PA
CBHW061024220326
41597CB00019BB/3322